ADVANCE PRAISE FOR
KINGDOM COME

Apostolics have a hunger for the supernatural. We want to hear God's voice and operate with anointing in the gifts of the Spirit. Many authors have endeavored to identify the keys to building a spiritual ministry, but in *Kingdom Come*, author Lori Wagner hit the nail on the head. She recognized that to be greatly used by God, essential elements must first come together.

To fully equip us, God, His Word, and the church each do their part, but there is one additional vital component: our willingness to allow God to mold us into a vessel of honor. *Kingdom Come* outlines this core principle—how to be spiritual and stay spiritual. Thank you for this book.

Jack Cunningham
Virginia District Superintendent of the United Pentecostal Church International
Pastor, Bible World, Chesapeake, Virginia

———

In *Kingdom Come,* Evangelist Lori Wagner challenges the status quo and contends with those who would take the path of mediocrity. Her transparency is evident throughout the book as she shares personal stories of visions and victories and also divine tools that will help so many to expand the kingdom of God. Her life of dedication and sacrifice bleed through the pages.

Make sure to take notes while reading. You will be blessed.

Victor Jackson
Evangelist

Lori Wagner, an anointed minister and prolific author, captivates readers with her new book *Kingdom Come*. As she follows the flow of the Spirit, she provides tools that will bring about spiritual growth and maturity. This exceptional resource details God's plan for His children to experience a greater dimension of freedom and empowerment beyond their natural abilities.

The book offers spiritual keys to help believers live out their faith in a real environment and be fully equipped as kingdom representatives. Amid negating circumstances and devastating experiences, Lori Wagner affirms the hope that anyone willing to commit to God and align with His Word can receive healing and wholeness. As we abide in Christ and apply kingdom principles, He bestows power from on high and we reflect His glory so that it might ultimately be revealed throughout the whole earth! For highlighting this reason alone, I rate *Kingdom Come* five stars!

Flo Shaw
Director, World Network of Prayer

Deep is calling to the deep in this incredible journey of revelation and inspiration. *Kingdom Come* is not for the faint of heart, but for those who yearn and pant after righteousness and the favor of God. In this book you will discover amazing insights and fresh understanding of familiar scriptures that are suddenly ablaze with deeper meaning.

How I pray for God's people to be keenly aware of all the possibilities and promises that can be experienced when we are kingdom-minded. I love books that captivate, challenge, and change you. Let this book take you there.

Mike Easter
Evangelist

If you desire a deeper understanding of how to be a conduit of the kingdom of God, *Kingdom Come* is a must read for you. Author Lori Wagner did an exceptional job addressing and clearly describing key aspects of God's kingdom.

A major strength of this resource is its thoroughness. The book is well organized, and I loved the author's frankness as she covered content and answered questions many born again believers have been asking for decades. *Kingdom Come* is full of spiritual nuggets that can help awaken and align you to reach your God-given potential.

Dr. Jenifer Williams
UPCI Ordained Minister, Licensed Professional Counselor, Pentecostals of Alexandria

---

Kingdom Come reveals the perfect synergy of a human spirit intertwined with the Divine. In this comprehensive work, Lori Wagner unlocks a powerful perspective on the wholeness that occurs when we meet Jesus at the altar of submission and self-sacrifice. As a counselor, I love the way she unveils the transforming power of the supernatural realm. When God helps us leave the baggage of our past behind, He deconstructs our wrong thinking and His healing light changes us from the inside out.

As an evangelist, I value her emphasis on the demonstration and power that Apostolic believers should routinely experience. This is stuff we can sink our teeth into and apply immediately. Live in victory! Share it with the world! Go!

Kara S. McCoy, MA
Founder, Genuine Apostolic

The spiritual insights contained in *Kingdom Come* will enrich your life, ministry, and walk with God. Lori Wagner writes with a grace and depth that encourage the reader to pursue the things of God. The material is meaty but written with such tenderness that it is easy to digest. So dig in. This book will be a blessing to you!

Ethan Hagan
Evangelist

KINGDOM COME

MOVE IN A GREATER DIMENSION OF LIBERTY AND POWER

LORI WAGNER

AFFIRMING FAITH
Clarkston, Michigan

AFFIRMING FAITH
8900 Ortonville Road | Clarkston, MI 48348 | www.affirmingfaith.org

© 2020 by Lori Wagner

All rights reserved. No portion of this publication may be reproduced, stored in an electronic system, or transmitted in any form or by any means, electronic, mechanical, photocopy, recording, or otherwise, without the prior permission of Affirming Faith. Requests for permission should be addressed in writing to Affirming Faith, 8900 Ortonville Road, Clarkston, MI 48348. Brief quotations may be used in literary reviews.

Scriptures, unless otherwise noted, are taken from the King James Bible, Public Domain.

Additional Scriptures taken from:
The Amplified® Bible (AMPC), Copyright © 1954, 1958, 1962, 1964, 1965, 1987 by The Lockman Foundation. Used by permission, www.Lockman.org.
The Amplified® Bible (AMP), Copyright © 2015 by The Lockman Foundation. Used by permission, www.Lockman.org.
Holy Bible: Contemporary English Version (CEV), Copyright © 1991, 1992, 1995 by American Bible Society, Used by Permission.
The Holy Bible: English Standard Version (ESV), Copyright © 2001 by Crossway, a publishing ministry of Good News Publishers. Used by permission.
The Holy Bible, New International Version (NIV), Copyright© 1973, 1978, 1984, 2011 by Biblica, Inc.™ Used by permission of Zondervan.
The Holy Bible, New Living Translation (NLT), Copyright ©1996, 2004, 2007, 2013, 2015 by Tyndale House Foundation. Used by permission of Tyndale House Publishers, Inc., Carol Stream, Illinois 60188. All rights reserved.
The Living Bible (TLB), Copyright © 1971. Used by permission of Tyndale House Publishers, Inc., Carol Stream, Illinois 60188. All rights reserved.
The Passion Translation® (TPT). Copyright © 2017, 2018 by Passion & Fire Ministries, Inc. Used by permission. All rights reserved. ThePassionTranslation.com.

Printed in the United States of America | Cover and Interior Design: Laura Merchant
Author Photo: Jonathan Main | Edited by: Kara S. McCoy

Library of Congress Cataloging-in-Publication Data
Names: Wagner, Lori, 1965 – author.
Title: Kingdom Come / Lori Wagner
Description: Clarkston : Affirming Faith.
Identifiers: LCCN 2020914672 | ISBN 978-1-7335517-2-4 (paperback).

Dedicated to the memory of
Eli Hernandez
(1960–2020)

Acknowledgements

Writing *Kingdom Come* has been an incredible journey. I'm so grateful to Rev. Kara S. McCoy for her help. From inception to completion, she contributed, and her fingerprints are in the fiber of the content. At the very beginning, as we sat around the table with pencil and paper, mapping and planning, she believed in the significance of this work and invested heavily in seeing it developed and brought to production. With a master's degree in counseling and current work toward a Ph.D. in Clinical Psychology, her educational background greatly assisted in fine-tuning sensitive components. She's proven to me the truth of the maxim, "two are better than one."

As always, I thank my husband and family for their encouragement; the Affirming Faith prayer partners for supporting this project and its writer in prayer; and the Lord Jesus Christ for His tremendous blessings and the privilege of knowing Him better through the writing of this book.

Contents

Acknowledgements... xi
Foreword... xiii
Introduction... xv
SECTION 1: The Kingdom of Righteousness 1
    Chapter 1: The Kingdom of our Lord 3
    Chapter 2: Kingdom Vision..................................... 11
    Chapter 3: Kingdom Components................................. 19
    Chapter 4: Kingdom Access..................................... 25
    Chapter 5: A Master Key....................................... 35
    Chapter 6: Kingdom Conduits................................... 43
    Chapter 7: Breaking Blockages 55
    Chapter 8: Getting Righteousness Right........................ 65
SECTION 2: Peace in the Temple of God 73
    Chapter 9: You are the Temple 75
    Chapter 10: Free Indeed....................................... 89
    Chapter 11: Wholeness in the Kingdom of Peace................. 97
    Chapter 12: Wilt Thou Be Made Whole?.......................... 103
    Chapter 13: Transformation in Progress 115
    Chapter 14: The Pivot Point 125
    Chapter 15: Distractions from Without and Within 135
    Chapter 16: Secret Weapons.................................... 149
    Chapter 17: Life Waves.. 159
    Chapter 18: The Dynamic Duo................................... 173
    Chapter 19: Pursue.. 183
SECTION 3: Joy to the World 195
    Chapter 20: Kingdom Ambassadors............................... 197
    Chapter 21: The Song of the Redeemed.......................... 205
    Chapter 22: The Divine-Human Partnership 215
    Chapter 23: Shine!.. 229
    Chapter 24: On Earth as it is in Heaven 241
Appendix i: *Kingdom Come* Diagram 257
Appendix ii: Diagram Explanation................................... 258
Endnotes 261

Foreword

From the first time I met Lori, I knew she was a "people changer." She is passionate about the Word, prayer and the apostolic faith. Every time I have read a book she has authored or have heard her speak, she exuded a love for truth and holiness. Lori embodies godliness and faith in a deep way.

Perhaps the greatest strength of *Kingdom Come* is Lori's unrelenting emphasis on the supernatural and how it cannot be supplemental but must always be integral to the Christian walk. This book will equip you to understand kingdom precepts properly and, on that firm foundation, commit yourself to it with confidence that God is willing and able to move in our lives.

The book addresses not only our identities and purposes but also the challenges we face in dealing with common distractions and enemies from without and within. Lori succinctly lays out the argument that only when we will what God wills are we able to complete the work of the Great Commission. We will then reflect the love and supernatural power of God in our world.

In *Kingdom Come*, Lori declares that when our temples are made "whole" and we unite in the purposes of God, we are prepared to serve as conduits to see salvation, healing, and deliverance manifest in the earth. All for His glory. All in His name. As He moves us into a greater dimension of liberty and power.

This book will not disappoint. Instead, it will encourage and empower the reader to do more, to commit more, and to serve the Lord whole hardheartedly! I highly recommend *Kingdom Come* to anyone wanting to access all that the Lord has for us through faith!

Lori, as always I am so proud of you and I am thankful we are friends.

Vani Marshall, MS Psychology, BCPPC
Counselor, Associate Professor of Psychology

Painting by Peter Louis Kalajian (1948–1997)

Introduction

Whispers swirled through the crowd as Jesus walked among the diseased men and women. The hum of the masses faded into silence when the Lord slowed and then stopped before a man lying on a pallet near the pool.

The sunken face of the feeble man lifted to meet the gaze of the One who stood before him.

Their eyes locked.

Jesus asked, "Wilt thou be made whole?"

During the last year of his life, my late husband, Pete Kalajian, painted a picture of the healing at the pool of Bethesda. The scene, brushed out in sepia tones on a stretched canvas, illustrated more than a miraculous healing. The larger top portion portrayed a divine encounter under beautiful arched porticos. At the bottom of the painting the reflection in the water mirrored the image above with one exception. Unseen in the natural world, an angel had already lifted the man for his healing.

During the months Pete fought cancer, his condition required admission for inpatient care at the hospital for one hundred days. When he was able to be home and felt well enough, he spent much of his time painting this work that he felt portrayed two worlds simultaneously. It revealed a significant spiritual concept: miracles experienced in the physical begin in the realm of the supernatural.

This concept is supported by Scripture. We see it even from the beginning of time. God first thought, and then He acted. He conceived the world in His imagination and then spoke it into existence. The Lord continues this pattern as He moves among us and also as He ministers through His Spirit-led ambassadors. The combined work of redemption at Calvary and release of His Spirit at Pentecost established that His kingdom would function with reciprocity. All power comes from God—and the Lord certainly moves at His discretion—but He also works with and

Introduction

through His people. He responds to their faith-filled petitions and intervenes on behalf of their intercessory prayers to release His glory on the earth.

God is our benefactor. We are recipients of His good gifts. He receives glory, honor, and pleasure when we, His dear children, function with the dignity and power He bestowed upon us. We show our gratitude by using these gifts to share His heartbeat with the world He loves.

When *Kingdom Come* began to take shape, I didn't immediately realize it would be the culmination of a spiritual revelation brought to light during my husband's illness. Not only would his painting take a significant role in the project, but one particular incident in a Detroit hospital also came into play. Mid-1996, I stood beside his bed listening to a conversation between him and visitors from our church. They were talking about Heaven, and their mention of a familiar verse caught my attention. "For the kingdom of God is not meat and drink; but righteousness, and peace, and joy in the Holy Ghost" (Romans 14:17).

In the past I'd considered this verse in a linear form—like an equation; A + B + C = D. But in that moment, God launched a new concept of His kingdom in my mind. Rather than seeing His realm as a composition of equally weighted elements lined up in a neat row (kingdom = righteousness + peace + joy), I envisioned a flight of stairs with a strong base supporting the higher elevations. These steps allowed both ascending and descending passage between Heaven and Earth—like the ladder or stairway in Jacob's dream (see Genesis 28).

Pete's painting and the word picture that came to me in the hospital regarding the kingdom of Heaven have become the foundational components of *Kingdom Come*. These, along with my studies over the last twenty-five years, have helped me identify what we'll refer to as spiritual keys. We know that keys generally symbolize power and government. It's significant that Jesus used the term metaphorically when He spoke of the authority He gave to His church. The keys Jesus supplied came with power to bind and loose, and open and close (see Matthew 16:13–20). I don't claim to understand all the aspects of the keys Jesus gave Peter, but I believe the concepts in this book will bring revelation to God's people. These insights have the potential to unlock doors for a revival of deliverances, miracles, signs, and wonders. This new level of operation requires that we, God's people, know who we are and how to use what He provides us in this divine-human partnership.

Peter was an ordinary fisherman who dropped his nets to follow the Lord. Along the way, a new spiritual awareness enlightened him to a fuller understanding of God's kingdom. Divine revelation activated his faith and inspired him to follow closely in the footsteps of Jesus. When he did, a wake of the miraculous trailed behind him and those who joined him on this journey of faith.

If God's people in our generation could truly grasp who Jesus is and the depths of the power He desires to give us, we could be used to affect greater change in our world. But so often Christians face life with an earthly mentality unaware of the emotional and spiritual pain all around them—invisible wounds just as real as the physical needs of those who once laid at the pool of Bethesda. As recipients of God's grace, we know His love is the only answer for the darkness that infiltrates our communities, our families—and sometimes even our churches. Despite the forces of evil at work, Heaven's light shines bright, and God calls you and me to shine His hope to those in our spheres of influence.

As we embark on this journey, we realize there's more to know than we have known. In *Kingdom Come* we'll examine the concepts of awareness, abiding, and obedience to discover their correlation to the righteousness, peace, and joy of God's realm. As we learn to see more clearly, connect more deeply, and demonstrate the Spirit of God more powerfully, we'll be better equipped to serve as conduits of the love, healing, and wholeness so desperately needed in the world today.

Jesus is the only source for true fulfillment. He alone offers salvation from sin, deliverance from oppression, and eternal life. The world has grown darker, but the power of God has not abated. Jesus disarmed Satan. Our enemy, though a cunning and experienced foe, has limited power in the life of a believer. Deception is his most powerful weapon. He whispers half-truths and accusations that stick like flaming arrows in our minds as he attempts to make us question our value and purpose. But I believe in these last days, God desires to clarify our understanding of who we are, what we have, and our roles in bringing the righteousness, peace, and joy of Heaven to Earth.

We pray, "Thy kingdom come. Thy will be done in earth, as it is in heaven," but for God's kingdom to come, His people must be one, whole, and mature (see Matthew 6:10). *Kingdom Come* is offered as a tool to help us grow and live in a greater dimension of liberty and power. As you read, expect God to open your understanding and draw you to deeper realms. He is looking for people whose hearts are open to new experiences, whose minds agree with His will, whose spirits commune with His Spirit, and who are willing to be vessels set apart to serve as He leads the way. God is well able to accomplish the many things you've dreamed of doing for His kingdom, but first, "Wilt thou be made whole?"

SECTION 1

The Kingdom of Righteousness

1

The Kingdom of our Lord

Thine is the kingdom, and the power, and the glory.
Matthew 6:13

The kingdom of God belongs to One. "The Lord hath prepared his throne in the heavens; and his kingdom ruleth over all" (Psalm 103:19). The Lord of Heaven is Lord of all, and everything originates with Him. "Thine, O Lord, is the greatness, and the power, and the glory, and the victory, and the majesty: for all that is in the heaven and in the earth is thine; thine is the kingdom, O Lord, and thou art exalted as head above all" (1 Chronicles 29:11).

This universal kingdom includes the heavens, the earth, and everything in between. Readings from Daniel 10 and Ephesians 6 indicate that within God's kingdom are subkingdoms governed by authorities who are granted varying levels of power and influence. Every subkingdom is subject to the dominant, higher realm.

The veiled world of the Spirit envelops the world we live in. Satan, also known as the "god of this world" and the "prince of the power of the air," has a sphere of power and a realm under his influence (see 2 Corinthians 4:4, Ephesians 2:2, Luke 4:6). Though demons or men rule in the visible or unseen boundaries of their domains, God maintains sovereignty. We see this exemplified in the Old Testament when God gave a king decrees from Heaven in a dream so "the living may know that the most High ruleth in the kingdom of men, and giveth it to whosoever he will" (Daniel 4:17).

Only by permission of the everlasting God can any power exist in the world. Before His crucifixion, Jesus told His disciples what was coming, "Now shall the prince of this

> Many of the principles and methods recognizable in the visible world, apply in the abstract workings of the unseen realms.

world be cast out" (John 12:31). After the resurrection, He said, "The prince of this world is judged" (John 16:11). By the time His Spirit was poured out at Pentecost, Jesus had subdued Satan and offered salvation to anyone who turned to Him desiring to be free. Accepting His offer means becoming subjects of His kingdom. As citizens of Heaven and members of the family of God, His power and authority enable us to withstand Satan's manipulations. Nothing can separate us from God—not death, life, angels, principalities, things present, things to come—and no creature (see Romans 8:38-39). Satan, our enemy, is irrevocably defeated!

Why, then, do Christians struggle? Why is there conflict and brokenness even in the church? Perhaps the answer lies in discovering the true identity of the "governing authority" in our lives. When we receive the gospel and respond to it, we accept God's lordship and governance (see Acts 2:38). We know that we should no longer follow the ways of Satan and sin, but what about the ways that seem right in our own eyes?

Our confession of faith and commitment to God require our continual rejection of rulership from any other kingdom.

This includes the kingdom of self (self-government) and the kingdom of darkness (satanic government). As we live as subjects of God's kingdom, we learn to align ourselves with God's Word. We no longer bow to the familiar idols of our own ideas and desires nor cave to the temptations of the enemy.

If we fail to follow in the ways of God, even though we may have the very best of intentions, our human tendencies will lead us astray. We will wander into enemy territory where we are vulnerable to the adversary, or we will trip over our own flesh. Either way, the resulting damage could disable us or even take our lives.

A significant key that enables learning, knowing, and following God is proper spiritual vision. Our limited faculty of sight at times persuades us to focus on the here and now, but what we see, even with our natural eyes, is connected to the unseen and eternal (see 2 Corinthians 4:18).

How can we gain spiritual vision so we can understand the things of the kingdom? First, we must be born again of the water and Spirit (see John 3:3-6). When Jesus spoke to Nicodemus He compared being born of the Spirit to the movement of the wind. Wind blows where it pleases. We don't see it, but we discern and feel its effects. We hear its sound even when we can't tell where it comes from or where it's going. Jesus said, "So it is with everyone who is born of the Spirit" (John 3:8)

Through the Spirit, it's possible to detect the movement of the wind of God who works how, where, and when He pleases. Human beings, using only their natural abilities, are unable to fully apprehend and follow the movement and ways of God that can only be spiritually discerned (see 1 Corinthians 2:14). But I assure you, it's God's desire that we learn to discern the ways His Spirit moves in the earth (see 1 Corinthians 2:9–10).

Kingdom Characteristics

Before we look at *how* to see the unseen, let's look at the Word of God to identify what we are looking at or for: kingdom characteristics. What types of resources and power may we access through faith? What spiritual features, available means, and what substance of the unseen world can we connect with to help us live victoriously in the here and now?

The King

God is incredible. God is infinite. God is more than you and I are able to comprehend. He wants us to know Him, but He also recognizes our inability to fully grasp everything about Him. Even the super-creative among us can only focus on one thing at a time. When we look at a picture, for example, we see the whole; but after a quick overview, our eyes move from one element to another to take in all the details. In the same way, we can only reflect on one aspect of God at a time even though (out of the corners of our spiritual eyes) we know there is much more than we perceive in the moment.

The language of Psalms reveals many nuances or facets of God's character. Our English word *facet* comes from the French *facette* which means "little face."

Consider the correlation between the facets (little faces or planes) cut in a diamond or crystal and the many expressions of God revealed to us over time. Each facet is a different face of God's single identity. Every "little face" demonstrates more of who He is and what He's like.

Some of those little faces, we love. Some scare us or confuse us. But no facet can stand in isolation from the whole. In fact, the facets should be somewhat symmetrical—well balanced. If we only focus on one facet (one aspect of God), we miss His full brilliance. A skewed perception of God develops unhealthy relationships.

Similarly, the study of the many names of God and their unfolding revelation of His character generates a more comprehensive understanding of Him. God introduces Himself to us as the God who alone created Heaven and Earth—who

Himself commanded the light to shine out of darkness (see Genesis 1:1-3). The Lord proclaimed that He is, and was, and ever will be, one God (see Deuteronomy 4:6).

God is eternal. He did not have a beginning, but on the first day of Creation, He wound and set time's clock. He created mankind to live in a system of sequential relations. One event succeeds another, and throughout time, God gradually communicated more of Himself to humanity. He does the same today with individuals like you and me. When we look back in the Word, we see God's progressive revelation of Himself in the ways He interacted with humanity.

Perhaps one of God's least understood facets is one that may be confusing. The God who is love also hates. Some struggle with this concept, but Billy Graham explained it this way. He said, "God hates sin just as a father hates a rattlesnake that threatens the safety and life of his child." God hates what hurts and separates, what wounds and takes.

Yes, the Lord is righteous. And though He is longsuffering and patient, He can also become angry and punish sin. I imagine most of us remember times in younger days when we thought our loving mom's or dad's anger was too severe even as we received a deserved correction. Perhaps at times a parent errs in disciplining a child, but God's wrath is never flawed. He doesn't correct out of vindictiveness or a "hate" based in self-indulgence or irritability. God doesn't have an angry character, even though He does get angry. It's simply another facet of His nature.

The glory of God revealed in the face of Jesus Christ is one of His most beautiful facets (see 2 Corinthians 4:6). Although we do not have the privilege of seeing our Savior's physical features, we know light is part of His essence. Jesus is "the true Light, which lighteth every man" (John 1:9). He is our eternal light and the Messiah who came forth from the Father of Lights. Jesus is God revealed (see Isaiah 53:1) and the "Sun of Righteousness" risen with healing in His wings (see Malachi 4:2). He is the God whose hand laid the foundation of the earth, and He made all things visible and invisible (see Isaiah 48:13, Colossians 1:16).

Jesus is not simply *at* the right hand of God; He *is* the right hand of God—the physical presentation of God in the world. Both human and divine, Jesus is the one foretold by the prophets: "For unto us a child is born, unto us a son is given: and the government shall be upon his shoulder: and his name shall be called Wonderful, Counsellor, The mighty God, The everlasting Father, The Prince of Peace" (Isaiah 9:6). One God is both the everlasting Father and Prince of Peace. One God is Savior as recorded in both the Old and New Testaments: "I, even I, am the Lord, And besides Me there is no savior" (Isaiah 43:11, NKJV, see also Acts 4:12).

Jesus came to Earth to save His people from their sins. Through His incarnation, He reestablished the connection between God and man and now provides all we need to do the work of the kingdom. The God who sees, offers spiritual vision. The God who supplies, grants provision. The God who is righteous, reveals the concepts that bring us into alignment with His character and purposes, and the God who is the Comforter extends consolation to and through His people. He is everything that anyone could ever need, and more.

Kingdom Constituents

God created angels as His first kingdom constituents (see Psalm 148:2-5, Colossians 1:16). He made a great many of these supernatural beings, the "host of Heaven," who move like the wind and appear as fiery flames (see Nehemiah 9:6, Hebrews 1:7). We don't know how many angels God made, but we do know they are the "mighty ones" (see Psalm 103:20). Angels can only present in one place at a time, but when they show up, they are able to use supernatural power against demonic forces (see Revelation 20:1-3). As spirits, angels don't exist in bodily form, although at times God may reveal them to us in bodily form. However they may appear, they maintain their supernatural power (see Numbers 22:31, Matthew 28:5).

Scripture describes an angelic hierarchy, a rank or order that outlines different types of angels and their purposes (see Jude 9, Daniel 10:13). Michael is noted to be an archangel, a designation that indicates he has rule or authority over other angels. Gabriel, considered by many to also be an archangel, is only indicated in Scripture as a messenger (see Daniel 8:16; Luke 1:19).

God sent cherubim to guard the entrance to the Garden of Eden, and God Himself is enthroned above these angelic beings (see Genesis 3:24, Ezekiel 10:1-22; Psalm 18:10). Two golden images of cherubim were carved into the golden cover of the ark of the covenant and their images were woven in the tapestries that created the inner chamber of the holy place of the tabernacle of Moses (see Exodus 25:22, 26:1).

Shining, six-winged seraphim appear around the throne of God crying out, "Holy, holy, holy, is the Lord of hosts: the whole earth is full of his glory" (Isaiah 6:3). We don't know much detail about seraphim, but we do see examples of these angels handling hot coals from the altar.

In a vision, Ezekiel described four sparkling "living creatures" as having four faces, four wings and hands, and feet like the sole of a calf's foot. When they moved, they looked like flashes of lightning (see Ezekiel 1:5-14). In a similar situation, four-faced, six-winged "living beings" are mentioned in Revelation 4:6-8. These are covered in eyes and never stop crying out, "Holy, holy, holy, Lord God Almighty, which was, and is, and is to come."

Some angels serve specifically as protectors and messengers, and all are servants and worshippers of God. In the earth, angels bring messages to people (see Acts 8:26, 27:23–24). They carry out God's judgments (see Acts 12:23, 2 Samuel 24:16–17), and they will accompany the Lord when He returns (Matthew 16:27). Angels have knowledge about the things on the earth and the things to come (see 2 Samuel 14:20, Daniel 10:14). Angels glorify God with their adoration and are "ministering spirits" that carry out the will of God (see Hebrews 1:14). The psalmist wrote, "Bless the Lord, ye his angels, that excel in strength, that do his commandments, hearkening unto the voice of his word" (Psalm 103:20).

In writing *Kingdom Come*, I want to fully acknowledge angels and their roles in God's master plan. They, like you and I, are created beings meant to glorify God, serve His purposes, and ultimately have their place in His kingdom.

Angels aren't the only kingdom constituents. We, as believers, even now, are "seated" with Christ and placed in a dimension of power with Him in the heavenly realm (see Ephesians 2:6).

> Jesus has enthroned us with Him in a place of shared dignity and dominion to rule over the powers of darkness in this world.

Because of what Christ has done for us, we no longer walk "according to the course of this world" (Ephesians 2:2). Yes, evil remains active all around us, but we now walk "in newness of life" with the power God has given His church. Christians aren't exempt from experiencing pain; but oppression and bondage—these can be broken. The effects of evil on the eternal soul of a believer are severed by the blood of Jesus. We can live in a realm of peace in the benevolent care of a God who is both sovereign in power and tender in compassion. He becomes our secret place—our refuge.

Kingdom of Light

God is light. He spoke light into darkness and imparts the "light of life" to us as we follow Him (see John 8:12). Jesus delights in rescuing us from the dominion of darkness and bringing us into His kingdom of light (see Colossians 1:12–13). He calls His followers "children of light" and makes us to be lights in the world (see Luke 16:8, Matthew 5:14).

In the summer of 2017, during pre-service prayer, I had a vision as I was praying for my church. I saw the members of my congregation as pieces of a stained-glass window. There were many different shapes and sizes and colors. It made me think of how the Lord created us as individuals and then united us to form a translucent mosaic of His design in the local church body. One by one, the Lord picks us up from our disconnected state. He cuts, polishes, and positions us, and then solders us together by His Spirit.

I've had the privilege of visiting many beautiful cathedrals, including Notre Dame in Paris before fire damaged the building in 2019. Its stained-glass windows were spectacular. During the day, visitors and worshippers inside the building saw sunlight streaming through the intricate designs. At night, deprived of sunlight, the windows were darkened. Imagine the scene outside the building if the light inside the cathedral was bright enough to illuminate the windows in reverse.

This illustration offers a portrait of God's intention for the church. The Lord shines on His people, and He means for those same believers to reflect His light out into the world. You and I were made to share His glory and take His presence into our communities—not just as individuals, but as His glorious, united church. We're called to share what we've received from the unseen realm of the kingdom of light. With its many facets and components, we shine the light of hope to those who reside in darkness.

2

Kingdom Vision

I pray that your hearts will be flooded with light so that you can see something of the future . . . that you will begin to understand how incredibly great his power is to help those who believe him.
Ephesians 1:18–19, TLB

Eyes of Faith

In Chapter 1, we discussed the character of the King and His kingdom, but what about the components of the heavenly domain? As kingdom constituents, what elements or aspects might we have access to? Isaiah, Ezekiel, Daniel, and John offer symbolism-rich pictures of Heaven. Ezekiel's first written words declared the heavens had opened and that he had seen visions of God (see Ezekiel 1:1). Ezekiel's spiritual vision opened his awareness of the unseen.

The discussion of open eyes is of primary importance. We must have an awareness and vision of the supernatural before demonstration occurs. With that in mind, we'll find it beneficial to study Ezekiel's experiences.

Chapter 1 of Ezekiel tells of a whirlwind coming out of the north and a great cloud with a raging fire engulfing itself. Brightness the color of amber radiated from the middle of the fire to all that surrounded it. The "amber" he mentioned was significantly smooth and refers to a kind of metal that is compounded of gold and silver. It gave off a remarkable brightness. As we mentioned in Chapter 1, from within this same entity was an appearance of four living, fiery creatures who sparkled like burnished bronze (see Revelation 1:15). These angelic beings connected to one another with unfurled wings under a spectacular crystal dome that stretched out above their heads. The KJV calls the dome a *firmament*, a term used to refer to the curve of the sky, especially when considering the sky as a solid surface. The same word is also translated *vault* which also implies an arch.

Under the dome, the four living creatures each had four faces making them capable of seeing in every direction. They only moved forward as directed by the Spirit, but they resembled flaming torches as they travelled. Above the crystal dome, Ezekiel saw what looked like a sapphire throne, and above it, a man. From the waist up, the man was the color of amber and looked like fire all around and within. From the waist and down was the appearance of fire surrounded by clear shining splendor that looked like a rainbow. Ezekiel called this brightness a vision in the likeness of the glory of the Lord.

Imagery

Scripture is filled with imagery. It's beautiful when God's Word speaks to us in pictures that impart revelation. Sometimes we see complex structures as far reaching as the universe. Other times we see characteristics or features of something much larger in a miniature form.

Scripture is also filled with symbolism. Conceptually, the physical mirrors the spiritual, but not always in apples-to-apples ways. Metaphors and analogies help us grasp the realities of the unseen. For instance, the Bible identifies the Lord as a shepherd and His people as sheep. While God is personally and interactively caring for His people, He's not limited to a caretaker's role. As we continue, let's keep in mind that much of Scripture was written in descriptive, figurative language. To properly understand God's Word requires balance. We shouldn't read too much into a passage, nor should we limit one thought or concept to a passage that might have more than one meaning.

The "Eye" Seen in Ezekiel

In a "still shot" of the scene recorded by Ezekiel, I see a representation of an eye. Of course, there's so much more, and we could spend an entire book fleshing out the concept, but to prevent from derailing from our theme of spiritual vision, let's look at a simplified view of the human eye.

In a human eye, the lens is a clear, transparent dome attached to muscles that move and adjust. As I read Ezekiel's vision, I pictured the firmament transported by angels as the lens of an eye. The throne rests on the firmament and the angelic activity beneath the dome (directed by the leading from above) caused the firmament to move. The dark center, the pupil, is actually a hole that immediately absorbs light rays as they enter into the eye.

In Scripture, God refers to His people as the apple of His eye (see Psalm 17:8, Zechariah 2:8). This phrase is a Hebrew expression that in the original language literally translates, "little man of the eye" and refers to the pupil of the eye, not a piece of fruit.

If you and I were to face one another and intentionally focus on each other's eyes, you could see your reflection in my eye, and I could see mine in yours. "The little man of the eye" is actually a person's own reflection in the eyes of one looking intently at them. This happens often in romantic relationships. Sweethearts say things like, "I see myself in your eyes." God wants to see Himself in our eyes. He wants us to see ourselves in His. This requires intimate, "face-to-face" communication.

> When God called His beloved the apple of His eye, He established our significance to Him.

The iris, the thin circular structure surrounding the pupil, determines the color emanating from the center of the eye. The Greek word *iris*, translated in Scripture as "rainbow," correlates to the arch of color radiating around the throne like a shining gem (see Revelation 4:3).

In October 2019, I had a unique experience in the evangelist quarters of a church in Santa Fe, Texas. As I knelt beside a bench praying and preparing to minister, I had a vision of Jesus. I wish I could say it was in great detail. The vision was more like a silhouette of the Lord seated on a throne surrounded by an arch of radiating light. The light diffusing from the throne resembled a rainbow, and I remembered Ezekiel's vision.

I made a rough sketch of what I saw in my journal. There was a horizon (a firmament), a man in the center seated on a throne, and glory all around. When I reflected on the drawing, it appeared to me to be the likeness of an eye. I "saw" drawn on my paper the "little man of the eye." A sweet presence of God swept into the room and I had a new awareness of God looking at me and me looking at Him. The vision also emphasized the significance of the rainbow in God's Word.

Ezekiel and John saw God's bow in brilliant color. I saw it in black and white. I would've loved to have seen the colors of Heaven. I expect them to go far beyond our limited color spectrum on Earth. But one thing is sure: there's a connection between the light radiating around the throne and the releasing of the light of God's kingdom in our world.

I've spoken for many years on the true nature of the rainbow. When we see rainbows from our perspective on Earth, we only see a part—an arc. But from Heaven's point of view, a rainbow is a full circle. I once had a friend who was an avid pilot. She has since passed away, but on a flight several years ago, she snapped a picture of a circle rainbow and sent it to me. That photograph is never far from my memory. It reminds me to look at life on Earth from a heavenly perspective.

Rainbows are symbols of a promise from God. From the earth we only see a portion. From our perspective, we only perceive part of what He intends to release in our lives, our families, our churches, and our communities. God said, "For as the heavens are higher than the earth, so are my ways higher than your ways, and my thoughts than your thoughts" (Isaiah 55:9). The apostle Paul wrote, "Now I know in part; but then shall I know even as also I am known" (1 Corinthians 13:12). We may never understand God's reasons or methods, but with eyes of faith we rely on God even when we don't have the whole picture.

> The throne of God sits inside a heavenly bow, and what issues from that throne, God intends to release in our world.

The Heavens

What do we know about the power from Heaven that poured out on the day of Pentecost? First, let's look at the word "heaven" itself. While we could never know everything about the heavens, we do know there's more than one. Jesus passed through the heavens (see Hebrews 4:14). Paul wrote about a man caught up to the third heaven, so we can be certain there are at least three heavens (see 2 Corinthians 12:2).

1. The first heaven is the atmosphere closest to the earth—the airspace in which the birds fly and the clouds form (see Genesis 1:20). In the New Testament, the same word translated "air" is also translated "heaven" (see Matthew 6:26, James 5:18).
2. The second heaven would be what we consider outer space—the habitation of the sun, moon, stars, and planets (see Deuteronomy 4:19, Matthew 24:29).
3. The third heaven (also known as the heaven of heavens) is the dwelling place of God and the resting place for the throne of God (see 1 Kings 8:30; Psalm 2:4; Hebrews 8:1, 9:24).

As we discuss the kingdom of Heaven, it is important to note this realm is not relegated to just one location. Heaven is the place where the presence of God manifests at the direction of His own will, just as we saw the Lord directing the throne in Ezekiel's vision.

It's human nature to ponder the amazing works of God in the heavens and His great mindfulness of humanity. We know that the same God who hung the moon and the stars also visited men and women on the earth (see Psalm 8:3-4). With David, we consider the heavens, God, and humanity, and our contemplation includes believers alive in our day. God included people in His divine plan. In the same way the rainbow forms a circle from an aerial perspective, God's perspective of the earth includes you and me.

> **Anywhere the King is, the kingdom is. And since the Lord is near to all who call upon Him, Heaven truly is at hand.**

There's one Lord, one faith, one God, one plan of salvation, and one bride (see Ephesians 4:5-6, Revelation 19:7). This is God's composite plan, figuratively tied together with His bow—a token of His covenant with humanity (see Genesis 9:13-16). The Lord revealed His bow to Ezekiel and John, and of course, to Noah, too. He continues sending His bows into the world in natural and supernatural ways, and we'll discuss this topic more in our chapter on the gifts of the Spirit.

The same God we see in Psalm 8 would one day be born to the earth in the form of man. In Jesus, God came to Earth to redeem it—all of it. Paul wrote, "For in him [Jesus] all the fulness of God was pleased to dwell, and through him to reconcile to himself all things, whether on Earth or in Heaven, making peace by the blood of his cross" (Colossians 1:19-20, ESV). Jesus's death inaugurated the restoration of sin-stained mankind and the earth to Himself (see Colossians 1:13-14). In an act that required both divine and human components, Jesus traded His life's blood for your life and mine. This legal transaction, initiated by the grace of God, offers regeneration to all humanity previously deadened by sin (see Ephesians 2:1, 4-5).

This is the kingdom of righteousness, peace, and joy. Paul wrote, "Therefore, since we have been declared righteous by faith, we have peace with God through our Lord Jesus Christ, through whom we have also obtained access into this grace in which we stand, and we rejoice in the hope of God's glory" (Romans 5:1-2, NET). This is the fulfillment of the prophetic words recorded by Ezekiel that God would take the initiative to give us a new heart and spirit (see Ezekiel 36:26-27).

Come into the Heavenlies

God's invitation is more than just a summons to the new birth experience. John paints another picture in Revelation in which Jesus addressed a church at ease—a church whose provision had lulled them into complacency and blinded them to their true spiritual condition. He urged them to buy pure gold and pure clothing and anoint their eyes so they could see what they hadn't yet seen. Jesus wasn't reaching for the unsaved, but speaking to a full-gospel, Spirit-filled church that had grown lukewarm. Because He loved them, He corrected them and told them to be zealous again for the things of God.

Jesus stood outside the door of the church knocking and issuing an invitation, "If anyone hears my voice and opens the door, I will come in to him and dine with him, and he with Me" (Revelation 3:20, NKJV). His next words, addressed to this same people, at first blush seem encouraging, but they also carry a warning. Jesus said, "To him that overcomes will I grant to sit with Me on My throne" (Revelation 3:21, NKJV).

What was it the people were to overcome?

In context, Jesus was addressing those in the church who would overcome their lack of spiritual thirst and hunger. These believers were active in their church and had need of nothing, yet the Lord found their behavior distasteful. In fact, He said He would spew them out of His mouth. These words poignantly illustrate that failing to overcome a lack of spiritual passion endangers a believer's opportunity to sit with Jesus on His throne.

Can we hear what the Spirit is saying?

Jesus said those who hunger and thirst for righteousness will be filled with righteousness (see Matthew 5:6). I pray God's church becomes hungry and thirsty for what is good and excellent in His sight. I pray the church heeds the Lord's request and applies the salve of His Word to our eyes—that we would remove anything blinding us from spiritual realities we see incorrectly. I pray that we would not allow ourselves to be satisfied with wealth—even a wealth of doctrine and knowledge—at the expense of the true love of God and an intimate relationship with Jesus. God sees not only our outward appearance (which includes our activities), but He looks at our hearts to see our faith (see 1 Samuel 16:7). The writer of Proverbs said, "As in water face reflects face, so the heart of man reflects the man" (Proverbs 27:19, ESV). God looks at the hidden man of the heart, because that is the essence of who we are—and that is who He loves. I believe He is looking to see His reflection.

All-Seeing Eye

God watches us, even now, with His omniscient eye. Omniscient means "knowing everything." God sees and knows all; past, present, and future. Thankfully, even knowing the worst in us, He doesn't turn His face away. He trains His attention on us, making those who keep His covenant the object of His divine notice. A Latin phrase, *coram Deo,* captures the essence of life lived under God's watchful eye. The phrase has different shades of meaning, including, "before God," "before the face of God," or "in God's sight."[1] *Coram Deo* encapsulates the overarching idea of living in God's sovereign presence, under His authority, and for His glory. It also refers to a face-to-face relationship with God in a posture of humility.

> **Whatever we do, we do in His presence.**

You and I live before the face of God. "The eyes of the Lord run to and fro throughout the whole earth to shew himself strong in the behalf of them whose heart is perfect toward him" (2 Chronicles 16:9). His eyes rest upon those who reverence Him (see Psalm 33:18).

As we enter into God's presence, the Lord may reveal to us supernatural activity occurring in His kingdom or in the demonic realm (see Ephesians 6:12). As we open ourselves to see and hear, we can be confident that any spiritual revelation from Him will always harmonize with the principles in the written Word. God never contradicts Himself.

I believe the time is now for God's church to open their eyes to the unseen. When the curtain over the supernatural is open, we can see the true spiritual influences behind what's happening in the world.

> **When we keep our eyes on Jesus, He exposes the works of the enemy and imparts what we need to live in victory.**

The Lord is willing to train and develop us in spiritual matters. He said, "I will instruct thee and teach thee in the way which thou shalt go: I will guide thee with mine eye" (Psalm 32:8). In this psalm, David expressed his confidence that God guides those who walk in agreement with Him on the right path—a path of peace that leads to righteousness and joy.

Part of our journey includes divine guidance, but what does that look like? Imagine having a face-to-face conversation and suddenly the eyes of the person you're speaking with move from your face to something over your shoulder. What's your first inclination? Mine is to look in the direction that drew the other person's attention.

If you and I keep our eyes on Jesus, communing with Him in prayer and reading His Word, we'll see what holds His attention. That is the mark we should aim for.

When we train our focus on His mark, we know where to shoot our arrows. In fact, the Hebrew word translated *sin* means "to miss, to err from the mark" or "to make a false step." If we don't know where God's attention is centered, we won't know His chosen path—the place to focus our ministry as His ambassadors in the world (see 2 Corinthians 5:20).

While we're not able to see the physical body of Jesus, we can determine how He looked at people and life in the gospels. And when we follow His line of vision, His eye will guide us to His will. Jesus is the *logos* of God made flesh—the plan of God come to life

> When we know Jesus through His teachings, His example, and in relationship with His indwelling Spirit, we see God.

A Healthy Pathway of Vision

Accomplishing the work of the kingdom on Earth requires spiritual vision. Referring back to the anatomical model of an eye, we can see how issues develop slowly over time. Scales and veils can form over spiritual eyes in the same way a cataract develops on a lens or a film grows over a cornea. Visual impairments may cause blurriness, wrong color perception, light sensitivity, and even double vision. Impaired vision in itself is not life threatening, but sight affects mobility and function.

Natural eyes consist of many components that work together to create a pathway of vision. This pathway carries electrical impulses from the outer world to the inner person, and into the visual cortex of the brain. The mind processes impulses so that objects outside a person can be discerned on the inside.

Visual stimuli travel through the eye on specific paths. The journey turns what is seen upside down, and then processes it to be right side up. This upside-down internal mirroring and reflecting resonates with *Kingdom Come* concepts we'll explore in coming chapters. We can learn to discern by God's Spirit if the things seen in the natural world are properly inverted and perceived correctly. God wants to train us to sense the true origins of what we deal with in life and ministry; what is issued from the heavenly realm, and what is from the powers of darkness.

God wants to fine-tune our vision so we can clearly see through eyes of faith. As the apostle Paul prayed for the Ephesian church, may our hearts be flooded with light so we can "see something of the future" and "begin to understand how incredibly great his power is to help those who believe him" (Ephesians 1:18–19, TLB).

3

Kingdom Components

And the God that answereth by fire, let him be God.
1 Kings 18:24

In Chapter 1 we looked at the King, the kingdom, and kingdom constituents. We also touched briefly on glory and light. In this chapter, we'll investigate components of the kingdom that will further open our understanding of God's nature. In God's Word He incorporated many different symbols, analogies, and figures of speech. He intentionally used natural objects and experiences to reveal spiritual concepts about His nature, His realm, and His creation. And He was prolific about it! Look at how many metaphors are included in just a single verse of one psalm, "The Lord is my rock, my fortress and my deliverer; my God is my rock, in whom I take refuge, my shield and the horn of my salvation, my stronghold" (Psalm 18:2).

Is God literally a rock, a fortress, a shield, and a horn, or are these metaphorical representations of His character, care, and capabilities? When the Bible says God is a rock, it doesn't mean He's literally a lump of minerals fused together. In His Word, He offers this as a comparison, so we recognize His solid, constant, stable nature. In fact, the word translated *rock* in one passage refers to a mountain in another, and in another, a quarry from which stones are hewn (see Exodus 33:21, Deuteronomy 32:18). Daniel wrote about God as a rock that would crush powerful nations (see Daniel 2:44-45). The various uses of this word help us to visualize the diversity of God's nature. He's strong, steadfast, and consistent. He's a provider and a refuge, a stronghold, shelter, and savior (see 2 Samuel 22:2-3).

When we read about Heaven, we see many of its elements and activities. These "kingdom components" disclose aspects of the atmosphere and nature of the kingdom of God. A full consideration of these components includes understanding them as the metaphors they are. The apostle John, also called John "the Revelator," authored both the Gospel of John and the last book of the Bible, the Revelation of Jesus Christ. These writings provide significant information beyond the details of what Jesus did. John saw who Jesus was. He unveiled nuances left unnoticed by other contributors to the Word. John pulled back a shroud and unfolded concepts with insight likely attributed to his close relationship with the Lord.

Living Word

In his gospel, John revealed Jesus as the living Word (*logos*) of God, made in flesh, to dwell among men (see John 1:1, 14). He specifically pointed out, "His name is called The Word of God" (Revelation 19:13). God's Word is alive, full of power, and active in our innermost person (see Hebrews 4:12). Jesus was the personification of the written and spoken word of God that in the beginning created the heavens and all the planets (see Genesis 1:1–3). As the living Word, Jesus physically and visibly, fully and completely, communicated God to the world. The living Word of God is still creating, correcting, instructing, and speaking life and judgement from Heaven to Earth.

Living Bread

When the Israelites lacked food in the desert, God caused grain to rain down from Heaven to Earth (see Exodus 16:4, Psalm 78:24). The people called the miracle bread manna, and this provision from God sustained them for forty years. Known as the "the staff of life," bread in its many forms is found in virtually every society. Even in those cultures where people don't cook or bake breads, grains serve as a basic food that supports life in general. John recorded Jesus's claim, "I am the living bread which came down from heaven: if any man eat of this bread, he shall live for ever: and the bread that I will give is my flesh, which I will give for the life of the world" (John 6:51). Jesus came not just to give bread, but to be bread—the only bread that truly satisfies. How do we eat the bread from Heaven? Jesus said, "Man shall not live by bread alone, but by every word of God" (Luke 4:4). Jesus, the Living Word is the Living Bread. His Word is still active and moving, and we must ingest it to live. We must read it, study it, and meditate upon it. It must become part of who we are to sustain our souls. The bread of life still comes from Heaven to Earth to feed whoever believes in Him (see John 6:35).

Living Water

Water, or as called by some, "flowing life," transmits life wherever it travels on the earth. Scripture uses water in several metaphors, but John portrayed Jesus as the only true source of living water (see John 4:10, 7:37–39). In Revelation 22:1, John also told of a river of living water as clear as crystal coming out of the throne of God.

Old Testament prophets had spoken of a fountain that would be opened to the house of David "for sin and uncleanness" and identified the Lord as the "fountain of living waters" (see Zechariah 13:1, Jeremiah 2:13). Ezekiel told of waters flowing from God's sanctuary that carry life and healing properties (see Ezekiel 47:1-12). The living water that originates from a heavenly headwater still flows and offers cleansing, renewing, and healing from Heaven to Earth.

Living Light

John declared that in Jesus was "the light of men"—the true light that gives light to everyone in the world (see John 1:4, 9). In a startling presentation, the apostle clarified for all that this light (Jesus) is a revelation of the glory of God (v 14). The light mentioned in John 1:14, as well as Revelation 21:3, can be understood as chosen by John to refer to "the Shekinah"[2]—a term which literally means "the dwelling" and is used for the visible presentation of God as light.[3] Jesus, the light that shone out of darkness, now shines in the hearts of people (see 2 Corinthians 4:6). Like the sun itself, Jesus radiates the light of life that purifies, guides, leads, and transforms. Jesus, the living light, still scatters darkness and reveals God's glory from Heaven to Earth.

Peace

The kingdom of Heaven is a realm of peace governed by the Prince of peace (see Isaiah 9:6-7). Peace involves more than a lack of striving, it includes "wholeness." Jesus offers us peace that goes beyond our sight and circumstances (see John 14:27, Philippians 4:7).

Without "wholeness," you and I would leak. Not only would we lose out on the power and full impact of what God wants to release, but we could possibly pollute the work He is doing through us. Wholeness enables us to become effective conduits that bring Heaven to Earth.

At Jesus's baptism, "the Holy Spirit descended in bodily form like a dove" upon the Lord (see Luke 3:22). The dove is considered a symbol of peace. The government of peace rules in the unseen realm but has made itself available in the here and now. The peace Jesus brought with Him from His kingdom is still being offered to His people on Earth.

Fire

From God's throne flows a river with many streams. If you're like me, you prefer to focus on the river of living water, but the Bible also describes a stream of fire from the same throne (see Daniel 7:9-10). Fire speaks of God's holiness and judgment of sin.

The book of Revelation mentions fire 25 times. In the Old Testament, God responded to prophets and kings by sending fire from Heaven (see Exodus 9:23, 1 Kings 18:38, 1 Chronicles 21:26). On the Day of Pentecost, God's Spirit fell on the believers. As they spoke in unlearned languages, tongues of fire from Heaven accompanied the release of God's Spirit on the Earth (see Acts 2:1-4). God sent and continues to send His fire from Heaven to Earth.

> God's breath releases both life and a fiery stream.

Anointing

Oil, a symbol of the Spirit, significantly finds its origin in Heaven in Jesus Christ, the anointed One (see Acts 10:38). The application of anointing oil sanctifies what was previously considered common. The anointing made everyday things and people sacred. In the Old Testament, oil applied to the prophets looked ahead to the coming Messiah. Oil used today in ordinations and to anoint the sick hearkens back to the One who came from Heaven and allowed Himself to be crushed in Gethsemane (which means oil press). Jesus endured the weight of our sins (see Mark 14:34). His sacrifice offered humanity the opportunity to be holy like He is holy.

The anointing oil symbolizes the healing presence of God. The anointed One, the "Sun of righteousness," rises unto those who fear the name of the Lord. He comes with healing and wholeness in His wings (see Malachi 4:2). This verse tells us that those on whom the "Sun of righteousness" arises shall go forth frolicking as well-fed calves. This connects to the foundational concept of *Kingdom Come*. It relates the presence of God with righteousness, peace, and joy.

The Temple

John wrote about the temple of God in Heaven (see Revelation 11:19). One of the most amazing components in Heaven's temple is God's original ark. God created the pattern for the ark of the covenant to mirror His heavenly throne (see Hebrews 4:16).

Chapter 3: Kingdom Components

The ark of the covenant represented God's habitation among His people—His mercy and His judgment.

Flow

As God's ambassadors, we share what He gives of His kingdom components. What flows from above, we tap into and disperse like the waters seen by Ezekiel that released life and healing (see Ezekiel 4:1, 9). We can become streams that channel Heaven to Earth.

We can't manufacture living water, living light, or living Word. We simply receive and give at God's discretion. First, we must drink the living water ourselves and experience it dwelling within us (see John 4:10, 7:38). Then, we become God's agents charged with seeing others who are thirsty and dry receive living water into their lives (see Isaiah 44:3). When God enlightens us, we gain for ourselves the light of life (see Job 33:30, Psalm 56:13, John 8:12). Our knowledge and experience help us help others receive light for themselves.

Jesus said, "I am the Light of the world. So if you follow me, you won't be stumbling through the darkness, for living light will flood your path" (John 8:12, TLB). The Lord promised that His light will continue to shine ever brighter until we reach the full light of the perfect day when the light of this life gives way to the full splendor of Heaven's radiance (see Proverbs 4:18). Meanwhile, fellow travelers are stumbling in the darkness (see Proverbs 4:19). Paul's admonition to the church echoes today. We, called out of darkness, join with the apostle in telling those among us to awaken, rise from the dead, and receive the light of Christ (see Ephesians 5:14).

Jesus is the answer for the world today. He's living water for the thirsty and light for those stumbling in the dark. He's bread for the hungry and our source for anointing and peace. And you and I must know who we are to properly receive and distribute the kingdom on Earth.

Elijah was powerful because he knew God, His nature, and His ways. He knew what he had access to as a man of God, and he availed himself of it. He made a declaration based on their relationship, and God honored it. Rain ceased for three and a half years, and it fell again when Elijah followed the Lord's direction and presented himself before the king (see 1 Kings 17:1, 18:1, 45). Elijah experienced a miraculous supply of provision when he was fed by ravens and later by a penniless widow (see 1 Kings 17:4, 14). God used him to do many miracles including raising the dead, prophesying, multiplying grain, and parting the Jordan.

When we understand the King, His kingdom, and the components of His kingdom like Elijah did, we can walk in the same boldness. The prophet of old declared among the people, "And the God that answereth by fire, let him be God" (1 Kings 18:24). I believe God will send the fire. He wants to demonstrate His power on the earth, and He wants to do it through people like you and me who stay connected, aware, and open to speaking with boldness and authority. Then we will see the components of the kingdom released in the earth so that God is known and served among the people.

4

Kingdom Access

Elisha prayed, and said, Lord, I pray thee, open his eyes, that he may see. And the Lord opened the eyes of the young man; and he saw: and, behold, the mountain was full of horses and chariots of fire round about Elisha.
2 Kings 6:17

The kingdom of God produces everything you and I need to thrive spiritually. We know the kingdom is near, but at times, God and His resources seem far away. How do we access living water, living light, or the power and peace of God right now when we need it? Knowledge alone isn't enough. Simply having desire doesn't open a spiritual faucet that releases Heaven's supply, so we must believe God Himself will show us how to fulfill His plan for our lives.

It would be wonderful if I could tell you I discovered an unfailing formula, a mystical method, guaranteed to work every time you need help from on high. *Just recite this phrase and end it with these three words, and the request is granted.* If only life were that simple. What I have discovered in the last twenty-five years is that, yes, there are principles to know and follow, but the key that opens the door to Heaven and its resources is only found when we know the God who *is* the door. Jesus proclaimed Himself to be "the Door," and He invites us to cross the threshold (see John 10:7). He already paid the price for our entry (see Hebrews 10:19). With the authority He imparts to His own, you and I have access to spiritual realms previously unknown to us.

When we think of a key, it brings to mind a small piece of metal shaped into two main parts: a bow (the usually curved and sometimes ornate top) and a blade (the metal shaft with ridges and cuts). An important thing to remember about a key is that it's made to match the projections built inside a specific keyhole. We could cut hundreds of keys with every good intention—keys that might even seem to slip into a lock but fail to turn it to an open position. To walk through the spiritual doors before us, we must know what fits the "Lockmaker's" keyhole.

The New Testament uses the word "key" metaphorically to indicate authority. When Jesus bequeathed the keys of the kingdom of Heaven to His church, He opened access to places that were previously closed to humanity. Peter's proclamation of Jesus's true identity triggered the release of the keys. God revealed to Peter that Jesus was not just a virtuous teacher who performed miracles. He was the anointed, the Christ, the Messiah, the Son of the living God (see Matt 16:16-19).[4]

I have spent years studying gates, doors, and keys. I believe I have some answers, but the most important thing I can tell you is this:

Accessing Heaven means knowing Jesus.

The first Passover and Exodus from Egypt served as a template of the true deliverance that would come through the sacrifice Jesus made at Calvary. The night before the Jews left Egypt, they participated in a ritual sacrifice. At the original Passover, while still slaves, Israelite families slew a lamb and applied its blood to the doorposts of their homes. God was about to release judgment and death, but He told Moses, "When I see the blood, I will pass over you" (Exodus 12:13).

At the appointed time—the same time of year the Jews participated in their annual Passover celebration—Jesus was crucified (see John 18:39). His blood stained the wooden beams of the cross on which He hung. Jesus, the Lamb of God who took away the sin of the world, gave Himself to open the way for those who would enter Heaven (see John 1:29).

The blood of Jesus did its work those many years ago and even now transcends time and circumstance. It continues to triumph, outstrip, and outdo the work of evil. The sacrifice Jesus made not only opened Heaven, it maintains access to Heaven for believers in our day and will continue until His second coming. Through the work of the cross accomplished by Jesus's death and resurrection, the Lord touched three dimensions at once—the earth, the air, and the heavens. When He cried, "It is finished," darkness filled the skies and the Spirit of Jesus stripped the prince of the air of the keys of death and hell (see Revelation 1:18, Colossians 2:15).

Christ's blood trickled to the ground (humanity's dwelling place) and a powerful earthquake suddenly and unexpectedly shook the earth. Rocks split and the veil of the temple was torn in two from top to bottom (see Matthew 27:51). The tremor struck fear in a Roman Centurion who said, "Truly this was the Son of God!" (Matthew 27:54). Through the work of the cross, Jesus offered pardon for His people. He entered the holy place in Heaven with the only consideration on which any person can receive pardon, His own blood (see Hebrews 9:12). I say again, the work of the cross touched three dimensions at once. In so doing, Jesus declared His authority and victory over the earth, air, and heavens.

Kingdom Faith

The unseen kingdom of Heaven is reachable only through faith in Jesus. Faith is a broad term that expresses a range of concepts including belief, hope, and trust. Faith is a fruit of the Spirit and a weapon of warfare (a shield). Faith is a virtue that originates with God, while being itself, a gift of God (see 1 Corinthians 12:8-9). Faith is each of these things, but it is, at the heart of the matter, a divinely inspired knowing or "faith perception" of what is not seen with the human eye.

God gave to each person a measure of faith. It's a small key, but it can open great doors into an unseen spiritual realm.

> Faith is a divinely inspired knowledge of Jesus.

Faith both believes and obeys God's Word for salvation and for life. Without faith, we can't access or please God, but with faith we know He exists and "He is a rewarder of them that diligently seek him" (Hebrews 11:6). Over and again, particularly in Hebrews 11, God's Word commends men and women for their faith made apparent through their obedience. Faith impacts our perspective. Believers look to the future and obey in the now. Through eyes of faith, we acquire personal confidence that God makes good on His promises even when we face challenges or can't see what He is doing.

Faith Factors

Everyone has an occasional struggle with faith. It's only human. Faith can falter when what we believe and what we're experiencing fail to reconcile. Thankfully, God knows our frames. He knows our emotions and offers grace when we stumble. Yet, we know faith is very important to the Lord. Jesus asked, "When the Son of man cometh, shall he find faith on the earth?" (Luke 18:8).

Could it be possible to love God and yet lack faith? Might the same people who regularly attend religious services lack the type of faith Jesus is looking for? Could a person's very sincere "spirituality" be based on superstitions or falsities that fly in the face of faith in the God who created the heavens and the earth? Could even the good members of the church believe in God but conduct themselves in ways unfaithful to their previously professed convictions?

Paul wrote that the three greatest virtues are faith, hope, and love; and then he specified the greatest of the three is love (see 1 Corinthians 13:13). Since love is the most important virtue, why wouldn't Jesus ask if He would find love in the earth when He returned? Perhaps the answer is found in the writings of Paul to the Galatians. He taught the church:

Faith works by love.

Paul's words above are also translated that faith works "by the means of love" or "on account of love." Faith and love intrinsically connect. Faith is confidence in God that displays itself in tender affection, warm thoughts, and devoted conduct, even in miraculous demonstrations of the supernatural.

Our hearts long to believe, yet we sometimes struggle with skewed perspectives. Instead of being led by the Spirit, we focus on self or allow carnal reasoning to dominate. Although struggles can cause our thoughts to stray, Isaiah reminds us that we have a heritage as servants of the Lord (see Isaiah 54:17). God delights in blessing His children. We can walk with confidence. We can rest assured that God provides the faith we need when we choose to follow Him. As we focus our vision on things above, we bring straying thoughts back into alignment. We remind ourselves that nothing can triumph over those who walk with the Lord. No weapon works. No accusation sticks.

Walking in the Spirit is another way of expressing the concept of living Christ-like faith. This means having a continual awareness of God's presence—a nonstop, God-consciousness that insists on pursuing the things of Heaven over the things of Earth. It's a type of faith that compels us to walk in new life with Jesus and demonstrate God's love and power to save, heal, and deliver.

Today's church should experience the same powerful demonstrations of faith as those performed by the 1st century church. The early church repeated everything Jesus did. Blind eyes opened (see Acts 9:8). The lame walked (see Acts 3:1-10). Not only were the dead raised to life, but the living dropped dead when they dared lie to the Holy Ghost (see Acts 9:36-43; 5:1-10).

The apostles' success directly correlated with their experience in the Upper Room. They believed in Jesus and obeyed His directions. They assembled themselves, prayed, and sought the Lord until He endued them with power from on high (see Luke 24:49; Acts 1:8; 2:1–4). These believers, men and women, knew Jesus through close, personal, spiritual encounters. Their faith led them to realize for themselves the truth of Jesus's words: All things are possible to them that believe.

Faith Governs

We see in both the Old and New Testaments that God's priority is and always has been kingdom first. He placed Adam and Eve in a Garden and gave them everything. Their only restriction in all the world was to one tree, but the serpent turned their attention away from God's perfect blessing to desire the one thing they didn't have permission to partake of. God's always held something separate for Himself so man would choose to honor Him. When men take what belongs to God, they choose the kingdom of self or the kingdom of the world (for themselves). God has always called His people to adhere to a "separateness" that intertwines with holiness. He said the gate to spiritual life is straight and the way is narrow (see Matthew 7:14). We see holiness expressed in the New Testament concept of "seek ye first the kingdom." When we honor the kingdom ways, we keep the flow from Heaven to Earth unplugged and unpolluted. When we seek our own, we plug, pollute, and dam the flow that could release healing into our world.

While walking in the Spirit is a moment-by-moment experience, spiritual laws govern God's kingdom. There are right ways and wrong ways to live, including in worship, fasting, and the ways we treat others. Scripture outlines these principles and then offers beautiful promises to those who live in agreement with them: "If you do these things, God will shed his own glorious light upon you. He will heal you; your godliness will lead you forward, goodness will be a shield before you, and the glory of the Lord will protect you from behind" (Isaiah 58:8, TLB).

In the same way that a river must have banks, our Spirit-walks necessitate governmental boundaries. If we learn the guidelines that govern the kingdom of God and walk in love, our faith will be set in motion and God will move on our behalf. When we keep ourselves "unspotted" by a continual washing of the Word, not only will healing waters flow, but we will grow in maturity and vitality as sure as the trees grew alongside the river in Ezekiel's vision. Those who delight in the law of God and meditate in it day and night become like trees planted by rivers of living water (see Psalm 1:2–3).

When we abide in the Spirit, in agreement with the Word, we find ourselves walking with an authority that needs no introduction. When Jesus came on the scene, devils trembled and people were affected. Some were attracted to the light and

> The closer we draw to Jesus, our passage becomes increasingly more narrow and straight, but greater yet is the resulting power and anointing.

others were repelled by it. When Jesus entered a room, the devils didn't confront Him, they got out of the way. Spirits know who's in charge. At the synagogue, Jesus met a man with an unclean spirit who cried out in a loud voice, "Let us alone! Are you come to destroy us?" Jesus rebuked the devil and he came out of the man (see Luke 4:33-36). Demons are real. I'm not looking to engage them unnecessarily, but we are confronted at times by demonic spirits. We don't have to be afraid. When we stay armored in the name of the Lord, demons know we have authority over them. They also know those who do not.

Our personal faith and relationship with God is more than a profession of formulas that worked for someone else. That idea turned out poorly for the seven sons of Sceva (see Acts 19:14-17). When we believe *in* God and recognize who we *are* in Him, we can speak what we believe in our hearts with our mouths, and demons have to flee. If we're not living in agreement with God's plan, we shouldn't attempt to cast out demons (refer back to the sons of Sceva), but if we're submitted to God, we can resist the devil, and he will flee (see James 4:7).

I want to take a moment to share something that happened the day I wrote this chapter. I'd taken a scheduled writing hiatus, so my mind hadn't been on any specific material for a few days. From a sound sleep, I awoke to the awareness of a dark presence in my room. I'm not sure if it was one demon or more, but I was paralyzed as I emerged from a foggy sleep to the sensation of being gnawed on by an evil entity. I can't really describe how the being looked, except that it was dark and creepy, and chewing incessantly on my left shoulder. The presence somehow paralyzed me physically, and I literally lost the power to move any part of my body. I couldn't speak. In my mind I began proclaiming the name of Jesus. Something broke.

Of course, I wondered the reason behind the attack. I do believe it was related to the writing of this book, but I can't say for sure. As I considered what happened, though, and what concepts I could learn from this event, several things came to mind:

1. <u>Power emits from our spirits</u>. Even while I lay on the bed unable to respond, something in my spirit moved into the spirit world that caused

the demon to let go. This is true in spiritual warfare, but it's also true in general principle. What we think about, allow our minds to dwell on and carry within us, emanates from us into the world around us. According to Proverbs, what resides in a person's heart issues forth from the inner person and transfers to the outer world like a gate opening to a passageway or a fountain flowing (see Proverbs 4:23).

2. <u>It's not always negative conduct that attracts demons</u>. I wasn't living in willful sin or rebellion. In fact, I was pressing into God and this work. Sometimes our positive, forward momentum attracts attention in the spirit world that we never intended to activate. I've heard stories of men and women used mightily by God who were approached by demons and even held conversations with them. An attack won't always mean we've done something wrong. It could mean we're moving into enemy territory and they're responding. Demonic spirits strike against us to thwart what they see coming before we see the spiritual progress we're making.

3. <u>God is greater</u>. The words "greater is He in me than He that is in the world" rang in my spirit as I thought about this encounter. Without uttering a word, without moving a hand, the Spirit within me overtook the spirit that had come against me. It was a decisive victory. We have power to defeat the enemy. We really do.

4. <u>The priority of the unseen</u>. This encounter emphasized a point we've been discussing in this book: things happen first in the spirit world. After merely thinking the name of Jesus in my spirit, I was able to speak and move. But it happened in the unseen realm first.

Faith Sees

We began this chapter with a discussion on knowing Jesus. Knowing necessitates perception—an awareness or seeing. Faith has eyes to see the unseen where regular vision is useless. We'll cover more on this subject in Section 2, but as it relates to kingdom access, it's through faith vision or spiritual awareness that God imparts revelation. God opens eyes and brings focus. He gives images, visions, and words. This faith perception is a primary tool to break the power of internal and external distractions that compete for our attention, our service, and even our devotion.

God has dreams for His people. Isaiah wrote, "For since the beginning of the world men have not heard, nor perceived by the ear, neither hath the eye seen, O God, beside thee, what he hath prepared for him that wait for him" (Isaiah 64:4).

Paul referenced this verse in the New Testament to affirm that human wisdom, based on human observation, logic, and reason, has value, but it can't compete with the wisdom that comes from knowing the hidden things of God (see 1 Corinthians 2:9, Isaiah 55:8–9). I once heard Eli Hernandez say, "Close your eyes, and you'll be surprised what you see." Jeff Arnold also addressed this topic when he said, "Look at the invisible to experience the impossible."

God opened Balaam's eyes to see spiritual events occurring around Him, and I believe He desires for your eyes and mine to open to a clearer vision (see Numbers 22:31). One morning, before I opened my eyes, I woke up mentally rehearsing the words of Psalm 19:14. I began to wonder how the words of my mouth or the meditations of my heart could be acceptable in the sight of God. Does God *see* our words? I turned to my concordance and realized the word translated "sight" means "presence."

God's presence is everywhere as we discussed in the segment on the "all-seeing eye." We live our lives in His presence. Not only is His eye on you and me, He wants us to be aware—to see and to know Him as He really is. This knowledge enables us to fulfill the mission of the church.

In Revelation 4:1, John spoke of a door open to Heaven. The apostle observed things you and I could hardly imagine. He witnessed interactions between God, angels, and mankind. Can you imagine standing at an open

> **God brings Heaven to Earth through the work of the church.**

door and peeking into Heaven? Inside we would see such beauty. There would be no sickness, not even fatigue. We would see only light and not even one shadow. No chaos, but peace. No anger, but love. We would see the glory of God and wonders no words could express.

The tabernacle of Moses had only one door. Within the sacred tent, a veil divided the space into two rooms: the holy place and the most holy place where the presence of God dwelt among the people. In the first temple built by Solomon, a veil was also erected between the holy place and the most holy place. We don't have detailed plans of the second temple, but Scripture clarifies a veil was hung in its interior even though the ark was no longer in the possession of the Israelites. When Jesus died, on His exit from Earth, something supernatural tore through the veil and ripped it open. Jesus displayed the emptiness of religious ceremonialism and revealed the absence of the presence of God. As His body lay inanimate in the grave, Jesus was at work in the spiritual realm. And when His Spirit reentered

His body on Resurrection morning, everything had changed. The power of sin and death were broken once and for all for them who would believe. After forty days, Jesus, the King of glory, returned to Heaven in bodily form. Angels rejoiced as He opened the door that signaled a transition from Earth to Heaven—like the door John had seen in His vision.

Yes, dark spiritual strongholds remain in the earth, and "gates of enemies" remain for God's people to topple, but greater is He that is in us. He is greater than any demonic spirit that vies for power in the church, and the church is destined to advance against the gates of the enemy. Jesus is coming back for a triumphant church. We are victorious because the Lord strengthens His people and makes us impervious to attacks, "strong like a fortified city that cannot be captured, like an iron pillar and heavy gates of brass" (see Jeremiah 1:17-18, TLB).

The principles exemplified in secular or satanic governments of this world are not those designed by God for His church. Neither Satan nor sin holds power over a believer's life unless the believer grants it. Satan doesn't "make" you or me or anyone do anything. Our own lusts lead us astray. When we give in to our desires, we create openings for demonic influence in our lives. The devil is an imitator. He copies the way of the Waymaker, but the door he opens leads to judgment and eternal separation from God. Our faith *is* our victory that overcomes the world (see 1 John 5:4). Our faith in Jesus makes us victorious right now.

Entering with Thanksgiving

We've discussed the access provided by faith and obedience, but is there a proper method to connect with the divine? The psalmist said worshippers should enter God's gates with thanksgiving and His courts (the place of His abiding presence) with praise (see Psalm 100:4). David wrote of the gladness in his heart at the mere invitation to go to God's house (see Psalm 122:1). He's also credited with saying that one day in God's courts is better than a thousand anywhere else (see Psalm 84:10). In fact, David valued God's presence so much he cursed his own wife when she devalued the ark and his worship of God.

Ingratitude offends God. Why? Because He's the source of all. Ingratitude reveals disbelief. When we're ungrateful, we must not really believe God's Word—that He has a plan for our good and that all things work together for good (see Jeremiah 29:11, Romans 8:28). Complaining expresses agreement with God's adversaries. Think of it this way: unthankfulness = unbelief = unholy, and unholiness breaks communion with God.

God honors gratitude. Gratitude reveals our faith in His goodwill toward humanity. Appreciation affects our atmosphere, and we want to bring the atmosphere of Heaven to Earth. When we thank and praise God it fosters greater faith. And as we've been discussing, faith walks us into the domain of the divine.

A Master Key

Out of the mouth of babes and sucklings has thou ordained strength because of thine enemies, that thou mightest still the enemy and the avenger.
Psalm 8:2

Psalm 8 is an incredibly significant portion of Scripture. It's a celebration of God's superiority that speaks of His glory as well as the glory of mankind. In it, the psalmist reveals humanity's position in creation and our God-ordained authority that reflects glory back to our excellent God. The content of this psalm may in fact serve as a "master key." A master key opens many locks, each of which has its own key, but which a master key can override. Psalm 8 reveals an overarching conceptualization of God, humanity, fallen angels, and man's destiny. Let's look at this master key cut by the psalmist's words and see how an awareness of its concepts might build our faith.

Psalm 8

[1] O Lord, our Lord, how excellent is thy name in all the earth!
who hast set thy glory above the heavens.
[2] Out of the mouth of babes and sucklings hast thou ordained strength because
of thine enemies, that thou mightest still the enemy and the avenger.
[3] When I consider thy heavens, the work of thy fingers,
the moon and the stars, which thou hast ordained;
[4] What is man, that thou art mindful of him?
and the son of man, that thou visitest him?
[5] For thou hast made him a little lower than the angels,
and hast crowned him with glory and honour.

> *[6] Thou madest him to have dominion over the works of thy hands; thou hast put all things under his feet:*
> *[7] All sheep and oxen, yea, and the beasts of the field;*
> *[8] The fowl of the air, and the fish of the sea, and whatsoever passeth through the paths of the seas.*
> *[9] O Lord our Lord, how excellent is thy name in all the earth!*

Psalm 8 provides an understanding of who we are and what our purpose in life truly is. So much hinges on our ability to grasp and live out the concepts in this psalm. When we embrace them, we're empowered to pivot into a more dynamic walk and ministry.

Verse 1

Psalm 8 is, above all else, a celebration of God. He's not just *the* Lord, but rather, He's *our* Lord. Our God is Lord over all of us and all things. His excellent name is His signature. He's signed His artwork which is all of the earth. His name, however, is more than an autograph or a title. It speaks to His character, essence, and what He's like. His name refers to the "person" of God and His multifaceted attributes including the glory He has placed in the heavens.

Verse 2

After rehearsing God's magnificence and greatness, David took what seems to be a random, sharp turn. His next words addressed babies, toddlers, enemies, and avengers. Seemingly out of the blue, David stated that little children have power against God's enemies. That is mind blowing. This is a key verse.

There are enemies in this world. And there is an avenger. This enemy cares nothing about us. He's God's enemy. It doesn't seem fair. We didn't enter this life with a chip on our shoulders against anyone; but when we were born, we had an enemy—this avenger. Satan attempts to get even with God through people. Because of Satan's pride and rebellion, God ejected him out of Heaven so fast his glowing form looked like lightning striking from above (see Luke 10:18). He's still angry and on the prowl, even though he knows he's been stripped of any long-lasting power or authority.

When the Bible speaks of babes and sucklings, it refers to more than newborns. It includes those still small enough to be carried in someone's arms. It refers to those who are naturally unable to accomplish much without the help of another. God's Word tells us that if we have faith and trust Him in the same way small children trust their mothers to feed them, He will still our enemies. He will silence them.

God takes young, undeveloped believers who simply love Him for who He is and makes them a force to display His true superiority to His enemy. God is gracious, good, and excellent, and He has an excellent plan for you and me. This verse tells us that God established this plan to show rebellious, high-minded, manipulative Satan and the fallen angels, a powerful truth:

God is able to defeat His greatest foe with the weakest and most vulnerable member of His family.

When the enemy sees the worship and childlike faith of God's children, there is nothing he can say.

There's a principle at work here that shuts down the enemy's accusations. When the Bible speaks about infants, at times it refers to more than the biologically young. When Moses spoke of God's children, he included people from any and every generation. In the New Testament John called these adult believers little children (see 1 John 4:4). How did grown men and women become little children? At Pentecost they were born of the water and Spirit, but not in infancy. Quite the opposite, they were brought into the kingdom as rational adults capable of making their own decisions to trust God with a childlike faith.

On the day of Pentecost, it wasn't the eloquent rabbinical teachers God filled with the Holy Ghost. He poured out His Spirit on those who were "young" in faith. The firstborn of the New Testament church were uneducated men and women—the first to utter the praises of God in languages unknown to them. God used humble, faith-filled men and women to establish a vibrant, healthy, and powerful church. As New Testament believers, we belong to this same church, and we have access to the same power over the enemy.

Satan's primary tactic to defeat God's people is to attack our faith.

Satan entices us to rely on our own know-how and power. He prods believers to function as mavericks rather than accepting with thanks who God made them to be. If he can convince us to be Lone Ranger worshippers, he can eventually isolate us, one by one, from regular fellowship with the community of believers. He plants thoughts that make people feel unwanted and tries to convince them that they don't belong in the church. He attempts to drive wedges between the people of God. We need to recognize this tactic for what it is and consistently join ourselves with other believers.

The accuser is still accusing. The enemy is still attacking, but when we carry God's Spirit, we take on stealth, spiritual gear—including a shield of faith that quenches all the fiery darts of the evil one. Does this guarantee us immunity to attack? No. But what Satan hurls at us is not going to take us down. Our shields suppress the impact of the enemy's weapons, and our childlike faith extinguishes the flames.

You and I can't take on the devil on our own and win. He's been around for at least thousands of years. We're just mortal people. We don't have the experience to take on this ancient enemy in our own strength. But if we turn to the Lord with childlike faith and adoration, our Father can do what we, on our own, cannot. This is the means God ordained to strengthen His people and give them rest. This is the method God uses to bring to an end the purposes of the enemy. It is faith—simple faith.

It's not faith in the simple, because God is complex. It's not simple-minded faith, because God is sophisticated, wise, and brilliant. It's a straightforward, uncomplicated, elementary faith in a God who's so big, so multifaceted, so "everything we need," that we can simply trust Him.

When we feel the need to still an avenger and stop the enemy from moving in our lives, we should pray in the Spirit. Worship in Spirit and truth. When we know who God is, who we are, and who the enemy is, we know we were created with a divine purpose. And that includes walking with dominion and authority.

Psalm 8 tells us the creator of the universe ordained a special role for humanity. When He created the world, He made human beings to have a certain place in His divine order just below the angels who serve around His throne. He didn't change His mind when Adam and Eve failed. God didn't change His mind about David when he fell and fell hard—more than once. God always knew humans would fail, and He knows we will, too.

God is bigger than our mistakes and failures. Jeff Arnold once said, "Your mistakes don't disqualify you from being mightily used of God. . . . Inside a mistake is a doorway to discovery. . . . You may have made a mistake, but you ain't one. You may have failed, but you aren't a failure."

God's plans are greater than our mistakes. His grace is greater. How excellent! If we'll humble ourselves and call on the Lord, we can fulfill the purposes of God and enjoy victory over our enemy. But to do this, we must double back and do an about face when tempted to act like Satan and do things our own way. We can't succeed by trying to take for ourselves something that was not created or intended for us. Instead of an earthly perspective focused on who we are *not* or what we do *not* have, we should celebrate who we are! Creations of God made with dignity and purpose.

Verse 3

When we look at the intricacies of creation and the complexities of God's design, we join with David who observed in awe the majesty of God. We wonder at the work He prepared and appointed. God created the moon and the stars and put them in their places. Imagine what it must have been like at the dawn of time. Envision God picking up Jupiter between His thumb and forefinger and placing it with a twist (so it would spin) right where He wanted it to be in the Solar System. Next, follow Jupiter with Mars, and then Venus, Saturn, the earth, the moon, and stars. God put each celestial body on its course and set each one in motion. Then He turned His attention to the earth. He carved out landscapes and sculpted mountains. He filled the oceans, and all He made reflected the vastness of His glory, name, purposes, and excellence. The handiwork of God in the heavenlies still silently speaks to the greatness of God's glory. It led David to contemplate how insignificant mankind truly is and the wonder of God's care.

Verse 4

After David considered God's work in the heavens, he asked the Lord, "What is man?" Just compare the magnitude of the universe with this teeny, tiny, wee little person. What is man? I think it's significant David didn't ask, "Who is man?" Pride asks, "Who am I?" Humility asks, "What am I? How can I serve?" Sometimes people get so caught up in discovering "who they are" they don't fulfill their God-given purposes.

When David mentioned man, he wasn't referring to one person. He included all of mankind, both men and women, who are fearfully and wonderfully made, but who are also frail and weak. This psalm includes you and me. It included David. And it even included Jesus. When David asked, "What is man? And the son of man?" who was he talking about?

David's beautiful question doesn't address the state of man at his creation. Instead, it refers to his fallen state. David was amazed that God looked at fallen man, past, present, and future; but He was also looking ahead to the "Man" to come. The Messiah from Heaven, a member of David's own earthly lineage would come to

Earth. He would return God's glory and humanity's dignity and position using means that He envisioned long before David's time.

Even though man failed, God cared and faithfully watched over him. God still had His eye on David, and He still has His eye on you and me. David contrasted man's pitiful state with the glory of all God is. What is man? What are mere mortals that God is mindful of us? That He would set His love and affection upon us and keep us in His merciful view? That He would care to visit us from generation to generation? No wonder David couldn't help but repeat himself, "How excellent!"

> God is mindful of us. He's willing to visit us today.

I'm so glad God hasn't forgotten us. We have so much more than a leather-bound letter filled with empty promises. Our God is a promise maker and a promise keeper. The Word says He made us a little lower than the heavenly beings, but then He crowned us with glory and honor. At one time, Satan also was crowned with glory and honor which reveals the necessity to recognize the significant roles humility and obedience play in retaining what God gives us.

We belong to the family of God. You and I are holy siblings, each with a holy calling. The power and pull of the things of this world are under our feet because the Son of man, Jesus Christ, visited the sons and daughters of man and restored what was broken. Jesus has already defeated every one of His enemies and put all things under His feet (see 1 Corinthians 15:27). Someday soon, everything will wrap up into one final, glorious victory. Until that time, we work to see His kingdom come and His will done in the earth as it is in Heaven.

In the garden of Eden, when God granted dominion over the earth to Adam and Eve, He transferred an invisible scepter from Heaven to Earth that fell from man's hands when he succumbed to Satan's deception. But God, in the very first book of the Bible, promised to crush the head of the enemy (see Genesis 3:15). God has His eye on mankind and His arms are open wide to us. Even when He sees darkness, hardness, and sin in our lives, He knows we're frail, and He's willing to come and visit us if we will turn to Him with the faith of a child.

He knocks at the door of our hearts and invites us in. He offers access and the freedom to continue in relationship with Him—into wholeness, peace, and power. It all comes back to faith. When we come to Jesus with simple faith, like children, babes and sucklings, we won't argue about what He asks us to do. We just do it because we believe He knows best. This should be such an integral part of our lives and evidence our childlike trust in the greatest parent ever.

This is the foundation. David knew it. The writer of Hebrews knew it. The apostle Paul knew it. Peter and all the apostles experienced it. With childlike faith and humility, we approach God and partake of His own majesty. By using the insignificant ones to defeat His enemies, God reveals His power and glory. He rules the world through the weakness of man, and that is excellent indeed. There's much more to discuss on the power of worship in chapters to come, but for now, know this: The enemy wants to capture God's people and make them trophies on his shelf, but God wants to use us to tread on the enemy and rule with Him now and in Heaven forever. He's given us the keys to unlock everything we ever wanted, but we have to pick them up, put them in the locks, and turn the tumblers.

6

Kingdom Conduits

*However, we possess this precious treasure [the divine Light of the Gospel]
in [frail, human] vessels of earth, that the grandeur and
exceeding greatness of the power may be shown to be from God
and not from ourselves.*
2 Corinthians 4:7, AMPC

In 2013, Doug Klinedinst saw waterfalls in the sanctuary of my home church; one on each side of the platform, and one huge waterfall at the back. Prior to that, Claudette Walker had a vision of many arrows coming into the church. She saw a geyser burst through and blow a hole in the roof and silver arrows (representing people) coming off of the fountain in the courtyard placed in honor of my late husband, Pete. Not long after, I saw a vision of a river running through the church altar. It reminded me of Ezekiel's vision of the stream in the house of God. These three visions, given in the same church building, share a common motif that correlates to the stained-glass window concept mentioned in Chapter 1. What happens inside the church is meant to have an effect outside the church.

When I saw the vision, I had an impression of God renewing the flow of water in the vessels of His people. I appreciate the blessings the church receives from God, and God means for us to enjoy them, but we also have a responsibility to distribute what we've been given: this treasure God placed within our earthly vessels. God designed humanity, you and me, to serve as walking wells fed by His lively spring.

In 1 Corinthians 2, Paul transmitted an incredible amount of information to the church at large. This one chapter includes great teaching on faith, the demonstration of God's Spirit and power, old God-secrets now revealed, spiritual discernment, and having the mind of Christ. In 1 Corinthians 2:9 Paul spoke of the things man had not yet seen or heard, but just three verses later he said, "Now we have received, not the spirit of the world, but the spirit which is of God; that we might know the things that are freely given to us of God" (1 Corinthians 2:12).

God desires to teach His people Himself. He's given to us a precious treasure: divine light carried in our human vessels. He gave us His Spirit, not that we would be puffed up, but that it would be evident that the light within us emanates from His greatness and power. Just as the living water comes from an unseen spiritual source (see John 7:37–38), the light of the gospel shines from the same source. Spirit-filled believers are meant to serve as conduits of the glory and presence of God.

A conduit produces nothing on its own. It simply conveys and supplies from one location to another.

A Current of Power

Within *Kingdom Come* we follow a pattern Jesus established: through the depth of many illustrations, we have an opportunity for greater understanding. When it comes to the subject of kingdom conduits, we look not only at examples of water, light, and oil, but also to electrical power. We see evidence of this electrical supply in the lightning flashes proceeding from God's throne.

In our natural world, lightning forms inside clouds in the earth's atmosphere. Ice crystals rub together to create a channel of negative electrical charge. It takes only a fraction of a second for an electric channel to originate and sculpt a complex, jagged bolt. The initial hop from the clouds to the sky (called a stepped leader) starts the process, but only goes so far before another leader forms, and then another, creating a magnificent, one-of-a-kind pattern. As a negatively charged channel descends, a channel of positive charge reaches up from the earth in attraction.

An average lightning bolt creates approximately one billion joules of energy. That's enough energy to power a 60-watt light bulb for six months. I don't know how often lightning flashes in Heaven, but Earth's atmosphere hosts about 1.5 billion lightning flashes each year. That's a lot of power!

Lightning becomes visible when the channel from the heavens meets the channel from the earth.

Not everyone has first-hand experience with the power of a lightning strike from the heavens, but each of us has likely experienced contact with a lesser-powered lightning bolt: static electricity. When we shuffle our feet on a carpeted floor, we pick up extra electrons. The charge we generate by the friction of our feet against the flooring moves up our legs. When we reach for a metal doorknob, the electrons we've accumulated jump to the doorknob creating a tiny lightning bolt. You might even hear a buzz (a mini-thunder) and feel heat which is always a component when electrical charges move.

Electricity is a form of magnetism. When one magnetic force senses a conductor approaching, it responds to the attraction by jumping in an arc to make contact with the conductor. This magnetism makes it possible, according to the Canadian Center for Occupational Health and Safety, for a person to experience electrocution without physically coming into contact with a power line. Proximity alone to an exposed power line may result in electricity arcing through the air and into a person on the ground.

The psalmist wrote: "The Lord looks down in love, bending over heaven's balcony. God looks over all of Adam's sons and daughters, looking to see if there are any who are wise with insight—any who search for him, wanting to please him" (Psalm 53:2, TPT). What attracts God as He looks upon the earth? Psalm 50:23 tells us true praise and righteous living honor Him and reflect His glory back to Him.

The Hebrew word for praise in this verse refers to an offering of thanksgiving. The root word, *yadah*, literally means to throw and relates to extending a hand. God wants us to know His hand is continually reaching to His people. And with His hand, He brings Himself, His possessions, and His power.

> To attract the power of God, we send charges of praise upward to the heavens.

Conduit

Scripture exemplifies the conduit principle in many ways. A vine is one of them. Vines differ from our previous examples of rivers, power lines, and lightning channels; but they share a commonality of purpose. Each draws from one source and transfers what it receives to another.

While at a ladies retreat on the Michigan campground, I switched on a microphone to lead pre-service prayer, but there was no sound. The controls were set. I checked the sound system, and then the power source. The main breaker was open and the mic switched on. People were praying, but there was no power to run the equipment. I didn't know what to do except move ahead until someone with more expertise than I arrived. I discovered later there was a connection issue with one of the circuit breakers.

Everything had appeared functional, but it wasn't. A necessary connection had been broken and no matter how prepared the prayer leaders were or how advanced the equipment, the amplification system was rendered useless.

My son does work in Information Technology. As part of his job, he recently spent several days installing conduit on a new construction site. One night as we sat chatting about his assignment, I said, "Stop talking. I've to get a paper and pen."

Conduit is a tube that creates a protective pathway for the IT wires laid behind the scenes. It's necessary for all the communication, computer, media, and other technology used in the building. It surprised me the amount of detailed forethought and planning required. Before any construction begins, plans are drawn that include consideration of future building growth, expansion, and maintenance. As my son explained his job, including climbing a ladder to install conduit hidden in the ceiling, my thoughts turned to *Kingdom Come.*

In the physical construction of buildings, flexible communications wires run through conduit planned for by an architect, implemented by builders, and ultimately used by a team working in the building. Despite the fact they're unseen by the employees, the conduit hidden behind walls and ceilings and under floors all powerfully connect them to one source. One access point provides the power that routes through firewalls, modems, and switches to direct communications from a global network to exact locations.

The Fountain

Linguists in archaic times used the word *conduit* to indicate a fountain. We've looked at the kingdom (the source) and now at the conduit (the vessel).

What opens the tap to release Heaven on Earth? We must will what God wills.

We will discuss this concept in detail in Chapter 14, but for now, consider the valve on the water lines in a house. Under a kitchen sink, a pipe connects the basin to the water supply. To turn the water on, simply open the lever on the valve. Water flow increases or decreases depending on the size of the opening created with the handle. A full 90-degree turn shuts it down completely or will open it to full capacity. I've had experiences at drinking fountains that either brought me in close contact with porcelain or left me wiping water off my forehead. One fountain, depending on the position of the handle, has the potential for zero flow, a trickle, or a projectile stream.

Life happens to each of us. We want to flow with the Holy Ghost, but distractions and sin can shut us down. Carnality and disbelief close us off. In full public confession, I share that I struggled during the writing of this book. Without warning, and right in the middle of the Covid-19 global pandemic, my already-chaotic life became a conundrum. Yes, 2020 slowed my travel schedule to a halt, but my family's foot traffic in and out the house took what previously moved like a winding country road on a Sunday afternoon and transformed it into a divided highway at rush hour. Not only was the house suddenly full of people who couldn't go to work, but I was pressed to find time to record video messages and other materials needed for ministry or speaking engagements. Social distancing restrictions required that we relocate a special family event that took months to plan. This created another list of unanticipated responsibilities. Sadly, to complicate the matter, the virus touched and even took the lives of people important to me. I struggled with balance, and to be honest, I didn't always maintain it "just so." In my frustration I cried out to God and received a surprising but very powerful answer.

> In the kingdom of God, dying to self-government opens the channel so righteousness, peace, and joy can flow out in pure ministry.

If *Kingdom Come* doesn't work in everyday life, it doesn't work at all.

My private time was suffering, too. I certainly love public worship gatherings and ministry, but I function best when I have sufficient quiet time with the Lord. I sit in my rocking chair, marinate in His Word, and saturate in His Spirit. I study and journal, ruminate and pray. It's so easy to hear God then and there. But what about in the distractions? Where we live? When the phone rings? When the demands of life hit us? When the storms rage? When the enemy comes against us? We must learn how to keep the tap open.

We addressed major blockages above, but what about the little foxes that come and eat away at our vines (see Song of Solomon 2:15)? Whatever form our predator takes, "foxes" left unattended will injure blossoms of faith that should be guarded. Little foxes spoil vines and waste vineyards. Little (and not-so-little) distractions damage the vine—a symbolic representation of our abiding communion with God. If we fail to contend with the little foxes, they'll bite off the shoots of new growth and chew away at the roots.

Over the last few years, my husband, a hobby poultryman, has lost several chickens to foxes. His temper flared one day when he discovered the remains of three of his "girls" in the yard. He had no qualms about taking out the fox that day. But in the spring when a momma fox had a litter under an outbuilding, the kits were so cute he didn't want to kill them. Instead, he threw a smoke bomb in their den, and after they ran out, he filled it with stones. That was several weeks ago, but in the last few days he spotted an adolescent fox coming boldly near the house. I'm not an animal control expert, and I'm not a hunter for sport or supper, but I do know a "so cute" baby fox grows up. Left unattended, it will harm foliage or fowl, now or later. We must take control over the little things that steal our time with God.

Walk in It

As we continue to journey with the Lord, we can't expect to remain in the same condition as we began. Believers should continually grow and mature, which means engaging with God in a process of spiritual transformation. As we walk with Him, God opens our eyes to new truths, and we share new experiences with Him. When the Lord gives a fuller revelation of Himself or a biblical truth, that doesn't mean we were "less" before, or that the truth we lived before was all wrong. But God wants to enrich our relationships with Him and mature us, so ultimately, walking in this Spirit-synced way means opening ourselves to change.

In November 2019, I'd just been having a conversation with a friend when I thought to pull out notes from a previous Landmark Conference message preached by Nathaniel Haney. His message included information on angels. He'd spoken of them traveling with people who fear God, and then he said preachers needed the revelation of who they are and what their job is—as both oracles of God and children of God. He spoke of the need of all believers, but especially those in ministry, to understand our partnerships with the invisible world. Immediately after reading my notes, I closed my eyes and saw three flashes of light followed by a sensation that felt like an electric blanket covering my entire back from shoulders to waist. It was an instant tingling that was so real, so vivid, and there was no physical explanation for it. Something happened. There was a supernatural visitation. I don't understand everything that happened to me that day, but I was strengthened, encouraged, and gained confidence from the encounter.

God's Two-Way Conduit

We know every good gift comes from above and that we have access to God because He first loved us. Everything originates *from* Heaven, but is there a way to draw Heaven's attention to Earth? Can we activate the flow? Prime the pump?

I grew up in a church where we often sang the song "Make me a Channel of Your Peace." The lyrics, potentially attributed to Francis of Assisi, can be found in a 1912 French publication. Following is the English translation I sang as a child:

Make me a channel of Your peace.
Where there is hatred let me bring Your love.
Where there is injury, Your pardon, Lord
And where there's doubt, true faith in You.

Oh, Master grant that I may never seek
So much to be consoled as to console
To be understood as to understand
To be loved as to love with all my soul.

God wants to make us channels—instruments of His kingdom where peace reigns. This is what Jesus referenced when He quoted the words of Isaiah (see Isaiah 61:1-3). Knowing God *desires* to use His people as healing and delivering agents, in the church, why don't we see more brokenhearted people embraced and healed by the love of God? Those captive by sin liberated by God's grace? Prison doors swung open? Grieving souls comforted? Ashes replaced with beauty, and mourning with joy? Praises offered to God as spirits of heaviness lift from those dealing with anxiety and oppression? If we position ourselves as intercessors, our prayers on behalf of the lost and hurting can generate a movement from Heaven to Earth.

The Bible tells the story of a man already tucked in for the night whose neighbor came banging on the door asking for bread (see Luke 11:5-8). The man didn't want to

> **Our compassion for others draws God's attention.**

answer and may well have allowed his neighbor to wait until the morning. But when the knocking neighbor revealed he was out in the dark asking on behalf of hungry travelers, the man with the bread inconvenienced himself to meet their need.

This parable reveals more than one principle, but I want to emphasize that compassion attracts God's notice . . . as well as a positive response. When could we possibly think we're being more Christlike than when we set aside our needs and wants to instead pray for those of others? This is surely one aspect of laying down our lives for a friend. God's love is powerfully demonstrated when we sacrifice our time and energy for the betterment of others. Of course, we show love when we provide for physical needs, but some issues can only be resolved by divine intervention.

When we give our time in intercession for others, it's like scraping wool-clad slippers across a shag rug on a dry winter day. If we touch a metal doorknob, we should just expect something to happen. We might even feel a sensation in our own hand as we reach out and minister in the name of Jesus. Our intercession creates a positive channel that magnetically draws the attention of the channel in the clouds and pulls down power from another atmosphere into this world. Our intercession can cause healing rain to fall from a heaven previously shut—even by the hand of God (see 2 Chronicles 7:13-14).

Atmosphere

Three months before his passing, Eli Hernandez spoke at my home church about the atmosphere of Heaven. His focus was on kingdom-mindedness. He emphasized that God wants our minds to match His throne so our prayers can meet the end-time needs. That doesn't happen naturally or even just because we want it to. It requires a process of transformation. He passionately preached that the more believers become like what's "in the throne," the more blessings will flow from Heaven to Earth.

He wasn't preaching a prosperity, name-it-and-claim-it message. He was talking about alignment. Attraction. Bringing Heaven to Earth. He even mentioned the scent of our prayers.

> "God wants to change the scent of our prayers."
> — Eli Hernandez

Consider this. Fragrances hold significance. I've worn the same perfume for years, and a couple of people have remarked, "That smells like you" when they smelled the scent on an article of clothing or in some other place. Fragrances transport our thoughts from the present day and hurtle us off into past places and experiences. It happens simply by catching a whiff of something familiar—the smell of baked bread, for example, or a certain holiday recipe from childhood.

God speaks of scents in Scripture. When He judged Israel, He said instead of sweet fragrances, they would smell a stench, and when He was upset with His people, He said He would refuse to smell in their solemn assemblies (see Isaiah 3:24, Amos 5:21). In other words, He wouldn't accept their offerings. In contrast, in the

New Testament, a gift from one believer to another was called a "fragrant offering, a sacrifice acceptable and pleasing to God" (Philippians 4:18, ESV). Christ's sacrifice was also called a "fragrant offering" (see Ephesians 5:2).

I promise to refrain from writing a thesis on the doctrine of smells, stenches, or sniffing; but there is a principle at play. There are pleasant smells that speak to favor and blessing, and unpleasant smokes and smells that irritate the nostrils of God (see Isaiah 65:5). Pleasant smells attract. Unsavory smells repulse. Eli Hernandez said that Hell has a smell like sulfur, and the book of Revelation backs his premise with its description of a lake of burning sulfur.[5] The same book reveals vials of sweet-smelling fragrance and identifies them as the prayers of God's people (see Revelation 5:8).

Can we determine a specific scent of Heaven, like roses or fragrant spices? Some claim to smell roses at times of supernatural activity, and I do count myself among those. But identifying the fragrance isn't as important as its source—our prayers. We can't help but notice as we read through the epistles, the fragrance of prayer saturated the atmosphere in the New Testament church.

Scripture doesn't specify the nature of the prayers. Were they petitions for needs, prayers of repentance, intercessory prayers, or even simply words of thanks and praise? I would imagine any true prayer offered with a pure heart is a sweet fragrance to God. The scents of our prayers bathe the throne with sweet smells. The depiction in Revelation gives us a peek into what true worship looks like from Heaven's point of view: The words and worship of our hearts travel through our lips, past the veil of the heavens, and into the presence of God.

Prayer manifests in Heaven as incense. Similar to floral scents that rise from the ground to bless our world, our prayer—our communion with God—rises to the throne where the Father captures it in golden vessels. He delights in our prayers in the same way we enjoy a beautiful bouquet of flowers. Our sighs and cries, our voicings and rejoicings, float upward.

> "What goes up must come down."
> — Sir Isaac Newton

If we send sweet smelling sacrifices upward, the laws of nature tell us we should expect a return to Earth of the same. In fact, Newton's quote above, "What goes up must come down," is actually a law of motion. We spoke in Chapter 3 about government and learning the protocols of Heaven. And we conclude this chapter with a restatement of some key principles.

We access Heaven by knowing Jesus, and we know Him through faith in and obedience to His Word. There's nothing more important than connecting and staying connected to God. If we're going to see Heaven come to Earth, each of us has a part to play. It's our responsibility to create an environment here that originated from the heavens. The Lord's Prayer began with "Our Father who art in heaven," and our prayers should also start with a heavenly perspective of God in the throne room.

As we spend time there, we steep in the atmosphere of Heaven like Esther who spent twelve months of treatments in perfumes. One can only imagine the scent that saturated her being, and the fragrance that aided her preparation in becoming "fit for a king." It's notable Esther prepared herself with nothing more or less than the king's attendant suggested for her signifying her yielding agreement with the expressed desires of the royal house.

The love of God has already been poured out in our hearts by God's Spirit (see Romans 5:5). To see more of God's glory released in the earth (and He does release His glory in degrees), we must prepare our hearts to receive more of Him. This happens when we apply the principles we've learned thus far about walking in a faith that works by love and thereby releases the operation of the gifts of God. This results in a greater demonstration of the glory of God. More love + more obedience should = greater glory.

> **If we stay connected to the throne room, we should pick up Heaven's scent.**

As people who have already received the glory of God, we should walk in a manner that indicates our true belief that we are sacred vessels—glory bearers (see 1 Corinthians 3:16). God's temple on Earth is a living, moving home within you and within me. We must walk the walk and talk the talk wherever we go. Since we've received the Spirit of God, we can't be the same as we were when we walked in darkness. There's no going back. This is our shift, and it's our season to turn the world upside down, preach the gospel, work miracles, signs, and wonders, and see the Lord add to the church daily such as should be saved (see Acts 2:47).

Perhaps you long to move into the deeper waters, but you've been standing for some time in waters where you still feel a measure of control. God wants to take you to a new dimension of faith—to deeper waters where He is in control. As you seek Him and His will—as you obey Him, He will take you to greater things. It will be the development of a greater capacity to maintain connectivity with God that allows you to serve in this new place with increased flow and fruitfulness.

> "We must act to align ourselves with what's ahead so we can become managers rather than seekers . . . align to what's moving among us, not just what's coming."
> —Eli Hernandez

Through you, God Himself will move from the supernatural realm to the natural in a breaking forth from the deep river that is already within you. You *can* do it because the conduit doesn't "do it" at all. Your job is to be a prepared vessel willing to partner with Jesus on His mission to reach the lost and gain a bride.

7

Breaking Blockages

A broken and a contrite heart, O God, thou wilt not despise.
Psalm 51:17

To be a free-flowing channel for Jesus requires a giving of self and a giving away of self. By the Spirit of Christ, Jesus provides all the power we need to carry out His mission of releasing the kingdom of God on Earth. To be a pure conduit for this divine flow requires the intimate, abiding relationship discussed previously, but in this chapter, we'll look specifically at some "conduit care."

While there are other factors to consider, my pastor, Marvin Walker, teaches that, "Living in the flow of the Holy Ghost should be the normal Christian life." Evangelist Lee Stoneking has often shared his similar thought, "God has got to have a channel to work through." If this is God's plan, it must be doable.

Just as natural wells are poisoned by pollutants, the well within can be tainted by sin. Spiritual conduits can become blocked by blight. In this segment, we'll look briefly at some concerns for a healthy flow. First, allow me to share an article, "The Flowing of the Spirit" by Simeon Young, Sr. (© March 3, 2014, by the *Pentecostal Herald*. Used by permission).

> Several years ago, Nona Freeman told me about a vision God gave her many years ago while the Freemans were serving as missionaries in Africa. The Freemans had been on an extended fast and were seeking God for revival. One morning during this season of prayer and fasting Nona was awakened by a presence in her room. As she recovered from the initial shock of this experience, she said she observed a being clothed with a long flowing robe from which emanated streams of light.

This presence approached her and said, "Don't be afraid. I have come to give you the secret to revival." The angelic visitor then unrolled a scroll containing the words of John 7:38—"He that believeth on me as the scripture hath said, out of his belly shall flow rivers of living water." The word *flow* was emphasized in a way that called her attention to that specific word.

The messenger told her that God's people were using too much human energy, that there was too much scheming and planning, and that human knowledge is a hindrance to revival. She was further told that revival comes when the Spirit flows through the church.

Nona asked, "What hinders the flowing of the Spirit?" God's messenger listed fourteen things that keep the Spirit from flowing. Nona recorded them in her Bible. At the time of my conversation with her, she did not have that particular Bible with her and could not remember all fourteen hindrances; however, she did remember ten things that stop the flow of God's Spirit. They are as follows: resentment, bitterness, criticism, judgmentalism, lust, complaining, rebellion, jealousy, ambition, and the desire to have a name of spirituality.

She said she was told that the Spirit would be made visible to her eyes. What she saw was a rainbow-colored light with the consistency of flowing water. As she beheld this, she was taken into a service in one of our churches. The preacher was preaching the truth and the people were saying amen. But as she watched this scene the angel asked her, "Do you feel the deadness and formality?" She acknowledged the deadness, and the Spirit carried her into another Pentecostal service. The preacher was preaching the same sermon the first preacher had been preaching. But there was a difference. Light was pouring into the top of his head and flowing out of his hands as he ministered God's Word. She observed this congregation was somewhat subdued in their response, but the light was pouring into them and then flowing out of them.

She told me that in this setting walked a man with a sneer that seemed to say, "You won't get me." He sat in the back of the room by a smiling older couple that made room for him. As the Spirit of God flowed out of the couple, it encircled the sneering man who cried out, "My God, I'm lost." He fell to the floor full length and was shortly filled with the Holy Ghost.

Sister Freeman said she saw the Spirit flowing in every direction from the church and that a woman outside the church was encircled by the Spirit and filled with the Holy Ghost.

As I recall that story that I first heard many years ago, I long for the Spirit to flow through me and through the people to whom I minister! I am reminded of the verse of Scripture that says it is "not by might, nor by power, but by my spirit, saith the Lord of hosts" (Zechariah 4:6).

We must not scheme or resort to human knowledge. If we have the courage to remove resentment, bitterness, criticism, judgmentalism, lust, complaining, rebellion, jealousy, ambition and the desire to have a name of spirituality, we will have revival.

Are you willing for God to cleanse your life of anything that hinders the flow of His Spirit? As you pray, ask God to reveal to you anything in your life that hinders revival in the church you attend. When God shows you something, be ready to faithfully and courageously deal with it. Allow God's Spirit to flow through you to the lost.

Before reading this article, I compiled a list of blockages I had uncovered in my own studies. There is certainly overlap, but the reasons I found for blockage include:

- <u>Lack of humility</u>: Jesus condemned religious leaders who exalted themselves above others (see Matthew 23:12). God resists the proud, but He gives grace to the humble (see James 4:6).
- <u>Disobedience</u>: When we know the will of God and don't do it, our prayers are unanswered. But when we are obedient, our conscience doesn't condemn us, and we can boldly look to God and receive what we ask (see 1 John 3:21-22).
- <u>Empty words</u>: The quantity of our words does not impress God (see Matthew 6:7). To be effective, we should pray thoughtful, specific, and focused prayers rather than heaps of empty, repetitive phrases.
- <u>Selfishness</u>: True spiritual breakthroughs come where giving thrives—sharing not only money, but ideas, time, property, and so on. When we give, God gives His blessings—the kind that make us truly rich (see Proverbs 10:22).
- <u>Self-centeredness</u>: When we esteem our own ideas and plans over God's Word or the objectives and suggestions of others, we exhibit a lack of genuine love. Scripture teaches that faith and the gifts of the Spirit work through love. When we prefer one another in love, we increase the flow of the Spirit (see Romans 12:10).
- <u>Self-pity</u>: Trials come to everyone, but when we have confidence God is going to use all things for good, we don't have to be crushed or discouraged. We can turn self-pity into something positive when we consider someone else's interests or troubles over our own (see Philippians 2:3).

- **Self-government**: Dying to self-government creates a channel to true righteousness and pure ministry (see Ephesians 2:8-10).
- **Family discord**: The husband-wife relationship can enhance or interfere in the effectiveness of our prayers (see 1 Peter 3:7). When our marriages model Christ and the church, we are sure to gain God's attention and response.
- **Wrong motives**: When we pray for our own benefit rather than God's glory, we ask amiss and will not receive (see James 4:1-3). If we don't know what to pray, it's always a good practice to pray in the Spirit.
- **Unbelief**: A person who has doubts is like a wave blown by the wind and has no reason to expect to receive anything from the Lord (see James 1:5-7). Pray in faith!
- **Lack of generosity**: People who shut their ears to the needs of others will have their own requests unanswered (see Proverbs 21:13). But when we give, we receive back in good measure (see Luke 6:38).
- **Unthankfulness**: God doesn't pour blessings into bags with holes in them, and unthankfulness is a sure way to turn His attention elsewhere (see Haggai 1:1-9). Believers should offer their prayers to the Lord with thanksgiving (see Philippians 4:6).
- **Unrepented sin**: If we harbor sin in our hearts, God won't hear our prayers (see Psalm 66:18).
- **Unforgiveness**: When we stand praying, we must forgive everything and anything we have against anyone else (see Mark 11:25-26). If we don't forgive others, we not only forfeit answers to our prayers, but can lose out on the forgiveness of our own trespasses.
- **Lack of reconciliation**: It's possible to forgive but not reconcile. We must make things right to the best of our abilities with our brothers and sisters before God will receive our sacrifices or hear our prayers (see Matthew 5:23-24).

As we consider blockages, some have wondered if demons are able to obstruct prayers. After all, there was a delay in the arrival of the angel sent to minister to Daniel. Scripture tells us, however, that God heard Daniel's prayer on the first day (see Daniel 10:12). Yes, there was resistance, but God answered. So, while demons may be able to hear our prayers, they also tremble at the words. We shouldn't be afraid to pray because a demon might hear. There's power in our prayers.

Nona Freeman once told a story about a time she was washing dishes and God directed her to do something out of the box. She felt impressed to go outside and wave. It seemed strange to her to wave—at nobody. She couldn't believe what God was asking, and so she didn't obey right away. But the feeling kept pressing her, and so she wiped her hands, stepped out on the porch, and smiled and waved at a passing car. A report came later that a man had been planning to commit suicide, but when he passed the woman waving at him, he realized there were people who cared. He changed his mind and made the decision to live.

In contrast to Nona Freeman's testimony, we read in Scripture of times God sent prophets to people He knew wouldn't heed His Word. Repeatedly, the people refused to hear and even conspired against and stoned Zechariah (see 2 Kings 17:14, 2 Chronicles 24:21). God's messengers were mocked and fought against (see 2 Chronicles 36:16, Jeremiah 1:19). They were imprisoned, stoned, and sawn asunder (see Jeremiah 37:15, Hebrews 11:37). So no, not every message from God is received well, nor every spokesperson either, but we won't dwell on that. Thankfully, most of us live where we don't fear for our safety. We may face mockery or ridicule, but our lives are typically not in jeopardy, and the gains of being a conduit of God's glory far outweigh any personal sacrifices.

Issues of the Heart

As we prepare to minister in our generation, we must recognize the lack of godliness in the world. Paul warned Timothy that the characteristics of the world would infiltrate the church. So, in addition to the list of known blockages above, we would do well to review Paul's admonition in 2 Timothy 3:2-9, for the issues we face in the world we sometimes also find in the mirror and in the pew next to us.

According to Paul, the attitudes and ways people conduct themselves reveal the issues of the heart. He identified the traits of the ungodly in 2 Timothy:

- Lovers of their own selves
- Covetous
- Boasters
- Proud
- Blasphemers
- Disobedient to parents
- Unthankful
- Unholy
- Without natural affection
- Trucebreakers
- False accusers
- Lacking self-control

- Fierce
- Despisers of those that are good
- Traitors
- Heady
- High-minded
- Lovers of pleasure more than lovers of God
- Having a form of godliness, but denying the power thereof
- Led away with divers lusts
- Ever learning, and never able to come to the knowledge of the truth
- Resisting the truth
- Having corrupt minds
- Reprobate concerning the faith.

I prefer to look to the positive, but we must deal with reality. Deep issues that block the flow of God can even be found within the church. Many years ago, T. F. Tenney preached a message about the necessary process of breaking before release. In reference to Genesis 7:11, he said, "The windows of Heaven are not open until the fountains of the deep are broken. There's got to be a breaking of the fallow ground." He went on to add, "We say, 'God, open the windows, open the windows,' and God says, 'I'm waiting for the fountains of the deep to break.'"

The anointing flows when we break from our selfish ways and turn to God. It may not look pretty. Others may not understand and might even misjudge us.

The woman with the alabaster box made a dramatic scene breaking the narrow neck or wax seal of her flask of oil at the feet of Jesus (see Mark 14:3). This beautiful vessel made of a soft, translucent rock used for carving decorative items was something precious and worth saving for herself. But instead, she chose to break it open and offer what she had to Jesus. When she honored Him, she released a unique fragrance into the world. As we release our hold on our own treasures and desires, and instead pour out our praise on Jesus, the aroma of Christ is released in the world. God sees you and me as the fragrance of Christ walking among the people of this world, those who are seeking salvation as well as those who are lost (see 2 Corinthians 2:15).

Anointing is costly. Communion with God connects us to the source. As conduits of the Spirit, we keep the tap open to minister life, strength, and healing to others and diffuse the sweet fragrance of Christ in our world. To maintain the flow requires a continual brokenness in the will of man. When that fails to happen, a re-breaking through repentance must occur so that the Spirit of God, once closed out by sin and selfishness, can again flood the soul, and reestablish communion with the Lord.

The brokenness Jesus seeks is the meek and quiet spirit at rest with God. Matthew Henry said, "Meekness is the silent submission of the soul to the 'providence' of God concerning us." As the man Christ Jesus brought His will into agreement with the will of the Father, He experienced a brokenness you and I emulate when we join Him in praying, "Not my will, but thine be done." Jesus allowed the breaking of His flesh. He's not asking us to receive stripes for our healing or have our bodies nailed to a cross to save our souls. His sacrificial death paid the ransom required to redeem us; and through His physical brokenness, we receive the spiritual wholeness of reconciliation unto Him.

The kind of brokenness that releases anointing in our lives requires laying down our will for the will of the Father. This is another way of expressing repentance. We'll discuss this more in Chapter 14, but for now, we need to recognize that repentance means accepting God's views and purposes for our lives and who He's called us to be. It means doing what He calls us to do day-by-day, month-by-month, and year-by-year.

When God touches us, He makes us whole. In our inner person, we experience an exchange, and the broken person becomes whole by the now-broken self-rule. This wholeness creates a conduit for currents of blessing, refreshing, strength, and power. God in Heaven appoints each man's work (see John 3:27, TLB).

Broken Circuits

At times we find ourselves uncomfortable in God's presence. We recognize our "undonenes" and feel tempted to hide like Adam and Eve. But then, more than ever, we should turn to God to receive the cleansing we need. The touch of God not only purifies us, it prepares us. In this exchange, when we see Him reaching to us, and we reach back, sparks can shoot out like a surge of electricity that sends bolts from Heaven to Earth. No matter where it strikes, what happens below remains connected to and dependent upon the initial "step leader" released from above.

King David knew his undone state as he pled for God's mercy. He couldn't forget his terrible sin and guilt. He knew that ultimately every sin committed is a sin against God, but David knew enough not to wallow in the grief resulting from his own poor choices. He turned to God who washed him clean—whiter than snow. He knew he needed a clean heart and the right spirit that only come from the presence of God. While he desired to worship, he recognized that in his current condition he must first offer the repentance that always gets God's attention.

David said, "The sacrifices of God are a broken spirit: a broken and a contrite heart, O God, thou wilt not despise" (Psalm 51:17). I believe David fully understood the complexity of brokenness. Yes, he had to break loose of sin. He sorrowed over his choices. He saw the destruction it brought. But he offered God his "broken spirit" knowing He could bring new life where he felt very dead and separated from the God he loved. David offered his broken and contrite heart. "Contrite" means on one hand "broken to pieces," but it also refers to a consciousness of guilt. David confessed a complete admission of guilt. He relinquished his passions and depended on the Lord to wash him so he could once again be in fellowship. He longed to experience the restoration of the joy of salvation and in response, he would be able to teach others who had sinned how to return to God (see Psalm 51:12–13).

> God has a magnetic attraction to brokenness.

David was anointed king early in his life. Five years passed before he defeated Goliath, and another five years before his appointment as Saul's armor-bearer. David experienced many ups and downs on his way to the throne. Twenty-five years passed after Samuel anointed him king and before he ascended to the throne in Hebron. There was no reign like David's. He united the kingdom of Israel, and in a decisive move, he returned the ark of God to Jerusalem. He was a worshipper and erected a tent for the ark of God. Israel expanded to its greatest reach. But twenty years into his successful, God-honoring reign, David sinfully indulged his lusts, committed adultery, and then engaged in treachery and murder (see 2 Samuel 11).

The nation of Israel benefited for years from David's intimate communion and righteous relationship with God, but his sin clogged the flow of blessing. As the Lord's chosen leader, he had served as a type of kingdom conduit, but as is often the case, one person's sin affects many. David's personal sin and separation from God weighed heavily upon him, but I can only imagine he must have known his conduct would negatively affect the people. Sin degrades and disgraces. Sin diminishes and brings shame; but integrity and virtuous character make a nation great (see Proverbs 14:34).

God has a history of choosing individuals to bless the multitudes. Just look at Abraham, Joseph, Moses, Esther, and David. Jesus chose twelve apostles and invested Himself in them expecting them to, in turn, serve as channels of His redemption to the world around them. The church today is called to serve as living conduits of God's redemptive work in the world.

Of course, it's possible for people to receive God's Spirit without human intervention. I received the Holy Ghost in a room all by myself, and I also know a man who received the Holy Ghost on a military ship out at sea. My husband received the Holy Ghost alone in his bedroom as he worshipped before the Lord. These types of experiences, however, aren't the norm, and I do know that both my husband and I had contact with believers prior to our private experiences. So while we can't put God in a box, His Word makes it clear that His plan to reach the world is through His people. Jesus said, "Truly, truly, I say to you, whoever believes in me will also do the works that I do; and greater works than these will he do, because I am going to the Father" (John 14:12, ESV). Paul wrote, "For we are his workmanship, created in Christ Jesus for good works, which God prepared beforehand, that we should walk in them" (Ephesians 2:10).

Now the God of peace, that brought again from the dead our Lord Jesus, that great shepherd of the sheep, through the blood of the everlasting covenant, make you perfect in every good work to do his will, working in you that which is wellpleasing in his sight, through Jesus Christ; to whom be glory for ever and ever. Amen.
Hebrews 13:20-21

David walked faithfully for a long time before his great failure. We learn from his life and the lives of many others recorded in the Bible about the importance of continuing to walk with God. The Lord is faithful to complete in us what He began (see Philippians 1:6). We have a responsibility to be faithful and abide with Him. Jesus said, "Abide in me, and I in you. As the branch cannot bear fruit of itself, except it abide in the vine; no more can ye, except ye abide in me" (John 15:4). When we stay joined to Him, He stays joined to us.

> "Whoever claims to abide in Him must walk as Jesus walked."
> 1 John 2:6

Spirit-Synced

In Section 2 we'll learn to identify sources of distraction and either deal with them or defeat them so we can freely access Heaven without restricting or cutting off our flow. We can learn to walk through storms, challenges, and even the shadow of the valley of death and keep our inner persons in tune with God. This is essential—alignment with God's will and Word—that creates a channel for the Spirit.

We'll experience setbacks along the way, but be encouraged. We can learn even in our losses. Peter walked on water, and then plunged into the same waves. I'm certain, however, that even though he sank, the experience changed his life and faith forever.

When Moses saw the burning bush, he chose to turn aside. And when he did, he received direction from God. Even Jesus allowed Himself an occasional derailment as He traveled from one place to the next to minister. Hurting people stopped Him, and He willingly turned aside, listened, and ministered to them. In the last couple of years God has been convicting me about being less hurried, slowing down, and living free from frenzy. That includes constant connection to social media. We can clog our spiritual hearing and numb our sensitivity when we're not focused. Instead, we multitask. We even multitask our time with God when He certainly deserves our full attention.

 I believe God wants His people to live what I call "Spirit-synced." This means "tracking" with Jesus. He sets the tracks, and we walk in them. It means dispensing what He would dispense if He were in our shoes. And He tells us just what He would do through the leading of His indwelling Spirit—if we listen.

God wants His people to live with a singular focus and undivided loyalties. We don't have the luxury nor the right to subdivide or compartmentalize our lives into spiritual vs. secular. This stops the flow from Heaven to Earth. Everything, after all, is spiritual. We also aren't authorized to determine for ourselves what's right and wrong. When we do, sin is a likely result. Sin causes alienation, which closes off our spiritual taps, while alignment with God breaks the blockages and opens the way for the flow of the Spirit.

8

Getting Righteousness Right

They shall speak of the glory of thy kingdom, and talk of thy power.
Psalm 145:11

Previously we discussed how to be open to the flow of God's Spirit. Let's look now at the kingdom itself. A kingdom is an area or territory ruled by a sovereign—in other words, an actual place that comprises the domain of a king. This realm is generally associated with the particular person who rules, and kingdom pertains to government.

The kingdom of God was a primary focus of Jesus's teaching, but His words weren't received by the majority of His own people. The Jewish leaders, in particular, were looking for a political savior. They looked for a Messiah to save the Hebrew nation from oppression so they could practice their religion. Jesus, however, represented an invisible realm in need of restoration. My friend, Stan Dyrdul, taught an excellent Sunday school lesson on the kingdom of God. Following are some of my notes from his class:

+ Religion divides, causes wars, and creates problems.
+ The Bible isn't about establishing a religion, but a kingdom.
+ Jesus spoke nothing that could cause a lack of peace within the kingdom, so what causes division in the church today? Man-driven motives.
+ Christians should make sure they can trace their roots to the book of Acts—to a type of worship that's God-driven, not man-driven.
+ God's original design was adequate then, and it remains adequate today.
+ Jesus purchased the church with His own blood (see Acts 20:28). Man doesn't have the right to establish any other church.
+ There is only one church (the original) and one kingdom of God.

In the introduction of this book we briefly touched on Romans 14:17, "For the kingdom of God is not meat and drink; but righteousness, and peace, and joy in the Holy Ghost." We looked at how this verse might appear at first glance to offer a linear concept, like A + B + C = D. I felt impressed with the idea that this verse revealed something more like a stairway. In this section we'll look at the bottommost step and first characteristic of the kingdom: righteousness.

An Attribute of God

Righteousness is not a "thing," and it has more than one component. First, it's one of the attributes of God. He is who He says He is, and He does what He says He will do. For you and I, righteousness has to do with being as we should be—in a condition acceptable to God. Let me give an illustration. If your bank statement reports a $250 balance, but your checkbook says $1,000, something is wrong. Barring any transactions in process, your register wouldn't be a righteous judgment of what is truly in your account. Righteousness, in another word, is reconciliation—like reconciling a personal bank book. If we don't reconcile, we might find ourselves writing checks that won't cash—which can, over time, land a person in jail. We need to know what's really in our account. Righteousness occurs when the two accounts match up, when they say the same thing. Righteousness, in this sense, is a legal term.

The truth is, none of our "spiritual bank statements" reconcile with God's holy register. We all fall short of God's glory (see Romans 3:23). That's why we need a righteous Savior. We can't be reconciled to God without faith in Jesus. His blood is the ink that revises our accounts. He paid off the bill we couldn't pay. He redeemed us.

Right Standing with God

Secondly, righteousness is the legal condition of being in right standing with God; being truly reconciled. Righteousness, in this case, is a "thing"—and that's "the doctrine concerning the way in which man may attain a state approved of God."[6]

I've heard more than one person say something like, "I've got my own thing worked out with the Lord." The flaw in a statement like this is the presumptuous "co-authorship" of the terms of the arrangement. We're in God's story, and as Author, He gets to craft the setting, scenes, and plot. Mere human beings have no authority during their moments in the sun—their vapor-long trips into time—to add or take away from the story written by the Author of it all. If you or I modify what God's written, the result differs from His story. It wouldn't be His story any more than if someone learned the password to your social media account and began re-writing your story according to their imaginations. With today's technology, a hacker could upload altered pictures and even edit your own previous posts. There are many hackers of the Bible today—those who would alter the story to fit their preferences—but we don't have the liberty to change the Word of God.

Righteous Conduct

Thirdly, righteousness has to do with ethical conduct: a person's integrity, purity, and virtue. It refers to a rightness or correctness in our thinking, feelings, and actions. The first reference to righteousness in Scripture belongs to Abram, the father of our faith, "And he believed in the Lord; and he counted it to him for righteousness" (Genesis 15:6). Before taking the first step into the kingdom, we must have faith.

When we believe, we act on it, like Abram. His faith was *counted* to him for righteousness. The term "counted" is similar to the term "reconciling" we previously discussed. In essence, God was saying about Abram, "I see his faith, so I'm going to go in my record book and make some adjustments on his behalf. I'll take his faith, add My grace, and that will equal righteousness to his account."

We see now that righteousness has three aspects that interlace and form what looks to me like a three-fold cord. One Bible dictionary said, "Righteousness is the sum total of the requirements of God."[7] This was referenced at the center of Jesus's Sermon on the Mount, "Seek ye first the kingdom of God and his righteousness and all these things shall be added unto you" (Matthew 6:33). It simply staggers my mind when I consider how many times I read that verse before I really caught its meaning. I understood about being kingdom minded and seeking the things of God, but are we, with the same fervor we seek His kingdom, seeking His righteousness? This refers to more than doing our best to live clean and pleasing to God. Are we actively pursuing His righteousness?

Seeking is a busy word. It makes me think of looking for my lost keys. Seeking requires action. It involves thinking, meditating, reasoning, and even asking questions; and it also means requiring, demanding, and craving. Did you ever get a craving you just couldn't get away from? How about a piece of homemade strawberry rhubarb pie with French vanilla ice cream? Or if that isn't for you, how about some salty potato chips or your favorite cup of Starbucks? Are we craving God's righteousness with the same or greater intensity we seek to satisfy our natural cravings? God's presence and favor reward those who seek His righteousness.

But remember this: the Righteous Lord loves what is right and just, and every godly one will come into his presence and gaze upon his face!
Psalm 11:7, TPT

Righteousness is beautiful. Greek philosopher Epictetus recognized humanity's fascination with righteousness in daily life. He taught that people are righteous through their own righteous deeds, and he noted mankind's tendency to praise those who are just rather than unjust. The disciplined over the undisciplined. The self-controlled over the uncontrolled. Righteousness is lovely, and generally seen as a positive attribute of society. We should aspire to have it in the civil sense, but even more, long for it as a spiritual attribute.

Our spirits require righteousness, and Paul taught God's people to think about it among the lovely things mentioned in Philippians 4:8 (the term *just* in the KJV refers to what is "right"). Jesus said those who hunger and thirst for righteousness shall be filled. In fact, they will be happy and blessed. A sacred wholeness comes to those who embrace and live out principles of righteousness. When we exemplify wholeness, it attracts others who are thirsty and hungry for God.

> **Righteousness and kingdom are inseparable. If we have no righteousness, we have no kingdom.**

Righteous Living

After meeting our righteous God and seeking His righteousness, knowing Him should positively affect our behavior. God living inside us inspires us to act in ways approved by or acceptable to Him. When we walk with Jesus on His narrow way, He leads us to broad places, but never by means of crooked paths. Consider the words of John the Baptist: "Every valley shall be filled, and every mountain and hill shall be brought low; and the crooked shall be made straight, and the rough ways shall be made smooth" (Luke 3:5). The prophet's teaching had nothing to do with the hillsides, terrain, or roads of Jerusalem. John was preaching about the hearts of men and women.

God's grace not only saves us. It teaches us to turn from godless living and worldly desires and instead live with wisdom, righteousness, and devotion to God right now in this evil world (see Titus 2:12).

Chapter 8: Getting Righteousness Right

By His grace, God reveals to us "mountains and hills" in our thinking that need to be brought into agreement with His kingdom. He so compassionately directs us to the words of truth that fill in the low places where our hearts fail to see who we are from His kingdom perspective. His Spirit smooths the rough places and reveals to us the crooked places that need to be made straight.

Yes, even though we're born again, in our flesh we may at times oblige thoughts and conduct contrary to God's Word—even wicked or perverse ways. We need our righteous God to transform our hearts so we can live rightly. That is a product not just of prayer, but accurately understanding God's Word. Paul admonished Timothy to study so he would rightly divide the word of truth, and in so doing, he wouldn't be ashamed (see 2 Timothy 2:15). Neither would others be led astray by his wrong teaching. A right understanding of God's Word leads God's people on righteous paths. We must get to a place that whatever His Word says, we do. We agree with it. We display it. We obey it. That's righteous living.

> "Grace reigns through righteousness, not around it."
> —Jeff Arnold

Eli Hernandez said, "I'm not trying to be right. I'm trying to be righteous." Being right and being righteous usually walk the same path, but not always. I love to serve and do for others, but I've experienced times that I reached my limit. In fact, sometimes my patience ran thin. Raw emotion has boiled beneath the surface, and perhaps, at least once, a fiery volcano of righteous indignation may have erupted when I found myself spinning too many plates while others weren't carrying their own. Even when the conduct of others may not be "right" from our perspective, we must still maintain a righteous response—and keep our cool. Keep our Holy Ghost. Keep the law of kindness in our tongues.

Living righteously almost always involves right relationships. Andrew Womack offered a layman's definition of righteousness as "right standing with God." This concept necessitates right relationships with people. Perhaps we might gain a more comprehensive understanding of applying righteousness in our lives by substituting the words "right relationships" in Scripture where translators have rendered "righteousness."

I offer this as an exercise for contemplation:

- If we hungered for "right relationships," we might set aside what we rightly expected and rather prefer others in love (see Matthew 5:6).

- ✦ We could say Jesus came to fulfill all "right relationships" (see Matthew 3:15).
- ✦ If we sought first the kingdom of God and "right relationships," we would have no problem fulfilling the Greatest Commandment or the Golden Rule (see Matthew 6:33).
- ✦ It's because the gospel offers us the opportunity for a right relationship with God, we're not ashamed to live and proclaim it (see Romans 1:16-17).

As Christians, God clothes us with His righteousness, but righteous character isn't imparted. It's developed. Our continuing growth and development in righteousness expresses true Christian character. The Bible gives stark illustrations on the lack of character development in the lives of men like Samson, Gideon, and King Saul. Their stories present an important principle. Gaining prominence for accomplishments or being given quick elevations can happen out of sync with a person's character development. Too many times we see magnificent "in the beginnings" followed by great collapses that bring reproach to the kingdom of God. These stories remind us of what can happen when success is accompanied by a lack of righteousness.

Our righteous or unrighteous conduct affects our lives, our homes, our churches, and our witness. John taught the church that the way to tell the difference between a child of God and a child of the devil was that a child of the devil "doeth not righteousness" or "loveth not his brother" (see 1 John 3:10). The children of God are called to live righteously and love their brothers and sisters.

God's Word is clear. We must be both righteous and loving, not one or the other. We can't swing to one side of the pendulum and believe, "It's all about love, love, love. Nothing else matters. Come as you are, stay as you are. God is just love, love, love." This in no way diminishes the reality of God's unconditional love. Any parent with a wayward child understands that even when our hearts are broken into a thousand pieces, we never stop loving. God never stops loving us, but we can take ourselves off the path of His blessing (see Psalms 5:12).

On the other side of the pendulum we find the "Church of the 3 Rs"—rules, rules, and more rules. The congregation looks like they were baptized in pickle juice. And what about the joy of the Lord? They know for sure that was an Old Testament scripture. Indeed, God established guidelines in His Word, but He did so for our benefit and because of His great love for us. Truth protects us from the harm that comes when we follow our own ways.

God is both righteous and loving—a God of grace and truth! Goodness and truth! Kindness and truth! Peace and truth! Faithfulness and truth! Mercy and truth! Psalm 85:10 is one of my favorite verses, "Mercy and truth are met together; righteousness and peace have kissed each other." Religion was never meant to be limited to a specific system of faith and worship. But instead it should be a pursuit of the amazing God who chose to bind Himself to flawed people. Our response should be to love Him and desire to please Him in return.

A Garment of Righteousness

In Scripture, righteousness often refers to items worn on the body. Job said, "I put on righteousness, and it clothed me" (Job 29:14). Revelation portrays the bride adorned in a fine linen robe fashioned of nothing else than the righteousness of saints (see Revelation 19:8, see also Isaiah 61:10). The armor of God includes a breastplate of righteousness that's not exclusive to the New Testament (see Ephesians 6:14). Isaiah wrote, "He put on righteousness as a breastplate" (Isaiah 59:17).

God repeatedly illustrated righteousness as something to be worn. In fact, Paul told believers to put on (or sink into) Christ who is our righteousness (see 1 Corinthians 1:30, Galatians 3:27). Whether a robe, a breastplate, or Christ Himself, righteousness covers us and protects us. When we walk with Jesus living lives of integrity and morality, the effect is like wearing a garment that has supernatural deflective power. The breastplate of righteousness is like a Satan-proof vest that covers our hearts—our innermost persons. Righteousness is more than a foundational first step in the kingdom of God. It shields us from the attack of the enemy.

When You Get it Wrong, Make it Right

All of us occasionally fall short in our efforts to live righteously. When we do, we need to remember the "right relationship" aspect of righteousness. Jesus told the believers in Ephesus to think about those times of their first love and how different they were to their present-day condition. He beckoned them to turn back to Him and do what they did then, or He would come and remove their candlestick from its place among the churches (see Revelation 2:4–5).

Jesus forewarned the church that if they didn't get their relationships right and do their "first works," He would move them from their current position of visibility and influence. In fact, they may find themselves in the dark. God is calling those who used to be more than they are presently to make a change. Jesus wants our relationship with Him—as well as our ministry efforts—to remain vibrant and vital.

The Lord God has told us what is right and what he demands: "See that justice is done, let mercy be your first concern, and humbly obey your God."
Micah 6:8, CEV

The Fruit of Righteousness

Righteousness works. In fact, Isaiah expressed it this way, "And the work of righteousness shall be peace; and the effect of righteousness, quietness and assurance for ever" (Isaiah 32:17). When we cultivate righteousness, the result is peace and security. James said, "And the fruit of righteousness is sown in peace of them that make peace" (James 3:18). We "make peace" for others by leading them to wholeness.

> When we plant righteousness, we will harvest wholeness.

The next level or dimension we'll discuss in Section 2 is Peace in the Temple of God. As we examine the topic, we'll find that the true test of any spiritual concept is found in our ability to put it into practice. *Kingdom Come* is nothing more than pages in a book if its principles aren't accompanied by the power of God to impact our everyday lives.

End of Section 1

SECTION 2

Peace in the Temple of God

9

You are the Temple

> *All of you surely know that you are God's temple*
> *and that his Spirit lives in you.*
> 1 Corinthians 3:16, CEV

In Part 1, we established the necessity of righteousness. After entering into a right relationship with the Lord and living in His righteous ways, we're now ready to step into the next dimension: the peace of God. Before we take that first tread, I want to emphasize that to access God's peace we must continually maintain our sturdy foundation of righteousness. If our foundation cracks, our peace won't have a stable base to rest on—and everything wobbles without a sturdy foundation.

Life brings with it internal and external challenges that threaten to sabotage our peace. At times winds and waves cause our ships to pitch and we reel at their impact. But we don't have to. Regardless of our circumstances, God can keep us in a place of peace.

When my husband was sick, the pieces of my mostly happy life seemed to swirl around my head. I didn't know where they would land. Would Pete die? Would he live, but be paralyzed? Would our kids be ok? What about the bills? What about the house? What about...? What about...?

One day as I drove to the hospital, the Lord dropped a little song in my heart. He reminded me that in every storm, there's an eye — a place of peace.

There is peace in the middle of the storm
Though the wind blows hard and long
In the dark of the night
Your Word's my guiding light
And I'll have peace in the middle of my storm.

Through this song, God reinforced to me the principle that peace rests on the Word—the righteous Word of God. If you're in a storm today, your spirit can find a place called peace. This isn't positive self-talk or something we manufacture. Jesus said, "Peace I leave with you, my peace I give unto you: not as the world giveth, give I unto you. Let not your heart be troubled, neither let it be afraid" (John 14:27). Jesus doesn't want His people to live burdened with trouble or fear.

Dwelling from Tent to Tent

For thousands of years, people have lodged in tents, especially those who weren't staying in any one place too long. In fact, when God first began His work on the earth, He stretched out what the KJV calls a firmament which refers to a great arch He called *Heaven* (see Genesis 1:6). The Lord stretched out Heaven like a canopy before He did anything on the earth below (see Psalm 104:2).

God designed Heaven, Earth, and mankind so He could have His own holy people in a holy world. Without getting into a lengthy study on holiness, for our discussion, we'll use its most base meaning: something or someone set apart for God. God created the first man and woman sacred, pure, and blameless. Made in God's likeness, Adam and Eve were spirit beings, but housed in flesh and covered with glory (see Psalm 104:1–2, Genesis 1:26).

> God made the earth for the habitation of humanity, but not just for people. His intention from the very beginning was to dwell with them.

What began so sweetly, went awry when Adam and Eve allowed Satan's trickery to influence them. What did the enemy tempt God's people with? He suggested they step outside the Lord's directives and gain for themselves the ability to decide what was right and wrong. He approached them with the same concept that brought him and one third of the angels into judgement: stepping beyond their own position of authority (see Jude 1:6). Their dissatisfaction and longing to self-govern caused them to sin against the God who made them (see Romans 5:19–20). The insurrection created division between Adam, Eve, and God. Mankind no longer had the same relationship with or access to the supernatural they once enjoyed.

From that moment on, sin alienated people from God and no man or woman could obtain God's favor or approval on their own (Romans 3:23). Because of His love for mankind, God initiated a reunification project. Part of His plan included the Law given to Moses and instructions to build a tent—a meeting place where He could dwell among the people (see Exodus 25:8). The sanctuary built at that time was called the tabernacle, which is another word for "tent." This dwelling place housed both the Word of God (the tablets containing the Ten Commandments) and the presence of God. The tabernacle's layout and function not only connected Heaven with Earth, its design foreshadowed the coming of Jesus and the sacrifice He would make to close the gap created by sin.

The Bible mentions the tabernacle in 50 chapters. The structure itself was basically a two-room tent made of skins and goats' hair surrounded by a linen fence. From the outside, the fence and tabernacle were simple in appearance. They featured no outer ornamentation. Inside the inner chamber were golden furnishings including God's earthly throne; the mercy seat, which sat on a gold-covered chest called the ark of the covenant.

There's so much we could talk about here, but I'll just make this one point. In the Hebrew language, the same word translated *mercy* is other times translated *lovingkindness*. Of everything the Tabernacle and its furnishings represent, God's lovingkindness extended to mankind is the most important. God established a place where He could sit with His people, interact with them, and share His favor and affection.

In the time between Adam and Moses, death ruled (see Romans 5:14). But another "Adam" was destined to come and bridge the sin-divide once and for all. The first Adam was made a living soul, but the last Adam (Jesus) was made a quickening spirit (see 1 Corinthians 15:45). The first man was of Earth, and the second *from* Heaven (v 47). Men are living souls who feel and think. Jesus had the same feeling and thinking capacities as a man, but because He was also a quickening spirit, He had, and still has, the power to bestow resurrection life. By the sin of one, death came to all, but by the sacrifice of one, those who receive the gift of righteousness through Jesus gain eternal life with God.

Every person misses the mark of holiness acceptable to God. Simply put, we can't make ourselves fitting companions of a holy God, but God can impart His holiness and splendor to us. This is what happens when we receive His Spirit at the time of our new birth. God comes to dwell in our hearts, and the more we know of Him and the deeper our experiences, the greater the weight of His glory we carry. When God fills us with His Spirit, we receive His favor. A rich spiritual vitality comes to us and we become His tabernacles (or tents).

 The good news of the gospel was never God's "Plan B."

The Bible tells us that Jesus was the Lamb slain from the foundation of the world. God's "Plan A" was that He (the holy God) would dwell with holy people in a holy place. This plan is still in effect, but because of sin, God rerouted humanity. He did it many times, moving from tent to tent. And even now, He's looking to expand His kingdom. He ever-increases His dwelling place in a spiritual "mitosis." While His Spirit remains in one "tent," He reaches out to embrace another.

God's presence is with us. His face and favor are upon us. Not only are we carriers of His glory, He commissioned us to build and grow His kingdom. The most important aspect of the temple is the presence of God. As we see in examples throughout the Old Testament, it's possible for a sacred place to become common, profane, and empty. To retain God's presence, we maintain our temples by honoring His holiness.

To dwell with God, we repent, we turn from doing things our own way. We access the blood of Jesus by baptism in His name which covers and pardons our sin. We're buried with Him in water and then raised with Him through faith (see Colossians 2:12–13). He cancelled our debts, and through baptism, He gives us a new covering, a pure covering of righteousness. We can be sacred, blameless, and pure, just like a tabernacle for a holy God should be. Our bodies become the temple of God on the earth (see 1 Corinthians 3:16, 6:19). We become members of a royal priesthood commissioned to minister to God and others (see 1 Peter 2:9).

When we look back on the tent of Moses we see how it moved from place to place as the Israelites wandered in the desert. God's people moved from tent-site to tent-site, from Gilgal to Shiloh to Nob to Gibeon. During their travels, however, Israel's enemies captured the glorious ark. For a time, priests continued to receive sacrifices and do their "God thing," but there was no presence of God among the people. It was formalism, ritualism. Modern-day Christians abide by the same principle. It doesn't matter how good our tents may look, how sincere we are, or how involved we are in religious practices if there's no presence of God among us.

Risking Everything

After David took the throne, He retrieved the ark from Israel's enemies. When the ark returned, David wanted worship to be expressed differently than it had been before. In Moses's tent, only the high priest could enter the room where the ark and God's presence dwelt. David, however, had an audacious relationship with God. At the risk of his own demise, he pinned his hopes on God's mercy and established a new tabernacle for the ark (see 2 Samuel 6:17, 1 Chronicles 15:1).

Chapter 9: You are the Temple

After thousands of years, God finally found someone after His own heart—someone willing to think "outside the box" and personally reach out to meet with Him. David appointed 4,000 singers and musicians to play skillfully and continually before the Lord, and he even created new instruments. He inaugurated 24/7 worship and prayer in an environment where anyone could participate and enjoy the presence of God. David's passion gained God's attention and favor.

> **David was willing to risk everything to experience for himself the presence and glory of God.**

After David's death, his son Solomon built a grand temple in Jerusalem. Following its completion, the ark was moved there, but the people's hearts drifted from the Lord. They didn't have David's passion. Hundreds of years before the birth of Jesus, when the Babylonians conquered the Israelites, the ark went missing. We don't know if the Jews hid it, or if their enemies took it. But what we do know is that once again we see in the temple a meeting place with no meeting. People came, but there was no presence of God.

This sad environment is what Jesus was born into. Yes, Jesus honored the temple. He called it God's "house" and His "Father's house" (see Matthew 21:13, John 2:16). He was protective of it, and got angry when people shopped and profiteered in its courtyards. Once He was so outraged He cast out the people who bought and sold in the temple and overturned tables and chairs (see Matthew 21:12). At the same time Jesus honored the building, He knew that a house made of stone wasn't as important as the relationships of those who gathered in it. He longed for people to experience something much greater than religious rituals.

Jesus called His body a temple—one that He would in fact raise up after His own people destroyed it (see John 2:19-21). We don't know what happened to the tent of Moses, the tent of David, or even the ark, but we know where the presence of God showed up on the earth.

In Jesus dwelt all the fullness of God. In the temple of His body, God fulfilled His prophetic words, "A throne will even be established in lovingkindness,

> **God presented Himself in Jesus.**

and a judge will sit on it in faithfulness in the tent of David" (Isaiah 16:5). Amos foretold God's promise to raise up the tent of David (see Amos 9:11). The prophet wasn't referencing a literal, physical tent with poles, but the type of connection God desired: a passionate, intimate relationship with His people.

Jesus, like David, created a way for humanity to access the presence of God. When the Lord poured out His Spirit, every person who received Him entered into a relationship with God without a mediator and without a veil of separation hung between them. When baptized the biblical way, covered entirely by water with the name of Jesus spoken over our lives, we're covered (see Acts 2:38, Galatians 3:27). We're "in Him," and when we receive the Spirit of God, He's "in us."

Before the building of the temple, God's dwelling hadn't been a house, but rather He'd gone from tent to tent (see 1 Chronicles 17:5). He moved from one tabernacle to another in a preordained plan. As He journeyed, He had you and me in mind. He never stepped backward to Moses's tabernacle even though it had been His own design. His glory had once filled Solomon's temple, but that was no longer His plan. God continually moves forward, and He wants His people to move forward with Him into a greater glory. From glory to glory, we transform in His presence as we walk in the light that comes to us through Jesus until the Lord comes again to bring us into the great canopy of Heaven.

God won't be restricted to a house made by human hands. His throne is in Heaven and the earth is His footstool. His desire is to live in the temple He made—the temple that is you and me. And some day, He'll eventually take us to His home in eternity. God's Plan A has always been a holy God dwelling with holy people in a holy place. He wants your heart and mine to be "that place"—a place of communion, rest, satisfaction, glory, and power. He wants us to delight in being with Him, and He wants those who have felt His presence to share the experience with others.

The Kingdom of Peace

Long ago, God chose Jerusalem, the city of David, as the place to establish His kingdom. Most commentaries propose that the ancient city is the same city called Salem, the realm of a priest and king named Melchizedek. The name Melchizedek means "king of righteousness," and this man ruled in Salem, which means peace.[8] Early in Genesis, Scripture presents to us a king of righteousness ruling in a city of peace, also known as Jerusalem.

The Bible tells us Melchizedek was the great high priest, specifically "the priest of the most high God" and ordained as priest after the order of the Son of God (see Genesis 14:18, Hebrews 7:3). He was without father, without mother, and without descent. Some take this to mean Melchizedek was a theophany (a visitation of God to Earth in the form of a man for a divine purpose). But those words don't necessarily refer to a lack of knowing who his parents were, rather they may specify the accepted process of serving as priest in that time. Being introduced without the acceptable evidence presented as proof to validate him, Melchizedek's historical priesthood broke what would become traditional protocol.

We only know what Scripture tells us, but it's important to note that this encounter between Abram and Melchizedek took place before the time of Aaron and Moses and the establishment of the official Levitical priesthood. What's really important here is that the future priesthood of the Messiah was prophesied to be one like Melchizedek's, not like the priesthood after the order of Aaron. Aaron was just a priest, but Melchizedek (the elder priesthood) combined the offices of priest and king.

Some propose that Melchizedek was, in fact, a pagan priest. But a pagan priest wouldn't have used the language he did when he spoke about the one true God. So, who was this man? Noah had three sons, Ham, Shem, and Japheth. Abram was a descendant of Shem (and all Israel—which makes them Shemites or Semites). Shem is considered to be a prophet in His own right, and some sources say He was the next prophet after His father.[9] It seems logical to derive as a conclusion that Shem was the great high priest of His day. After the washing of the world with water and then starting over, God used Shem's line to bless the world through Abram and eventually Jesus.

According to the genealogies recorded in Genesis, Shem was alive in Abram's day (Genesis 11:32, 12:4, Acts 7:4). Only one great, high priest can serve at a given time, and Shem clearly functioned as the great high priest during His lifetime—the same time frame in which Melchizedek lived. We know Shem inherited the land of Salem, and Melchizedek was the king of Salem. If Shem was indeed Melchizedek, then Melchizedek wasn't his name, but his title: King of Righteousness. This king-priest blessed Abram before Abram gave him any offerings. He may well have been conferring the order of the priesthood to him. An "ordination" of sorts.[10]

There's a lot of information here, a lot of history, symbolism, and foreshadowing. We're looking at a habitation of peace in a royal city that came to be known as the City of God. We see in Jerusalem a representation of a heavenly kingdom and a city whose name scholars believe translates "possession of peace."[11]

Although no ark resided behind the veil when Jesus gave up His life on the cross, the torn fabric represented a new era marked by personal worship. The footings of this "tabernacle" then expanded from where they were laid in Jerusalem to Judea, to Samaria, and are still reaching for the uttermost part of the earth. One day, it will move even further beyond into Heaven.

The cross of Christ sank the first peg of David's new tabernacle. The glory that filled the Upper Room on the day of Pentecost raised the roof.

God dedicated this new "dwelling place" with fire from on high. No longer restricted to one building, God made men and women His own, individual, mobile temples. James told believers in his day they were witnessing with their own eyes the restoration of David's tabernacle (see Acts 15:13-20).

The tabernacle of Moses plotted a path from Earth to the unseen realm of God. The way continued to Calvary and is open to all today. Like the many colors of the rainbow encircling

> David's tabernacle foreshadowed the New Testament, Spirit-filled church.

Heaven's throne, God invites whosoever is willing to take this spiritual journey to gather around Him (see Psalm 117:1, Hebrews 4:16). He welcomes members of every tribe and tongue to join Him. Beneath the pavilion of His presence, He oversees His beloved in intimate personal worship of the type established by David. The people divided into Jews and Gentiles now intertwined like a wild olive tree—branches from differing backgrounds now nourished by one root (see Romans 11:18-24, Zechariah 2:11-12). An authentic picture of God's church includes people from all nations.

All this history reveals the connectivity from the origins of the world, through the flood, through the "ordination" of Abram by Melchizedek (Noah's son, Shem), to the establishment of the nation of Israel and the

> Salvation comes from the Jews, but Jesus offers restoration to all who worship in Spirit and truth (see John 4:22-24).

holy lineage of Jesus, son of David, who is both king and priest of Jerusalem.

Melchizedek, David, and Jesus revealed God's plan for the invitation of all people to His kingdom. His inclusivity reached beyond any limitations of lineage, social strata, or ethnicity to "whosoever will."

The Favor Indicator

The presence of God indicates His favor. As we covered in Chapter 2, we are the apple of God's eye. His affection is on us. He delights in us and we bring Him satisfaction. He sings over us with joy (see Zephaniah 3:17).

Those who have God's Spirit, have His favor. The psalmist wrote, "Surely, Lord, you bless the righteous; you surround them with your favor as with a shield" (Psalm 5:12, NIV). God doesn't punch in and punch out on the job of shielding His people with favor. His mercies are new every morning, but His favor surrounds His people and keeps them safe. God continually looks for someone who is reaching for Him with desire, and searches for opportunities to pour out His blessing and favor (see Chronicles 16:9).

"May the favor of the Lord our God rest on us; establish the work of our hands for us" (Psalm 90:17, NIV). Noah found favor with the Lord (see Genesis 6:8). Esther found favor in the eyes of all who saw her (see Esther 2:15). Daniel found favor with his captors, and Mary was favored above all women (see Daniel 1:9, Luke 1:30). God's favor can reach us wherever we are. It knows no boundaries, and He will find us when we delight in Him. When we seek His kingdom as our first priority, we position ourselves to receive favor that can, in turn, result in increased influence, spiritual breakthroughs, and open doors.

> Imagine what we could accomplish if we truly recognized God's favor and goodwill that continually surround us like a shield.

How is this possible? Because there's a connection between favor and anointing. As God looks to see who He can bless, He chooses to anoint certain individuals for special purposes. The prophet Samuel took a horn of oil and anointed David in the middle of his brothers. When he did, "the Spirit of the Lord came upon David from that day forward" (1 Samuel 16:13). How did this happen? While David served in the humble position of shepherd, his sincere love for God and pure worship drew God's attention. When the Lord poured out His favor upon David, his life was never the same.

A House of Prayer

Prayer is a place. It's a meeting place with God where we present ourselves to Him, and we tuck ourselves in the secret place under His wing.

> "To pray is to descend with the mind into the heart, and there to stand before the face of the Lord, ever-present, all-seeing within you."
> —Theopan the Recluse

Prayer is an inexhaustible subject. I spoke at an event once with a woman who'd written 26 books on just this one topic. So, while there are methods and concepts to share on prayer, I want to bring out what I believe is its most important aspect: communing with God. Prayer is a lifestyle, not just something we do. It's connectivity with the Spirit that abides in us as we abide in Him. Prayer entertains and acknowledges the Spirit of God which is always present and everywhere.

Of course, there are diverse types of prayer—from petitions to praise, repentance to intercession. All are important, but what could be more important than hearing from God? It's so easy in our world to be loud and distracted by all the noise around us. When it comes to prayer, volume doesn't equal power, and God doesn't give us points for style or presentation. God didn't scream the world into existence. He spoke it in simple sentences. While there's time for exuberant worship, powerful petitions, and eloquent words, we must also make time to be still—to hear God's voice, to embrace alone-time with Jesus to pray and meditate and listen.

Jesus spoke about a prayer closet. It's wonderful when we have a certain place and time for prayer—a place where we close ourselves off from the world in private interaction with God. Often when praying in public, I bury my face in my handkerchief to shut out the distractions around me. The noise is just as loud, the people just as close, but that little hanky serves as a portable "secret place" that helps me connect in a deeper way. I once faced a season when my family and other matters seemed to constantly preempt my quiet time. Even in my usual place of prayer, I couldn't keep my mind from the distractions running to and fro. In desperation one day, I picked up a prayer shawl I'd received as a gift, and completely covered my head with it. Beneath the fringed cloth, I was able to "shut the door" on the distractions of my life and close myself in with God. He met me with a completely new experience.

The truth is, we have access at any time to God's presence. We just aren't always aware. In February of 2018, I awoke with a vivid remembrance of a detailed, God-given dream. In the dream, I walked up the stairway of our home. I heard my son breathing as he slept in his room. I remember hearing him whisper "Jesus" and begin to speak in tongues in his sleep.

Suddenly, I became aware of an attic door I'd forgotten about. The passage wasn't easy to get to, but I navigated my way to it and opened the door. Inside I found a suite of rooms stunningly decorated in blue and white tapestry brocade. They reminded me, although less ornate, of Napoleon's castle. I was in awe, and I wondered, *How could I have forgotten this place?*

In the dream, I realized I wasn't alone. As I moved from place to place, I chatted with another being about what we were seeing. I said, "This is amazing. I can come back here and make this space into part of my office where I can read and study."

The memory of the dream haunted me throughout the day. As I contemplated its meaning, I thought how the revelation of that room related to prayer—prayer at a new level. I had access to this unseen, forgotten place whenever I was willing to take the time. As I reflect on it now, I'm reminded of the tapestries that covered the holy place in the tabernacle on its sides and ceiling. I recalled feeling my companion was an angel, and the blue and white décor being significant representations of holiness and purity.

Yes, this was a dream. There's no physical suite of blue and white rooms above my house. But there's a place I can go any time if I choose to take my eyes off the lower level and access the higher one. It's up to me, because this is my house, my tabernacle, and God's dwelling place.

Powerful Prayer

Prayer is so powerful. Perhaps that's why Satan does everything possible to keep us from it. When we have a place of regular prayer, we can create heavenly access points. In these places where we regularly meet with God, the atmosphere seems always ready and supernaturally charged. Not unlike Jacob's experience at Bethel, where angels traveled up and down between Heaven and Earth, we can establish a spiritual access point for ourselves in prayer. My husband and I have hosted two men recognized as prophets in our home. On both occasions we received confirmation of angelic activity. One man said our prayer room was "packed" with angels, and the other said it was "easy" to pray there and sensed a waterfall flowing.

When we position ourselves regularly in a place of prayer, we can find ourselves the recipients of heavenly marching orders, divine intelligence, and the assistance of heavenly beings. When we consistently involve ourselves in prayer, especially during the first part of our days, we should expect to see an increase in spiritual activity.

Madame Jeanne Guyon, an influential French woman devoted to prayer, believed that union with God is the key to perfection and happiness. She said, "The way to become perfect is to live in the presence of God." Madame Guyon, whose written works fill 40 volumes, believed that walking *before* God is what enables a person to be blameless, and prayer is what brings us into His presence (see Genesis 17:1).

In prayer, we don't just give, we receive so much. God strengthens us, fortifies our minds, and connects us with His realm of peace and power. When we simply speak the name of Jesus, light enters darkness. Peace overtakes chaos and settles our minds and spirits. Strength returns, and we can soar like eagles.

In His presence, He raises us to a place—a stable place—an established kingdom—higher than our natural circumstances. He renews us and makes us whole in Him. He's the lifter of our heads, our burden bearer, our center, and our world. In Him, we discover a holiness that silences our boastful swagger. By His Spirit and through His Word, He imparts to us who He created us to be.

God's voice can be heard by all who welcome Him into their daily lives. He's our teacher, guide, and prophet. We must discipline ourselves to be intentionally aware of His presence, and when we are, we remain ready vessels. Ready to hear, receive, and share God's love with others in any way the Lord wills—with power, demonstration, healing, miracles, deliverance, glory, and joy.

Worship in the Temple

As the habitation of God, we are privileged to entertain His presence. We were created to worship, and there's incredible power in our praise. I believe in the power of prayer. There's nothing like it, but we also need to recognize that worship is prayer. Worship is warfare. Worship is victory. It's common to evaluate our prayer lives, but how healthy are our praise lives? We must worship in our temples, and when we do, we'll see amazing things happen.

> "Sometimes we fight when we just need to shout." —Rema Duncan

When we worship God, He who is already everywhere manifests Himself among us. And where He is, He brings victory. When we worship, we activate freedom, for where the Spirit of the Lord is there is liberty (see 2 Corinthians 3:17). When we worship, we acknowledge and honor God, but worship isn't only about what we give to Him. He gives back to us strength, joy, victory, power, and blessings. Not only that, but His presence refines us. A tremendous power and performance of God moves among us when we give ourselves to praise and worship.

God designed everything to give Him praise, and when we worship together in unity, we enter into agreement in the Spirit.

When Adam and Eve sinned, what was "that" which was lost? We could say many things, but at its core "that" which was lost was unbroken communion and worship.

True worship isn't just praise with lips or hands. It's not only separation from worldliness. It's not simply reading and knowing His Word in our minds. It's more than intercession, giving, and serving. It's even more than loving God.

True worship is *living* God. This is a key to being a conduit in the kingdom. We must have our ears and hearts attuned to God who lives within, so we connect Him to our world.

> **God wants us to move into a new destination, a realm of peace.**

Peace is a Place

Peace is a place where we can live. We don't have to move from peace to chaos when life pushes against us. One of the enemy's tactics is to use our God-given emotions against us. He attempts to engage us in the realm of feelings and drag us right out of peace like a string of shoes tied to the back of a car. Knowing this, when we feel our emotions escalate, we should stop ourselves, evaluate our situations, and refuse to be engaged on an emotional battleground that cripples us with fear, doubts, and "what-ifs."

God didn't promise to protect us from all of life's challenges and sicknesses, but instead, He gives us the power to overcome. Fear moves us from peace to torment because it corrodes our confidence in God's goodness, but Jesus is the Prince of Peace. His kingdom, therefore, must be a land or realm called Peace. Peace is the dwelling place for kingdom subjects to reside—not just visit every now and then.

Peace isn't simply the absence of turmoil or trouble. It's a state of tranquility and order that comes with the presence of God. The Lord Himself said, "I will extend peace to her [Jerusalem] like a river, and the glory of the Gentiles like a flowing stream" (Isaiah 66:12). This passage directs us back to our focus of being kingdom conduits—whole, strong, and tools in the hand of God. The Lord intends to release rivers of peace and healing in us and through us, but like waters that run downstream, we must let peace have its way. Paul reminded those who walk with God to let the inner calm that comes from His Spirit guide their decision making (see Colossians 3:15). This passage takes me to one of my life verses. "I will make peace your governor and righteousness your ruler" (Isaiah 60:17b, NIV). These words give us wisdom when we face everyday life. They tell us two important things to consider when making a choice to take action:

1) God will make peace our governor, and
2) God will make righteousness our ruler.

When we face a decision, remember that a governor serves as the head of a state. Life presents us many opportunities to enter into a variety of "states." Sometimes I'm in a state of confusion, other times a state of distress or a state of distraction. When I find myself slipping into one of these states, I purposefully turn my focus from the disturbance and let peace become my "head of state." Literally, peace becomes my governor—the one in charge and giving direction. When God's peace resides within us, we can defer to its leadership and direction. That peace is God Himself helping us make the best decisions even in difficult situations and especially when we feel out of control.

In the second part of this passage God said He'll make "righteousness your ruler." We've discussed righteousness at length, but remember that righteousness—our morality, our integrity, our living in right standing with God—is meant to rule us. The word for ruler in this passage means to apply pressure. What's righteous should be our driving force—like a taskmaster, our motivator—it tells us what to do. When God's peace governs and righteousness rules, we have confidence in God's guidance. If we don't have peace, we don't change direction. If a decision is not based in righteousness, we don't move an inch.

The phrase "in peace" is found throughout Scripture in 55 locations. When Jethro told Moses to "Go in peace," the older man knew his son-in-law wouldn't be facing a bed of roses. Many challenges lay ahead. When we face the testing of our faith through

> **Peace isn't something to "get" and carry around, rather, peace is a dimension to live in.**

the trials and stresses of life, knowing the Prince of Peace makes all the difference. Regardless of the situations we face in our homes, schools, churches, or jobs—our spirits can continue to walk in a place called peace. We can depart in peace, return in peace, come in peace, lay down in peace, get up in peace, die in peace, sow (or plant) in peace, and be in peace. And it's all because we have the right foundation.

10

Free Indeed

If the Son therefore shall make you free, ye shall be free indeed.
John 8:36

You and I are absolutely free. We've been forgiven of our sin and liberated from shame. Several years ago, God gave me a message for the church that I've preached many times domestically and internationally. He placed within me a burning desire to see God's people released from the paralyzing effects of shame. Two verses form the foundation for this message, "The Scarlet Letter." "Fear not; for thou shalt not be ashamed: neither be thou confounded; for thou shalt not be put to shame: for thou shalt forget the shame of thy youth" (Isaiah 54:4). "There is therefore now no condemnation to them which are in Christ Jesus, who walk not after the flesh, but after the Spirit" (Romans 8:1).

We've clarified that believers filled with God's Spirit serve as His temples on the earth. God's enemy isn't happy about this plan and does everything possible to break our awareness of God's presence. He attempts to shut down the demonstration of the kingdom of God through us, and one of his primary methods is through accusations calculated to breed self-condemnation. The enemy's lies, however, contrast starkly with our true condition. He accuses hoping to hamstring the church. Those he can't convince to give up on God, he tries to stop short of their potential and hobble around impaired by a misperception. God wants to shine His light on Satan's dark lies. He wants you to know that you are free so that you can live in and lead others to freedom.

Illusions

One day while preparing to speak at a conference in Michigan's Upper Peninsula, I experienced an absolute lack of direction as to what message I should share with the ladies. Scheduled for months in advance, I'd been praying all along and for several days specifically seeking, but I kept coming up empty. I remember staring at the blank computer screen and praying, but it was no use. I couldn't get my thoughts together, so I decided to take a break and eat lunch.

I carried my food into the living room and sat in a chair. I ate, staring out the window, mindlessly watching the chickens free-range in the yard. Mentally, I "blanked out." It was like a "reboot," and was I ever glad God came through with a download. One thought came to mind. Three words that I didn't intentionally think dropped into my consciousness: The Scarlet Letter.

The Scarlet Letter was required reading when I was in high school. It was written in the 1800s by Nathaniel Hawthorne. It's a complex book written in the setting of a Puritan settlement in 17th century Boston. The main character in the story, 16-year-old Hester Prynne, was forced against her will to marry an older man. Not only was her situation unhappy, her husband sent her across the ocean to America to set up house for them. Years passed and he never joined her. He was assumed lost at sea.

Alone, and not knowing if her husband would ever arrive, Hester unwisely fell into a relationship with a man and became pregnant. She gave birth to a baby girl she named Pearl, but she refused to identify the father. Her conduct was unacceptable in the Puritan community. Hester was shunned by the people and as her punishment, forced to wear a scarlet letter, the letter A, as a badge on her chest. The "A" Hester wore signified that she was an adulteress. It was a symbol of shame, and she wasn't allowed to appear in public without it.

The story took many twists from there, but the point I want to make is that the scarlet letter was a badge of shame. Shamed. Disgraced. Dishonored. Everywhere she went everyone knew. She heard the ladies whispering as she walked by. She saw the pointing fingers of the children and the reproachful glances of the men. Shame. She wore it literally as a badge whenever and wherever she was in public.

So back to preparing to speak. I realized that the idea of *The Scarlet Letter* hadn't generated simply in my own mind. God had given me direction, and I was thrilled. I filed the thought away and started packing, accompanied by music streaming through my iPad. When the words to an old hymn came on, I stopped packing and stood still. Tears formed instantly as the words of G.T. Haywood's song filled the air, "I See a Crimson Stream of Blood." A picture flooded my mind—a scarlet letter A being drenched in the blood of Jesus.

> *I see a crimson stream of blood,*
> *It flows from Calvary,*
> *Its waves which reach the throne of God,*
> *Are sweeping over me.*

The blood of Jesus washes away every trace of sin. When He cleanses our lives, there's no stain where sin used to be. There's not even a smudge or a grease mark. He makes us whiter than snow.

After I listened for a moment, I knew I had to take notes of what was coming to me. I walked to the kitchen and wrote on my shopping list, "Jesus carried your shame, your sin. It was nailed to the cross, so you don't have to carry it anymore." I felt such power in the truth of that statement. I knew it could help many people change their mindsets and position them for a greater spiritual transformation in their lives. God wants His people perceptive and aware so He can release what He has for them, not only as individuals, but also the whole of the church.

During an evangelism tour of New Brunswick, Canada, I had a brush with perspective. As I drove a rental car from one church to the next, I noticed something on the hilly roads. It had rained the night before, and as I drove, I kept seeing what looked like water shining on the pavement ahead. But when I passed through that place, there was no puddle. What I was seeing was a phenomenon that tricked my brain. Scientifically speaking, the optical illusion was the effect of the refraction of light while passing through varying temperatures of air.

Ironically, I'd recently read about the sinking of the Titanic. After nearly fifty years of research, investigators finally concluded an optical illusion was the cause of the sinking of the "unsinkable ship." The weather and atmospheric conditions caused those on watch to see a smooth horizon instead of the iceberg—until it was too late. An optical phenomenon that simply bent light created a mirage that convinced those on watch that all was clear.

I believe God desires to radically change lives, remove dangerous misperceptions, and set His sons and daughters free once and for all. He wants us free from the things of the past that have held us back and free to spring forth with new life in a new season.

> Believing an illusion can result in devastating consequences.

The Power of Perception

Job knew the power of perception. When he was at his lowest, he compared his lot in life to that of a tree that had been cut down. He believed a sawed-off tree had a better hope of recovery than he, because a tree can sprout again even if the root is old and the trunk dies in the ground. Job said, "Yet through the scent of water it will bud and bring forth boughs like a plant" (Job 14:9).

The words "through the scent of water" in this passage drew my attention. Technically, water doesn't have a scent. And trees certainly don't have noses. What this verse reveals to us is that at the perception of water—the realization there is a source of water—God can cause new life to burst out of a hewn down stump.

Hope leaps in our souls when we understand there is a source that offers new life. There is a fountain of living water available for even the driest of souls. Our perception is the means by which we are able to walk in a new liberty and fulfill our destinies.

I love to talk about healing and hope. Why? Because, at times, I've felt broken and desperate, and I can tell you from personal experience that our God is a God of healing and hope. But the truth is, if God heals you or me from life's wounds and gives us the hope of Heaven in our hearts, we may still have a wrong perspective of ourselves. We might know that Jesus paid the price for our sin, but have we stopped to realize that He took the shame, too?

 Sin and shame are not the same thing.

Jesus didn't suffer the cross only for our griefs and sorrows. He didn't come just to heal sickness or disease. He took our shame. Once our sin is under the blood, we never have to feel ashamed again.

So many people profess to believe God's Word but aren't able to let go of shame. It's easy to allow emotions to override what the Bible tells us, but I'll be honest. I've had to grab myself by the scruff of my own neck and say, "Emotions, you're not the boss of me." When emotions heighten, sometimes we have to speak to them and tell them they aren't allowed to govern us.

> **Shame paralyzes and condemns, but the Word of God says there is no condemnation to them that are in Christ Jesus.**

Shame is a powerful thing. It's a straitjacket you and I were never intended to wear. When we understand how truly free we are, we can take off any negative perception that hinders us and walk in true liberty. Don't misunderstand. It's right to have shame for sin, but when we repent of our sins and are baptized in His name, Jesus separates us from sin and shame. It's gone forever! And for those of us who haven't been perfect since our baptisms (and who has?), God still offers access to His mercy and forgiveness to settle any shame problems once and for all.

The Gift of Repentance

While it's true that we have access to innocence, there are times we must acknowledge any ongoing errors. The gift of repentance offers us the opportunity to silence the voice of our accuser. When we confess our faults, the wonder-working power of the blood continues its work. The sin that causes us to feel distant from God, is once again removed, and we become comfortable in God's presence—ready to commune with Him and be His instrument in the world.

When we experience salvation, we're born again, but not every habit is necessarily instantly transformed. God doesn't want us to feel condemned when He shows us patterns and habits we need to work on. He convicts our hearts by showing us the evidence of things we need to change, but He doesn't condemn. Maturity recognizes that we're still growing in His process. We need to remember the grace that God provides at every stage of development. There's a constant source of victory, even when we stumble along the way.

In this world, we have both human and spiritual natures that tug and pull us in different directions. But when we're born again, we begin a new, Spirit-empowered life in which we choose, choice by choice, the satisfaction of pleasing the Lord over the temporary, guilt-inducing entertainment available to those who bow to the kingdom of self. If we see ourselves from God's perspective, we're filled with accuser-conquering, delivering, healing, regenerating power.

Indeed

The blood will never lose its power. Jesus went to the cross for all sin—past, present, and future. If something in our lives is wrong, He can make it right, and once it's done, we're free indeed. I love that God put the word *indeed* in Scripture. It's like a verbal exclamation point that means, truly we are free, in reality we are free, it's a point of fact we are truly free.

After writing the note on the grocery list, I returned to the bedroom to continue packing and another song began to play. Again, I was moved to tears by the words:

> *There is a fountain filled with blood,*
> *Drawn from Immanuel's veins,*
> *And sinners plunged beneath that flood*
> *Lose all their guilty stains:*

> *Lose all their guilty stains,*
> *Lose all their guilty stains;*
> *And sinners plunged beneath that flood*
> *Lose all their guilty stains.*

The writer of Hebrews tells us that Jesus, who is both the Author and Finisher of our faith, endured the cross and despised its shame for the joy that that lay before Him (see Hebrews 12:2). What does it mean to despise the shame of the cross? It means Jesus disregarded the shame. Shame had no power over Him. What He had in mind was far greater than any disgrace or dishonor. He saw you and me instead and said, "I think they're worth it."

Jesus went to the cross with joy for you and me. The people spat in His face, brutally abused Him, and hung His naked body on the cross. He was punished so we could be forgiven. He was wounded so we could be healed. He was rejected so we could be accepted. He was cut off so we could be joined in. He was made to be sin so we could be made righteous with His righteousness. He carried our shame so we could carry His glory.

We may have been disgraced. We may have done disgraceful things. But when we're in Christ, walking not after the flesh, but after the Spirit, we no longer bear reproach for the things of the past. There are too many people tormented with a sense of debilitating humiliation. Sometimes it's the discomfort or embarrassment that results from their own sin. But I'm on a special mission to call out the devil for the despicable way he deceives innocent people who experienced a wounding by others.

> **We cannot carry shame and glory in the same package.**

The accuser whispers lies into the ears of those who were victimized. He makes them feel ashamed for something that a selfish, self-serving person perpetrated upon them against their wishes. It's time for God's people to stand up and say, "I refuse to be ashamed for what someone else did to me." Not only for the physical injustices, but shame from the actions of others we're not meant to bear. It's time to stand up and declare, "I refuse to be ashamed for the things my kids have done. I refuse to be reminded of what Jesus has already forgiven. I refuse to be ashamed of past mistakes." We must not let shame stop us from being who we are. We can't let misperceptions block the flow of God in our lives. We're meant to be kingdom conduits and share the Spirit of liberty with others.

A Blood-Washed A

The devil doesn't want us to walk in the magnificent power that freedom brings. He wants us to wear "scarlet letters" on our chests. Oh, he doesn't care if no one else sees them. He just wants us to know they're there. When we do, we begin to convince ourselves that God can't really use us. It's hard enough to even hold our heads up or lift a hand in worship. So, while we may not wear a literal badge, we wear our "scarlet A's" like hidden emblems, painfully visible to our own hearts and minds. The "A" the devil pins on us represents his accusations. The accuser of the brethren calls us, "Accused" to make us feel ashamed and unworthy (see Revelation 12:10).

When you sense an accusation, notice its origination point. The enemy's indictments don't come from our spirits—the place where God lives. The enemy whispers perception-bending allegations in our minds. We don't even realize at the time they are coming from an external source, because we know what we did. We know where we failed. If we listen long enough, the enemy's lies can become part of the way we think about ourselves. Then, like the effects of an optical illusion, our consciences become programmed to believe the enemy's lies. We begin to heap on ourselves condemnation when we should be exercising the power we have through right-standing with God. We need to stand up to the accusations and agree with God's Word. We don't want to agree in our own thought lives with the devil.

The devil may have been right in the past. Yes, we were accusable because we were guilty, but now God's word tells us He washed our "A's" away with His own blood. From God's perspective, that "A" no longer stands for "accused." It stands for "acquitted." We've been cleared, exonerated, discharged, and released. Jesus says our verdict is, "not guilty." We've been set free.

11

Wholeness in the Kingdom of Peace

The law of the Lord is perfect, restoring the [whole] person.
Psalm 19:7, AMPC

The three major components of humanity; body, soul, and spirit, often feel as if they're in a colossal tug-o-war. In every tussle, a winner emerges. Will the body, soul, or spirit gain the victory and lead the person? The one that dominates becomes the leader by default. The strongest component holds the advantage. The one we nurture most will develop and grow.

God knew this world would require all three components to work together for our survival. He gave us bodies to relate to the physical world. They house our souls which were intended to process what we received through a God-filtered connection. The Lord could have created robotic beings to offer Him worship, but instead, He intentionally designed each of us. True worship includes seeking God and together discovering our destinies in Him.

Although Adam and Eve's bodies didn't house God's presence as living temples as we do today, their pure human spirits stayed connected to the Lord. The first man and woman enjoyed uncontaminated dispositions. All they considered and did was influenced by God and God's nature. As the seat of our minds, emotions, and wills, our souls harbor our strengths and strongholds, our wisdom and weaknesses. Looking back to the Fall, we see mankind's greatest battleground lies within. Like Adam and Eve, any issues we have with God, self, or other humans, most often pertain to our souls.

The health and survival of any thought, feeling, or character trait depends on the power of the leader.

Minds reason. Emotions feel. But the will decides our course of action.

C.S. Lewis said, "You are a soul. You have a body." Our souls were created to serve our spirits and God. Because of sin, Adam and Eve turned from serving the logic (*logos*) of God transmitted to them Spirit to spirit, and instead became independent thinkers. Instead of living out God's supernatural order in which everything was filtered by His Spirit before being processed by the soul, their choice corrupted God's plan. As Spirit-filled Christians, we have the opportunity to go back to the original plan. Rather than following our intellect and desire, we allow God's Spirit to filter every thought, purpose, and passion.

Paul wrote about this way of living to the Romans when he urged them to present their bodies and dedicate every part of themselves as living sacrifices (see Romans 12:1–2). God's people were never meant to conform to the way of the world led by its superficial values, selfish practices, or individual ideas of right and wrong. This happens in a progressive transformation as we mature spiritually. Renewing our minds and bringing our thoughts into agreement with His feeds what leads us in the right direction. We can be certain what the will of God is and do what is good, acceptable, and perfect in His sight.

Not all logic is corrupt, but logic that disagrees with God's *logos*, fleshly desires, or unbridled emotions can bring us out of step with God's plan.

Paul continued in Romans 12 warning the people not to think more highly of themselves than they ought. Instead, they needed to have sound judgement (see Romans 12:3). Paul's choice of language refers to "the body as a whole, the instrument of life," and is used at times to refer to "the complete man" (as in Romans 12:1, see also Matthew 5:29, 6:22; James 3:6). When we allow God's Spirit to lead our whole being, we become the person God designed—a living being, holy and wholly connected to Him. We know Him and serve Him with all we do and think.

The Passion Translation renders these verses this way: **"Beloved friends, what should be our proper response to God's marvelous mercies? I encourage you to surrender yourselves to God to be his sacred, living sacrifices. And live in holiness, experiencing all that delights his heart. For this becomes your genuine expression of worship. Stop imitating the ideals and opinions of the culture around you but be inwardly transformed by the Holy Spirit through a total reformation of how you think. This

> When we allow God's Spirit to lead, we win.

will empower you to discern God's will as you live a beautiful life, satisfying and perfect in his eyes" (Romans 12:1–3, TPT).

The call to stop imitating the ideals and opinions of the culture around doesn't infer our every thought is wicked or our desires evil. Every thought and urge just needs to first run through a filter comprised of His Spirit and His Word that removes anything impure, unnecessary, or even ill-timed. We should ask ourselves, "Am I agreeing with God about who I am? My purpose? My lifestyle choices? About what is holy and delights His heart?"

Holiness unto the Lord

Holiness is a major topic of Scripture. God is holy, and He expects those who receive the deposit of His Holy Spirit to go beyond the sphere of the ordinary and become holy like He is. Holiness means being His, but it also includes being complete and perfect, powerful, and pure. Through the Spirit, God brings Heaven to Earth in our innermost beings. For those willing to crown Him Lord of all, He extends the offer to be made whole.

Holiness requires dedication to God's kingdom. As citizens of Heaven, we subordinate our self-images or self-interests and place God on the throne of our hearts.

When we surrender our entire selves on God's altar, the Lord consumes only what hinders us and then gives us back what's best. We no longer trust any reflection that doesn't agree with who God says we are. Ridding ourselves of the self-limiting opinions of others, we surrender our past, present, and future to His design for our lives. It's part of the process of becoming the man or woman God intended from the beginning—a person made in His image.

It would be wonderful if we could instantly switch the looking glass of self for the looking glass of God. But this transformational process takes time, just as the "ugly duckling" in Hans Christian Anderson's tale endured the process before coming to understand his true identity. The duckling knew right away something was wrong. Through no fault of his own, others mocked, taunted, and bullied him. His reflection told him he was ugly because he was different, and the world around him—even his family agreed and made fun of him. The issue wasn't his condition, but his perception. He wasn't a duckling. He'd never been a duckling even when he lived in a duckling world.

He felt awkward and rejected, but after a season of wandering and isolation, he found himself at the edge of a lake where he experienced an incredible revelation.

He could hardly believe what he saw staring back at him from the clear water. It wasn't the reflection of a dark, gray misfit, but a graceful, beautiful creature. It wasn't until the swan realized he was never meant to be a duck that his self-perception was truly made "whole." Nothing changed about his DNA, but the revelation of his identity changed him from an unwholesome view of self to a sense of wellbeing he'd never experienced before.

The word *wholesome* derives from an Old English word *hal* that means "healthy." The swan wasn't healthy until he saw his true reflection. In Anderson's story, the swan looked into the lake, but in God's kingdom, we look into His Word. We set our gaze deeply into His perfecting law of liberty. As we respond to its truths, we experience God's blessings in all we do (see James 1:25).

The more time we spend dwelling on God's Word, marinating in it, letting it saturate us, the more understanding we receive and the greater its transformational work manifests. When we first hear or read, the concepts crowd in with so many others; but as we dwell on them, God's ways become part of our subconscious. The Word not only tears down destructive strongholds, it builds new fortifications around our minds. Regularly ingesting God's powerful living Word displaces, brick by brick, the foundation of the enemy's strongholds. Instead, it raises a garrison of truth that accomplishes God's pleasure as He sends it to you and me to make us whole, holy, and more like Him (see Isaiah 55:11). The law of the Lord is, in itself, perfect, and in turn restores us, making our inner person whole (see Psalm 19:7).

> **As wholeness for the person depends on agreement with God, so the integrity of the Church requires unity among its members.**

Holy Whole

In the Gospel of Matthew, the writer quoted Jesus's reference to the Old Testament command "be holy as I am holy" as "be perfect, therefore, as your heavenly Father is perfect" (see Leviticus 11:44, Matthew 5:48). Biblical scholar David de Silva believes Jesus chose the word *perfect* "as a new but related term . . . given that *holiness* often denotes 'completeness' and 'wholeness' (and not just something set apart from the ordinary) in the Torah."[12]

De Silva made the case that "God's perfection consists of God's completeness." And as we unite with Him and filter our thoughts through His filter, we become holy and whole. We think like Him. We act like Him. We acknowledge His lordship. So while each of us is comprised of body, soul, and spirit (reflecting the outer court, inner court, and holy of holies), the "wholeness" in our temples determines the reach and effectiveness of our ministries.

> When we choose to have our flesh serve the kingdom instead of our passions and desires, we can truly shine.

A major focus of *Kingdom Come* is to help people see themselves as kingdom conduits. To be an effective conduit requires soundness and wholeness.

A garden hose with leaks wastes water and can be difficult to use. A hose pointed in the wrong direction or spewing a polluted substance can do more damage than good. As a garden hose wouldn't be used to put out a fire in a high-rise commercial building, and a fire hose would uproot plants in a garden, a conduit must be prepared for its purpose. Spiritual conduits prepare by connecting to the headwaters of Heaven and then transmitting what Heaven is sending: water, fire, or light—the power of the kingdom. In these types of spiritual transactions, wholeness is essential for the safety of the conduit as well as those receiving ministry.

> "The world needs Jesus, but Jesus needs you to manifest His power. Release the unstoppable Spirit" —Jena Grech

The Mind of Christ

After Adam and Eve's fall, God made a covenant with them that included putting enmity between the serpent and Eve. I've heard people say "enmity" means "hatred," but when I looked it up, I found it interesting the Hebrew word translated "enmity" in the KJV actually means a "hostile mind." When I think about Jesus, I don't think about hostility, but Scripture tells us the Savior who was to come from the seed of the woman was going to have a "hostile mind" toward evil.

Paul clarified in his letter to the Corinthians that this same mind of Christ is the possession of God's holy people (see 1 Corinthians 2:16). You and I are supposed to have the mind of Christ (which is a mind hostile to anything that opposes God).

Consider these contrasts:

- Jesus brought glory to God, while Satan sought glory for himself.
- Jesus came to seek and save the lost, while Satan seeks to devour and kill.
- Jesus exemplified humility and servitude, while Satan rallied God's own angels to rebel against their Maker.
- Jesus displayed compassion to the hurting, while Satan tempted the Lord when He was at a very weak point.

When we agree with God, the resulting "wholeness" God works in our lives can affect not only the way we see ourselves, but also the way others perceive us. We can join the ranks of those who turned their world upside down for the cause of Christ (see Acts 17:6).

> **The mind of Christ and the mind of the enemy directly oppose one another.**

12

Wilt Thou Be Made Whole?

When Jesus saw him lie, and knew that he had been now a long time in that case, he saith unto him, Wilt thou be made whole?
John 5:6

In the process of becoming whole, believers must not only deal with sin, but the baggage of negative, unprocessed emotions from past experiences. Emotional baggage and its accompanying, learned coping mechanisms affect our lives and work for the kingdom.

One of the most important actions required to become whole is for the believer to allow—even invite—the Lord to uncover any dark things hidden inside. We must grant Him access to areas that have generated fear, planted roots of bitterness, or made us feel rejected so we can confess, forgive, and break free from strongholds that formed over time. This is vital, because what we don't open to God for healing becomes an access point for the enemy. Scripture tells us we shouldn't give place to the devil (see Ephesians 4:27). The word *place* comes from the Greek word *topos*, which is the root of the word topography. We can't give him one inch of ground in our lives. If you and I close our wounded areas off from God, we give a foothold to the enemy that could develop into a stronghold of demonic influence.

> The enemy wants to keep us trapped in the past, but God wants to reveal our need for healing.

Many times, forgiveness is the key to closing the door on Satan, even if we've been wrongfully hurt by others. Jesus knows how that feels. Think of how He handled suffering inflicted on Him when He was innocent of any wrongdoing. Jesus didn't threaten others or sulk. He didn't internalize pain or carry hidden malice or ill will. Instead, He committed Himself to God who judges rightly (see 1 Peter

2:23). Forgiveness shuts the door on the devil and opens the way for healing and restoration. God always meets us where we forgive. It's there, in a moment of forgiveness, we see facets of His nature being formed in us. This is where the rubber meets the road. We surrender our thoughts and feelings to God one at a time, and as we do, our willful laying down of self plays an integral part in our being made whole.

We can't make excuses for ourselves and allow things that happened in our pasts to "justify" today's poor responses, resentments, or self-centered choices. In breaking harmful emotional ties to our pasts, we destroy the fetters intended to restrain us.

One of the sad aspects of emotional pain is that it causes people to build invisible walls around their hearts. While not true in every case, some build walls because they can't face the reality that they bear a measure of responsibility in a hurtful situation. There are certainly times innocent people become victims through no fault of their own, but we also can contribute to our own problems. When that happens, we should take personal responsibility and admit our roles without excuse—regardless of any legitimate reason we could claim that our actions were caused by someone else.

Wall-building is understandable, but it isn't really logical. The hurt gets protected instead of the heart being healed. While existing within these artificial "safe places," people become isolated and lose their sense of community. God wants to heal these hurting people through you and me. To do so, we must be whole ourselves. It might seem scary to ask God to help us dismantle our walls, but if we want to help others, we must.

When it comes to emotional healing, it would be nice if we could have a "Jericho wall" experience—one shout and they're gone. But emotional damage most often didn't happen in just one day. An incident may have occurred in a moment, but the toll of the damage grew over time. Taking the wall down brick-by-brick requires a process, but it will be worth the effort. Patient persistence in the presence of the Lord helps us to become more like Him.

Every person enters adulthood with baggage—some of us with more than others. Of course, life is filled with complexity. We never know what may change tomorrow, but just for an example, let's contrast the lives of two infants with radically different upbringings. There's an adorable

> "Being more like Him means being less like me." —Jeff Arnold

Chapter 12: Wilt Thou Be Made Whole?

little girl in my church. We'll call her baby number one. Not long after her birth, a fan club formed around her. Every time she entered the building, people smiled and waved and stretched their arms out to her. Her delight was their delight. Contrast the story of this loved little one with a child born into a family where the mother suffered with depression. Baby number two, often left in a playpen, saw few smiling faces. Her cries habitually went unanswered or simply resulted in being handed a bottle. Without the comfort of even basic diaper changing, she learned to accept the loneliness and silence as part of normal life.

Now imagine both girls as teenagers. Both are filled with the Holy Ghost and baptized in Jesus's name. Both are experiencing the love of God, but their outlooks, estimations of self-worth, and expectations for the future are still influenced by the experiences of their early lives. Baby one expects the best. Everyone's happy she is around. Because her childhood afforded her many positive interactions, she considers her input valuable and that people want what's best for her. Baby two, because of her lack of support, often anticipates rejection and struggles with feelings of unworthiness and fear. Her early experiences set her up for lifelong insecurity. Right now, someone reading this book may have a similar story to tell—someone who's experienced the love of God but still faces emotional issues due to life's unforeseen circumstances. Perhaps ways of thinking and coping with life have been affected. Those parts of us also need to experience God's transforming power.

God is gracious, and some things He just wipes away, like an instantaneous deliverance from a nicotine habit. But the reality of spiritual growth means a process of renovation. Emotions can get damaged, just like physical bodies can be injured, but if we'll work with God, He'll help us put aside old grievances and heal old wounds that plug up our spiritual conduits. God has destined us for victory, not defeat. We're part of His kingdom intended to rule and reign with Jesus, but first, we must lay aside the weights so we can run the race with endurance (see Hebrews 12:1–2).

We spoke in Chapter 10 about victimized people being free from the shame of what someone else did to them. The truth is, most any type of injury can cause emotional pain that runs far deeper than we might expect. The old saying that sticks and stones break bones, but words never hurt—that's a lie. To complicate matters even further, sometimes people with damaged emotions don't even know the reasons for their feelings, or why their perspectives differ like baby one and baby two in the example above.

Emotional injuries are sometimes caused by physical experiences, but also by negative words, actions, and attitudes inflicted on a person—usually by someone significant to them and often during formative childhood years. I have no educational background to validate what I'm about to say. This is only my observation, but I believe a mother's emotional health can transfer to her child at some level. We've heard of children exposed to addictive substances while in the womb. The term "crack baby" reflects the child born with a physical addiction to the same substance their mother abused. What about a child routinely exposed to the chemicals released in the brain upon the onset of anxiety, for example? I'm not sure if there is such a thing as an "anxiety baby," but the feelings of stress experienced in the womb may impact the baby even into adulthood and affect the patterns of life they establish. While this is a stark revelation and paints a picture of even greater unseen and unaddressed emotional needs, I believe whatever traveled with the blood of the mother to the child can be restored by the blood of Jesus.

Emotional injuries can happen at all points in life. At times they're linked to a single traumatic event or result from a pattern of abuse over many years. They can result from rejection, criticism, and a sense of being unloved or unwanted. Subjection to a loveless authority crushes and abuses the spirit. Parental indifference can produce a sense of worthlessness in a child, and grief from a loss such as a death or divorce can cause emotional damage as well. Painful memories often haunt innocent victims of physical, sexual, or emotional abuse, and have the potential to cripple their ability to create healthy relationships. Often, they are left feeling unworthy and ashamed.

Sadly, many Christians bury their memories and try to stuff their emotions far away in their hearts where they don't have to face them. They believe they should automatically be made whole when they've been born again. While some emotional problems are related to chemical imbalances of a physical nature, some are rooted in the culture or experience of neglect, abuse, or other types of suffering. God offers wholeness to the brokenhearted. He sees the lingering pain from the scenarios of life and will take action on behalf of those who present themselves to Him, openly and honestly. Though the process may be painful, we can trust His intention is never to hurt us. His desire is that we would gain true freedom.

Wonderfully saved brothers and sisters, living sanctified, productive, Christian lives may still face their life circumstances and emotional processes with pain and struggle. Many times, it may be due to emotional wounds or circumstantial problems. Dealing with an emotional challenge

> **If we bury our emotional problems, we bury with them the possibility of true emotional healing.**

doesn't make a person any less of a Christian. It just reminds us that we all live in a human condition in a fallen world, and sometimes everyone needs a little help to get through.

Life experiences program our brains to automatically take action in response to threatening or unacceptable events. Deep inside, our response mechanisms warn us, "Remember! When this happens, you should _____. When you feel afraid, you run, or you fight, or you eat, or you shop, or you bully." These patterns can be broken, and new ones established. Jesus went to Calvary not only for your soul's salvation, but to make you emotionally and behaviorally whole. I believe God wants to bring healing to His church, but we must bring out of hiding the unresolved issues and face them with His help. If we could fully know how much God loves us, that knowledge would displace our fears, and we would feel safe in allowing Him to work in us and make us fully sound in our minds, our thoughts, and our emotions. Instead of living with fear or feelings of rejection or inadequacy, we can live in a realm of love, peace, oneness, and wholeness with God.

The Love of God Does the Work

The Hebrew view of people didn't divide men and women into body and soul. Their perspective was to see an individual as one, whole person. When Jesus walked through the Holy Land, He healed all of the peoples' many diseases. Diseases are more than physical maladies. A disease can also be "a particular quality, habit, or disposition" that adversely affects a person or group of people. The word *disease* comes from an old French word formed from two other words that means "lack of ease." A lack of ease means a person has pain, feels disquieted, or has a burden that causes them to suffer in some way.

Jesus did more than heal infirmities, He helped people—even the "untouchable" ones. A woman with an issue of blood was made whole (see Matthew 9:21-22). Scripture bears no record of any person touching the hem of Jesus's garment for healing before the woman pushed her way through the crowd, but her act of faith brought healing for her and opened a new avenue of healing for others as well. Just a few chapters later we read that others believed if they could touch the hem of Jesus's garment, they could receive healing as well (see Matthew 14:36).

On another occasion, a woman who wasn't of the Jewish faith stopped Jesus while He was on His way to another city. She begged him, "My daughter is vexed with a devil." How did Jesus answer her? First, He ignored her, but when she wouldn't give up, He said, "It's not right to take the children's bread and cast it to dogs."

Despite His harsh reply, the woman answered saying, *I know it's true, but even the puppies under the table get to eat the scraps that fall to the ground.*

"Then Jesus answered and said unto her, O woman, great is thy faith: be it unto thee even as thou wilt. And her daughter was made whole from that very hour" (Matthew 15:28). This woman's daughter had a condition that caused her "dis-ease." A "lack of ease." It wasn't a physical condition, but it affected her physically. Of course, not every physical illness or condition is caused by an inner emotional or spiritual condition, but sometimes they are. The good news? Jesus has power over *all* disease.

There are so many beautiful things we can learn from this story. One of them is how Jesus referred to healing. Jesus called the deliverance and healing the girl needed "bread" for the children of God. Our loving Father provides bread for His children. *Give us, this day, our daily bread, Lord, Make us whole—complete in You.*

> **Wholeness is a gift from God for His children. It shouldn't be a surprise. It's not the exception to the rule, but God's desire.**

Undisturbed Communion

Life can be tumultuous, but when we remain connected to the presence of God, we can experience undisturbed (or at least lesser-disturbed) communion with Him. When we abide in God, what we struggled with in the past, what we once lacked the willpower to control, doesn't seem as hard as it once did. We find ourselves complete in Him (see Colossians 2:9-10). His nature, character, love, mercy, and grace fill us up. That's what complete means; to fill to the top so that nothing is wanting.

Jesus said, "Peace I leave with you, my peace I give unto you: not as the world giveth, give I unto you. Let not your heart be troubled, neither let it be afraid" (John 14:27). When we experience wholeness and peace, we can learn to truly release offenses, resentment, anger, and the need to control. This is the way of the Spirit. This is the way of love. This is a way that clears, rather than blocks. It opens the channel of unity rather than division, peace rather than chaos, contentment rather than anger. "For to be carnally minded is death; but to be spiritually minded is life and peace" (Romans 8:6) "Let us therefore follow after the things which make for peace, and things wherewith one may edify another" (Romans 14:19).

We're Mature When We're Broken

Ephesians 4:11-13, a familiar passage, affirms that we not only have God's Word and Spirit to teach us, But God provides trainers for His children. We want God to use us, and so He gives to the church apostles, prophets, evangelists, pastors, and teachers for the specific purpose of equipping believers for service in building the body of Christ. And He's fully committed to us as we strive to reach our potential. He's going to continue working in the church this way until everyone is in unity in faith, in the knowledge of Jesus, mature and has measured up to the full and complete standard of Christ. As we seek to grow, we submit ourselves to the teaching, guidance, and instruction of the ministry God has placed in our lives.

What does it mean to measure up to the full and complete standard of Christ? The Amplified Bible says it is "manifesting His spiritual completeness and exercising our spiritual gifts in unity." Unity is essential to the wholeness of the church.

Consider Ananias and Saphira (see Acts 5:1-10). This couple died when they acted deceitfully. Why were God's consequences so final? We read right before this incident that the people were of one heart and one soul. It was this unity that caused the believers to sell what they had and share it according to their needs. In fact, directly before this encounter with Ananias and Saphira, Barnabas is particularly mentioned as having land, selling it, and bringing all the proceeds to the apostles.

Although Ananias and Saphira were believers, something was amiss. They didn't have to sell their land. There was no mandate to do so. They could have given an offering to support the community without pretending what they gave represented all the proceeds of the sale of their property. But the couple wanted to appear to be as the others in their community (see Acts 4:32). Powerful ministry was going forth and great grace was upon them all. Until. Until the deception.

God judged Ananias and Sapphira so harshly not only because they attempted to deceive Him to look good among their brothers and sisters, but because their act broke the unity of the church. The story correlates with the Old Testament encounter between Achan and Joshua. In both accounts, the people were moving forward in victory until selfishness and deceit threatened to break the flow of God's blessings on the entire faith community. In both cases, God's people were at places of new beginnings and the corporate body was in danger of suffering. Peter revealed the root cause behind the deception. He said Satan had filled Ananias's heart (see Acts 5:3). The enemy was trying to stop the work of God by breaking the unity, the wholeness God was blessing. God's work goes forward with power when His people live in unity.

Scripture offers a paradoxical concept for living the abundant life with Jesus:

To live whole, we become broken.

We know God wants His people to be whole, but I hear teaching and preaching about brokenness. How can we be both whole and broken? And who wants to live in a state of brokenness? How could brokenness coexist with being at peace? I've given this a lot of thought, and to answer the question we must first examine what was broken in the Garden. We touched on it earler: Relationship. When Adam and Eve chose their way over God's way, they experienced brokenness in their relationship with Him.

Now consider with me, what did the cross restore? When Jesus, the second Adam, laid down His life for others and accepted the will of God over the desires of His own flesh, He restored the opportunity for relationship between man and God. In His humanity, Jesus didn't want to face the pain of the cross. His flesh cried out, "O my Father, if it be possible, let this cup pass from me" (Matthew 26:39). Guiltless, innocent, and knowing what was ahead, Jesus gave Himself to the will of God. He turned away from His human desire to live and avoid the agony of death by crucifixion. He knew that without His sacrifice, Heaven's door would never be open for you or for me.

Jesus brought His will into agreement with God's purposes. It cost Him something, but He did more than lay His life down. He resurrected with power! He exited the grave in great victory. When we bring our wills into agreement with God's purposes, even when it costs us something, we will also rise to a new level of experience with God.

Our brokenness—our agreement with God's will for our lives—is the path to wholeness.

We will look at this in more detail in Chapter 14, but for now, recognize that God designed us to walk with Him in the Spirit. If we fail to do so, we may set ourselves in opposition to what is best for us. To accept His path means granting

Him sovereign permission to guide us. Charles Spurgeon said, "There is no attribute of God more comforting to His children, than the doctrine of Divine Sovereignty." He also said,

> "When you go through a trial, the sovereignty of God is the pillow upon which you lay your head."

Wholeness in our broken world is available only to those made whole by Jesus Christ. After my first husband passed, a friend took me out of town for a weekend runaway. I enjoyed the change of scenery. The simplicity of the Amish community was soothing, but one moment touched me deeply. Walking through an outdoor display of handmade crafts, a sign caught my eye that said, "God mends broken hearts, if we give Him all the pieces." Whatever fragmented parts we have—our hearts, our minds, our hopes, our dreams—if we give God all the pieces, He will make something beautiful. It may not look exactly the same, but He knows what's best. He picks up the broken pieces and restores our souls.

I served as part of the National Day of Prayer Task Force for several years. Second Chronicles 7:14 has been a cornerstone verse in this organization for decades: "If my people, which are called by my name, shall humble themselves, and pray, and seek my face, and turn from their wicked ways; then will I hear from heaven, and will forgive their sin, and will heal their land." One day when I was praying at the altar, the Lord impressed me with a thought: "You're the land." I didn't get it at first, but then the thought came to me, "What did God make Adam from?" The answer, of course, is dirt!

My mind flooded with a revelation hidden in 2 Chronicles. If God's people will do the things He says, He will heal us . . . our land . . . our dirt. My "land" and your "land" become whole when we acknowledge God's sovereignty, humble ourselves, commune with Him, and reject the wicked ways of self-rule. This passage provides a key to healing and wholeness, and when we're whole, we can impact our world for the kingdom of God!

Wilt Thou Be Made Whole?

Just as some people "never grow up" and fail to mature emotionally, it's possible to be born again and continue to live "less than whole" in this world. Not everyone wants to be whole. Not everyone in the Bible was whole. Some settled for just a blessing or an experience. We see an example of this when Jesus healed the ten lepers (see Luke 17:11-19). Jesus healed ten, but only the one who turned back to worship and thank the Lord received true wholeness. Jesus said specifically that the leper's faith had made him whole (see v 19). This leads us to wonder how the leper exhibited his faith in a manner different from the others? All ten cried out for mercy. All received a blessing, but the one who turned to Jesus, worshipped, and gave God glory and thanks—he was made whole. When the leper realized what happened, he left his companions and turned his face to Jesus.

What does "whole" mean in this encounter with the leper? Jesus saved the man from the disease and also the effects of the disease. Leprosy brings numbness, muscle weakness, and eye problems that can lead to blindness. It causes disfigurement and paralysis. He did more than stop the leprosy and heal symptoms like skin sores or ulcers. More than just a surface healing, when Jesus made the leper whole, He restored everything the man had lost. He removed the effects of the disease. Where there'd been numbness, God restored feeling. Where there'd been weakness, God renewed strength. If vision had been lost, God gave 20/20 sight.

Jesus Christ is the same yesterday, today, and forever. He still offers this type of full restoration for people with all types of diseases—whatever causes them "lack of ease." Whatever a disease takes, God can give back. He's willing to do more than deal with symptoms from the pain in our lives. He does more than "stop the bleeding" from our past wounds. He wants to take away the effects and the emotional damage we experienced.

Seeing leprosy is easy. Those men had skin splotches. They may've been missing digits or dragging body parts. Emotional issues are inner ones and not always easy to see. Someone may look put together on the outside but have serious cracks on the inside. Those who want healing must do what the leper did. Find Jesus and ask for mercy. Acknowledge all He has already done with thanks and praise! Then watch and see what He restores.

Imagine how the leper felt. His leprosy had isolated him from loved ones, public worship, and society. It probably took him awhile, even with all the joy he experienced, to learn to integrate with his world again. To give a touch, and to receive a touch. To stop speaking with his own mouth, "Unclean! Unclean!" when the people came near. It must've taken some time for those words to stop replaying in his head.

The leper received healing, but I can't imagine he ever forgot what he experienced during his affliction. It's possible to suffer, find healing, and leave the pain of the memories behind even though they remain part of our human experience. I can look back on things that hurt me deeply in the past and say, "That doesn't hurt me anymore." How? This is the health and wholeness we're talking about. This is being free. And it includes freely forgiving those people and situations that hurt you. Even forgiving God for allowing those things to happen.

The lepers offer an example to us of people suffering for reasons completely out of their control. The Prodigal son gives us a different type of example. This young man, injured by his own selfish choices, enjoyed a good life at his father's house, but he wanted to see what the world had to offer. He partied away everything his father gave him and found himself starving as he slopped pigs in a filthy, disgusting pigpen. The young man, feeding animals considered unclean, had fallen below the worst of the worst, but one day he recognized the true state of his pathetic condition and "came to himself" (Luke 15:17). The son remembered how much better the servants of his father's house lived with proper food and care. He came to his senses, stopped opposing himself, got up out of the pigpen, and went immediately to his father's house. He was ready to throw himself on his father's mercy and humble himself to be a servant, but he received mercy—just like the leper did.

Scabs Vs. Scars

Any wound we have suffered in our lives God can redeem and use. Our hurts make us sensitive and compassionate toward others who have suffered in similar ways. When we share from our woundedness, God so many times releases His healing power through us.

One of the requirements for being a priest was that the body couldn't have scabs on it (Leviticus 21:20). A scab is an unhealed wound. Unhealed wounds keep people from getting close to us in the areas of our injuries. This physical requirement for priesthood brought to mind the unhealed wounds that many people bear in their spirits. Spiritual scabs can disqualify a person from important ministry.

Scars may remain on a body, but their sensitivity differs from that of a scab. Our wounds must heal. We must seek to resolve the past offenses that God allowed into our lives. When we overcome, we'll receive authority over the thing that wounded us and become vessels of healing in similar situations. I believe God can take every kind of suffering that a believer endures and redeem it for a kingdom purpose.

I once experienced a very deep wounding. It hurt more than I thought I could bear. I suddenly understood how people could die from the trauma of emotional loss. It felt like a semi had parked on my chest, and the only way I could relieve the weight was to say over and over, "Lord, I release this to You. Lord, I release this to You."

I was hardly able to pray, but as I sat quietly in my office, I had a mental image of myself ground to fine powder. There I was, a pile of dust on a rug in the middle of my living room floor. But after just a few moments, I saw the particles on the perimeter begin to lift and spin. In a matter of moments, the entire powder pile came roaring to life like a cartoon version of a spinning Tasmanian devil. I later shared my experience with my pastor's wife, and she told me a few days afterward the Lord had given her a vision of me. In the vision, God was taking the crushed powder and loading it into bullets—bullets she said did damage to the enemy line.

I've ministered out of my brokenness—but from a position of wholeness. God did show up and help me through that incredibly painful season. It changed me. Forever. And because of that pain, I not only have a new level of compassion, but also an authority to minister to those who are suffering in the same way.

Feelings are real, but that doesn't mean they're always true. When they're based on wrongful perceptions and past experiences, our emotions may be heartfelt, but not based in reality. The more time we spend in God's presence and reading His Word, the more our perceptions and thoughts align with His. In His presence we see that we don't have to remain victims of our pasts. As new creatures in Christ, we can break free—even from the effects of the past. God wants to deliver some people from yesterday, set them free to really live an abundant life, and use them as ambassadors for His kingdom.

He's opening doors of opportunity, doors of utterance, doors to realms we've never known before. He's inviting us into a greater experience, and it's up to us to walk through the doors. We can't resist or shrink back, but instead maintain our confidence in God. Yes, there are weights to lay aside, cares to cast away, and imaginations to be brought into obedience, but today is the day. It's time to refuse to accept the status quo and answer the call of Jesus: *Come! Go!*

13

Transformation in Progress

And we all, with unveiled face, continually seeing as in a mirror the glory of the Lord, are progressively being transformed into His image from [one degree of] glory to [even more] glory, which comes from the Lord, [who is] the Spirit.
2 Corinthians 3:18, AMP

God loves you just as you are, but the "you" you are right now isn't the full vision of who He intends you to be. Transformation is His objective for each of us, and not just the metamorphosis of our souls. He wants to see all of us—spirit, soul, and body—completely new, wholly consecrated (see 1 Thessalonians 5:23).

Jesus's first miracle was turning water into wine—now that was a transformation, and just the first of many signs of who Jesus was and the work He came to do in the world (see John 2:11). I can't believe it was mere coincidence the first miracle happened at a wedding. Marriage is one of God's favorite symbols of the covenant He offers to His people. Jesus is, after all, the Groom who will one day marry His bride, the church.

In the miracle at Cana, Jesus had the servants fill large vessels with water. He used the available vessels (large stone pots that held the water used for the purification of the wedding guests) and transformed their contents into an abundance of fine wine, a symbol of God's blessing (see Proverbs 3:10). This first miracle is revelatory indeed. The Lord can take common, everyday vessels and use them for something exceptional. At the wedding, Jesus not only provided what was needed, He miraculously produced far more than the amount required to satisfy the thirst of the wedding guests. Jesus is a transformer and a creator of "more than enough."

Although the Gospel of Mark doesn't include the account of Jesus's first miracle at Cana, he and two other gospel writers do record a teaching early in the Lord's ministry on wine and wineskins (see Matthew 9:16–17, Mark 2:21–22, Luke 5:36–39). Jesus taught that new wine must go into new vessels (bottles or wineskins). If poured into old ones, the rigid containers could burst, and everything would be lost. Jesus's parable referred to the relationship between His teachings and the Pharisee's view of traditional Judaism. To receive Jesus's words required a flexibility this strict religious order lacked. For those of us who are spiritually thirsty—who desire God to pour something new in our lives—we must be flexible like the new wineskins Jesus spoke of in His teachings.

Jesus offered more than a salvation experience that brings us into eternal life. Every miracle He performed was intended to draw our gaze to a future beautiful day when all of His people will join Him at an incredible marriage feast. After our supper with Jesus, we'll live forever in His kingdom in a realm where there's no sickness, sorrow, hunger, oppression, or death (see Revelation 21:4–5). Jesus is already making good on His promise to make all things new. When He filled us with His Spirit, the process immediately began.

> "We need God to transform our 'wineskins' into new, so He can put new wine, new anointing in us."
> —Nathan Stirnemann

Works in Progress

As new creations in Christ, we're no longer what we used to be. We're walking forward in His process, going deeper, with an ever-open invitation to experience more. I remember a day not long ago when, after a time of study and prayer, the Lord took me to a deeper place of praying in the Spirit. He asked me to surrender another part of myself, and something began changing in me. I'd been praying and serving God for over thirty years, but in that moment, I experienced something powerfully new.

I thought to myself, "If after 30 years I can't truly surrender all, when will I be ready?"

In that sacred encounter with God, I acknowledged some malformations in my thoughts due to circumstances out of my control. I confessed that I still felt some residual damage from issues of the past, but I also professed my belief that God can heal even the scars left behind from old wounds. I asked the Lord to completely heal my mind, my thought processes, my self-image, and my emotions.

> The time is now because the need is now.

We talked about brokenness and wholeness in Chapter 12, but let's look at what it takes to move forward with victory in our attitudes and mental realities.

A Reality Attitude

Dealing with reality requires backbone. It can be hard to face our own weaknesses, not to mention accepting the flaws of other human beings, too. Nobody passes all of life's tests the first time. Even the most gifted and capable among us navigate learning curves, setbacks, and even failures that can make us uncomfortable or insecure. Knowing that every person shares this common condition should encourage us. Learning is a dignified thing to do. God calls us to walk worthy as one of His chosen—to measure up to the standard He sets (see Ephesians 4:1). To achieve this maturity requires God's people to be humble, gentle, patient, and tolerate one another in love (see Ephesians 4:2). To walk worthy includes accepting who we really are, celebrating our progress, and courageously facing areas of change God brings to our attention.

At one time, neither my husband nor I had experience caring for farm animals, but when we moved to a new home with a chicken coop and shed right on the property, we thought we would try our hand at farm living. We read online how to care for our animals and did our best, but we made mistakes—fatal mistakes.

I had a veterinarian friend who made house calls. She helped us when we first got chickens and even performed autopsies on three pullets when the young, healthy-looking birds died one after the other for no apparent reason. Each of the autopsies revealed the same issue: crop obstruction. I did some research and discovered that the raw oatmeal we'd been giving them as a treat likely killed them. Apparently, the uncooked grains stored in their crops, absorbed water, and then caused the impaction. Oatmeal is a great treat for chickens—but if it isn't cooked, it can kill. I just didn't know it.

We also tried our hand at goat keeping. My husband purchased a pregnant female and a companion goat for her with visions of fresh goat milk and cheesemaking. As the time of the delivery drew near, it was clear something was wrong. My friend came and checked the momma goat. I still remember the expression on her face that told me she knew more than she was saying. We failed or missed something important in caring for momma goat, and she died the morning after giving birth. Bill ended up burying the goat he bought for milk, and we both became nanny goats bottle-feeding the twins around the clock with formula purchased from the local farm supply store.

Obviously, animals get sick, but I believe my friend held back information because she didn't want me or my husband to feel bad. But if we were going to continue caring for farm animals, we needed to learn how to avoid future issues.

I don't fault my friend's motives in withholding information. She was an incredibly encouraging person, and she truly cared about me, but friendship is only true friendship when it tells the truth.

King David recognized that he had blind spots. He said, "Who can understand his errors? cleanse thou me from secret faults" (Psalm 19:12). In Chapter 7 we discussed David's brokenness when he willfully sinned. In this psalm, he asked

> **Be a true friend to yourself. Tell yourself the truth.**

God to consider him innocent for his actions taken in ignorance. Hidden things inside of him had caused him to err. His son Solomon wrote "God will bring every deed into judgment, with every secret thing, whether good or evil" (Ecclesiastes 12:14, ESV). The author of Hebrews said, "No creature is hidden from his sight, but all are naked and exposed to the eyes of him to whom we must give account" (Hebrews 4:13, ESV).

God is light, and in Him there's no darkness at all. John told the church that if people claim to be in relationship with God but walk in darkness, they're lying to themselves (see 1 John 1:5-6). I'm not trying to put a guilt trip on anyone. None of us are so Christlike that we've eradicated all darkness from our souls. Yet God's Spirit shines His light on us from the inside out to help us discern not only between good and evil, truth and lies, but also the areas we may not see our own need for improvement (see 1 John 1:8-10). Through the Spirit, God gives discernment to help us realize and amend any inflated views of our own righteousness (see Matthew 7:3-5). He teaches us His word and grants us good judgement so we can walk in step with His ways (see Psalm 119:66). As a loving Father, He gives us what we're able to bear: milk for the young and strong meat for the mature (see Hebrews 5:14). He teaches us to sense what is vital and prize what is excellent so we can be pure, blameless and sincere—not stumbling in our own approach to God or causing others to stumble either (see Philippians 1:10). Facing our issues is important for us, but also for others. What we might not see in ourselves, others do—in the church and out. So besides damming the flow of the Spirit in our lives, issues hidden deeply within, even hidden from our own awareness, can cause offenses and stumbling blocks for others.

Transformation is Character Development

In God's kingdom of righteousness, practicing spiritual disciplines develops righteousness in our spirits through character formation. This transformation is the increase of the nature of God within us that occurs when we purposefully arrange our lives in ways that seek spiritual growth. Through both personal and

Chapter 13: Transformation in Progress

interpersonal spiritual disciplines, we learn to cooperate with God regardless of our current circumstances. We read our Bibles, pray, gather in fellowship, worship and more to train ourselves in godliness (see 1 Timothy 4:7). John Ortberg said, "To grow spiritually means to live increasingly as Jesus would in our unique place." In other words, what would Jesus do if He was me? How would He act in my house, my church, on my job? Studying how Jesus lived should challenge us to live the same principles in our day-to-day lives.

We began our chapter discussing Jesus's miracles, and while He certainly did amazing things, He never transformed a baby into an adult. Why? Because spiritual growth mirrors physical growth.

In living organisms, growth takes place over time. The Bible often compares men to trees. Consider with me that a tree is not merely *from* a seed. A tree *is* a seed that has matured.

Life begins when water awakens a dormant embryo within a seed. The rudimentary plant begins to grow, swelling inside and then breaking the outer shell to allow for its expansion. Although parts of the seed fall off, the seed doesn't die in the way we might imagine. Rather, as it sprouts and develops, it stretches higher and further to grow into what was in its DNA all the time. It dies to being only a seed.

God gave me a word at the end of 2017. I spoke it twice over the pulpit and it was confirmed by a visiting minister who quoted it almost verbatim. When he spoke the same words God had given me, I laughed out loud. I was so excited for that confirmation. What was the word? That God was going to awaken and reactivate dormant seed. When the minister said those words, I felt something break inside me.

When I pondered the prophetic word spoken three times over the same pulpit in one month, I considered the different types of seed in the world. My first thought was to those who'd once served God, but for some reason walked away. These people had been filled with His Spirit, but the seed they received is now dormant. I thought of the unsaved and the measure of faith God placed within them that's just waiting to spring to life. And I also thought about mature believers who have yet to realize their full potential. No matter what kind of experience we've had in Christ, there's always more. I pray as I write these words that dormant seed is activated in your life and that God animates within you a vibrant, exponential growth for His kingdom.

Spiritual growth results from an expanding, increasing process that develops the mind of Christ in believers as they live in relationship with God. Educators use a term, "a spiral of learning," that applies to spiritual growth, as well. Although at times we feel we're experiencing setbacks or having to relearn the same lessons, as long as our spirals keep ascending and expanding, we're making progress and learning more of God than we knew before.

In the Darkness

Sometimes the work of transformation seems as if God is "sending us to our rooms"—in the dark without a flashlight. We feel isolated in the shadows. We aren't alone in these types of experiences. Joseph endured the rejection of his family, being thrown in a pit, sold into slavery, and wrongfully imprisoned before his elevation to the palace. In his younger days, Joseph rejoiced in his God-dreams, but perhaps his character lacked the formation needed before he was ready to see those visions from God fulfilled.

There are times God hides himself in darkness or stretches out the darkness to accomplish His purposes (see Psalm 18:11, Exodus 10:21). We undergo seasons in which we feel God has hidden Himself from us.

 Even in times we feel lost and languishing in some obscure place, isolation doesn't mean rejection. Wherever we find ourselves, God has promised to be our helper and keeper, even when we're in tight places (Psalm 121).

"Suddenly sometimes comes slowly."
— J. H. Osborne

Lasting Change

In June 2017, I traveled to Canada for a ministry trip in Elliot Lake, Ontario. As I passed over a bridge near the Soo Locks, I remembered my experiences with locks when I was a little girl living in Kentucky. I was nervous when our family used to get from one lake to another. Navigating into the chamber from a lower level brought our little vessel into an enclosed, dark, dripping place where we had to come alongside a steep wall and tie to a mooring line. As the waters rose, things brightened, and when the transition was complete, we were at a new level, a new horizon, a new place to move about, explore, and enjoy.

Sometimes God directs us into scary, dark places, like the locks I recalled from my childhood. And sometimes God uses those experiences to bring us out into new places where we can move and operate at a higher level. It takes the process to make the move, but there are some occasions God allows us to completely transition from one place to another and we never have to go back to the other level again.

Practical Steps

Theories are wonderful, but how can we apply the concepts we're learning and truly experience spiritual transformation? The first step is to invite Jesus to speak to us, to grant Him "all access" into every part of our lives. We need to be real with ourselves and with the God who already knows our issues and shortcomings (see Luke 7:39). God sees our struggles and even knows the times we feel He's not come through on His promises. He's very aware of the places in our lives we need healing and even the occasional doubt that causes us to question our ability to hear His voice. It's always best to be honest with God. After all, He abhors hypocrisy but responds to openness and humility.

Next, we can ask the Lord to develop our ability to better hear His voice. We need His "right now" words—His instructions, insight, and guidance for our daily lives and ministry. Sometimes people hear God's voice before anything happens visibly (see 1 Kings 18:1-2, 41). What we hear in our spirits can be more accurate than what our eyes observe.

After humbling ourselves before the Lord and asking Him to show us where we need to improve, what we don't "hear" or "see" through prayer or revelation often comes to us as we read His Word. For instance, when we prayerfully read Galatians 5:22-23, the Lord can walk us through a "fruit inspection" in which He shines light on areas we need to grow. Whether we see something glaring, or the Lord ever-so-gently brings something to our attention, we should acknowledge, confess, and devote ourselves to making the choices necessary to open a path for godly growth. When we evaluate ourselves against His ideal (His Word), the Lord can open our awareness of which fruit is most lacking or what might be hindering the flow of His Spirit in our lives. Confession is a key in the transformation process. With our words we speak agreement with God's Word. We speak what His Word says about us and release that agreement into the atmosphere. Our spoken agreement with God's Word can activate His promises and principles in our lives. With our own mouths we can nurture our own souls, and God will do the work. Our job is to be patient, and when our patience is in full bloom, then we will be "ready for anything, strong in character, full and complete" (see James 1:2-4, TLB).

While God aids us as we seek spiritual development and wholeness, the enemy tries to trip us up. I thought about this as I passed a field that had piles of rocks and debris lined up along its edge. I wondered where the rocks came from, but I knew the field was a well-established field—in use for many years. So why, suddenly, had these giant rocks appeared? They had been there all along, but only over time and use did the stones begin to surface and impede the farmer's ability to plant his crop.

> "I must allow God to work in me what I have never dreamed of, so that I may become a prepared vessel whom He can use." —Watchman Nee

What kinds of stones appear in our hearts that block growth? At times, anger springs up and wreaks havoc. Anger can stem from many issues, but it often reveals our own condemning judgment and feelings of self-righteousness. We also get angry when we feel out of control, when really we have no right to superimpose our priorities, convictions, or expectations on others.

Pride, at the root of so many of our issues, is another stone that must be plucked from the field of blessing and wholeness. Time in God's presence can help us overcome its negative effects. Isaiah 6 reminds us that every person is undone without God, and each of us is equally dependent on His mercy for salvation. In His presence, we nurture the meek and quiet spirit God finds so beautiful (see 1 Peter 3:4). And as we turn our faces toward Him, He transforms us over time to become more like Him—with ever-increasing glory. The KJV says we move "from glory to glory," and I sometimes feel God is moving me from "Lori to Lori." The process includes putting away childish things which may be another type of stone in our fields (see 1 Corinthians 13:11). God helps us remove the childish responses and hindrances that we picked up throughout our lives.

> "Anger is close to sin." —Watchman Nee

Resent or Refine

In the very early hours one morning, the sounds of my husband snoring woke me. I wanted to go back to sleep, but not only was Bill snoring at my head, the dog was snoring at my feet. I was lying there not wanting to get up, even tempted to resent the fact that Bill was in deep sleep mode at the same time he was keeping me awake. But before I opened my eyes to check the time, a written word appeared in my mind: *refinery*.

I quickly got out of bed and forgave my husband (who I realized later had served as an instrument of God). As I walked from the bedroom to the prayer room, the words came to me, "Don't resent the refinery." God allows the refining process in our lives to transform us even while we're already saved and working for His kingdom. Wherever we are in the process, He loves us, but He takes us through difficult seasons that teach us—so we can learn, grow, and change.

I usually think of refining as it relates to gold and silver, but that morning I thought of oil. Refining removes impurities. It would be lovely if we could be refined just once. If we were metals, we could get away with that, but we're not metals, we're dirt. The "stuff" of a lifetime that has settled into our dirt comes out in layers over time—like the rocks in the field. When refining comes, it's because God wants to deal with another layer—because we need pure oil for today.

Natural oil requires refining, but the oil of the Spirit contains nothing impure, nothing crude. The oil, however, is transported in earthen vessels. In order that we might share with others the pure love of God, we must make sure our flesh doesn't contaminate the message. Our distribution channels must remain clean, and this requires that we face His refining process, whatever form that takes.

> "For God's revival to happen, He needs a vessel to come through."
> —B. H. Clenendan

Oil refining occurs through a distillation method that heats and separates its components. The heat serves a purpose—purging out impurities. Fiery trials can have the same transformational result in our lives when we don't resent the refinery, but rather embrace the process that allows the Spirit to freely flow. That's what *Kingdom Come* is all about.

When Jesus stood in the synagogue and said, "The spirit of the Lord is upon me," He was sending a message. "I've got the oil!" What He started with His oil, we're supposed to continue. We're anointed with the purpose of sharing the good news, binding the broken, proclaiming liberty, and opening prison doors . . . right now. Today is the acceptable time for these wonderful things to happen through you and through me.

God refines us so we can help others by sharing His comfort and joy with them. The process prepares us to minister His Spirit to hurting people, beauty to those who know only ashes, and hope to the broken. As we serve as conduits of His Spirit, we'll see powerful things happen in our lives and the lives of others; people established in their faith and God glorified, desolate places rebuilt, and wasted things repaired. Our work will be directed by the Lord in truth, and we'll enjoy everlasting covenant with God (see Isaiah 61:8). Everything a believer could ever want is here—designated for God's anointed, chosen servants: direction, covenant promises, relationship with God, and even blessings for the children. These are the blessings of the refined—the transformed. So let us not resent or resist the refinery, but respond. We'll be glad we did.

14

The Pivot Point

And he said to them all, If any man will come after me, let him deny himself, and take up his cross daily, and follow me.
Luke 9:23

Evangelist George Bennard, after being heckled by several youth at a revival meeting in 1912, had a vision. In it, he said, "I saw the Christ and the cross inseparable." Inspired by that vision, the preacher wrote the beautiful hymn, "The Old Rugged Cross."

> *On a hill far away stood an old rugged cross,*
> *The emblem of suff'ring and shame,*
> *And I love that old cross where the Dearest and Best*
> *For a world of lost sinners was slain.*
>
> *So I'll cherish the old rugged cross*
> *Till my trophies at last I lay down;*
> *I will cling to the old rugged cross;*
> *And exchange it some day for a crown.*

I admit, it's painful to think about the realities of Jesus's death on the cross. I don't like to think of all He suffered, and I've never found any pleasure in viewing, reading, or thinking about the action, the gore, or the horror in media portrayals of it. In our world today, a cross is a symbol for our faith, but it wasn't until after the 4th century that the cross became a widely-used emblem of Christianity. Prior to that time, it symbolized the gallows of a criminal. Consider how we would feel if an electric chair was offered as the emblem of our faith.

The cross was an instrument of the most cruel, humiliating, and contemptible punishment. It originated with the Phoenicians and eventually became used by the Greeks and Romans. The cross was not for petty offenses, but for the guiltiest, the robbers, the basest of the base, the authors and abettors of insurrections. It was an instrument of capital punishment, the greatest irrevocable penalty.

Growing up I saw crucifixes on display, and I understand why some people hang them in their homes and houses of worship. They remind us of Jesus's horrific death, and we do need to remember that. We need to retain in our memories the reality of what happened. The Lord began dealing with me a couple of years ago about looking at the results of Jesus's victory through the right lens. He led me to look at glory, victory, spoils, authority, and spiritual gifts through the crosshairs of Calvary.

Crosshairs are fine wires or threads in the focus of an eyepiece of a weapon that help us be sure we're on target. We "sight" through crosshairs, and sometimes sights need adjusting. If they're off, the target may become lost. A key to remember, however, is that we're not aiming for the crosshairs. They line us up with the target so we can hit it, but first, we must identify the target. As we discussed in Chapter 2 the Hebrew word for sin means "to miss the mark." It also means to "miss the path." If we want to hit the mark, we must narrow our focus.

The phrase "in the crosshairs" is used figuratively to describe someone or something being targeted. Crosshairs also refer to marks used in print work. They assist in positioning and superimposing images for correct alignment. When images run through a printer more than once, the crosshairs help each layer remain centered properly on the frame.

Each of us "runs" through life at different times, and each of us must align ourselves with the crosshairs of Calvary, or our eventual image will be incorrect. Lining up doesn't mean being a cookie-cutter version of someone else, in fact it means the opposite. Each of us was designed to be a wonderful, unique creation intended to be "in line" or "on the right path" with God.

A crosshair is formed when a pair of perpendicular lines intersect—and the axis of their intersection is called the origin. An origin is the first stage of existence, a beginning, a source. Similarly, Calvary's

The cross is the pivot point.

cross creates an intersection, an axis. In prayer the word *fulcrum* came to me. A fulcrum is similar to an axis. It's a support or point of rest on which a lever pivots. A fulcrum plays the central role in an activity, event, or situation. It's the movable component of a hinge, joint, or spine that allows motion back and forth.

The Cross

We've established that the cross marks the way. It was a pivotal point in time. We understand some of what the cross meant to Jesus—the suffering and the death. The cross is featured in so many songs and sermons. Images are printed on t-shirts, hung on walls, and engraved on Bible cases. But what does the cross mean to a believer today? What does it mean to you and me?

One thing the cross is not is an object of worship. Christians shouldn't worship *the* cross. Instead, we worship the Lord who endured it. Because of the cross and Jesus's shed His blood, we have access to Heaven. In addition to all the meanings of fulcrum listed above, it also literally means a "post." Jesus said He was the door. He was the gate, but that door wasn't open until it was hung on the hinge of Calvary. Doors are hung on posts. Gates are hung on posts. Figuratively, Calvary was the hanging of a door on a post. And it's the only way you and I can enter into the kingdom of Heaven.

As I meditated and studied this topic, I thought about how the fulcrum of the cross is our support. The fulcrum of the cross is our point of rest. We don't labor for salvation. We rest in the work of Jesus. The fulcrum of the cross was the pivot point for all humanity, and it became a personal place of turning when we met Jesus there ourselves.

It's the cross of Christ that gives us access to God. It's the ground where we enter His presence with thanksgiving and praise, but an entrance is just a beginning. The cross means more than access. It exemplifies the culmination of Jesus's perfect example of a life of service and sacrifice. You and I are invited to join Jesus in living lives of purpose—but not our own purposes. The cross symbolizes dying to our own ideas and agreeing with the Father's kingdom purposes.

In Christ, God became human and stayed human, even though it was an incredibly humbling experience (see Philippians 2:6-11). Yes, Jesus worked miracles, but He did those for others. He never claimed any special privileges for Himself. He never took a pass on a temptation or trial because He was God. He lived a selfless, obedient life; and then died a selfless, obedient death.

> **The cross exemplifies selflessness.**

The Bible tells believers to choose to think of themselves the way Jesus thought of Himself—to think the same way He did (see Philippians 2:5). We should look to Him as our example, and His example was selfless humility. Calvary's cross was a capital punishment. What it meant to Him, and what it means to you and me today is death to "self" or "self-denial."

Of course, we as Spirit-filled Christians, believe in abundant life, the blessed life, and living an overcoming life right now with joy and peace. But we have to keep the right focus: through the fulcrum of the cross. Jesus personally carried the load of our sins in His own body so we might live for righteousness (see 1 Peter 2:21). Jesus went to the cross so we could follow in His footsteps, and what did He do?

According to 1 Peter 2:22, He didn't sin. He didn't speak cunning, crafty words to deceive anyone or for His own selfish purposes. He never spoke contemptuously or abusively even when that was how people spoke to Him. When He suffered, He didn't threaten retribution, though He could have, and had every right to. Instead, He said, "Father forgive them," and He laid His life down.

Notice how Peter described believers in this portion of Scripture. He said, "we, being dead" (v 24). Jesus went to the cross for our offence, but unless we are dead to the same offence, we are unable to live righteously, or in a right relationship, with God and others. And what was that offence? Was it lying, cheating, stealing, or something worse? What was the original offence? We touched on this in Section 1. Adam and Eve loved God, but they wanted to be more than God made them to be. They wanted to be like God—to choose for themselves what was good and what was evil—what they could do and what they chose not to do.

What was Satan's offence? He wanted to be "like the most High" (Isaiah 14:14). Satan wasn't trying to displace God. He wanted to be like Him. The offence of sin isn't lying or stealing or doing what we shouldn't.

The offence of sin is wanting to be like God— deciding for ourselves what is good and evil.

We want to be like God, but we know, according to the Word, doing what is right in our own eyes is wrong and leads people on paths of destruction. The willfulness to govern ourselves must die. We can't look to our own judgments to determine the best course for our lives. We must look to the cross for the right focus.

Oh, yes, salvation is free. We could never pay for it ourselves. It comes through the love and grace of God alone, but our response to what God has given us should never be ho-hum, lackadaisical, or nonchalant. Some time ago, I jotted down a phrase someone said, but I failed to note who. It was a preacher, though, who said, "If it wasn't a cheap cross, then it's not going to be a cheap response."

> **As long as we are committed to the Word of God, God is committed to us. Anointing comes from the Word. It's not an emotion. —Jack Cunningham**

The Measurement of our Lives

Through the cross we enter the kingdom of Heaven, and it's by the fulcrum of the cross we measure our lives. It's both our reference point and an axis. It functions like the beam on a balance scale to measure our souls. Do we have the right balance of truth and compassion, righteousness and peace, justice and mercy?

Because of the cross you and I are able to pivot in our extremes to the will of God and cultivate lives of worship in Spirit and truth. Jesus told His followers that each of them must carry his or her own cross (see Luke 9:23). I know we sing about clinging to the old rugged cross, and I believe in that metaphorically, but we must cling to our personal crosses, as well.

What is my cross? What is your cross? It's not a thorn in the flesh. It's not a temptation. It's not a trial.

> **My cross and yours is the intersection of our wills and the will of God.**

Consider the vertical beam (the Y-axis of the cross) as a representation of God's will attached at a pivot point with the horizontal beam (the X-axis) that depicts our own. As long as we vertically align our wills with His, our beams run parallel. There's no conflict. When we seek a different way, the weight of that decision tips at the pivot point like a teeter-totter, and we actually create an intersection of wills. When we accept God's will, there's no disagreement—no cross. When we agree with God, our burdens seem lighter. Our "yokes," symbols of submission and the implements of our service to God, become easy.

 The cross is the place you and I put aside any personal desires or conveniences we would choose for ourselves that conflict with God's Word or the direction His Spirit is leading. When we do, we can keep close to Jesus and follow Him—past the cross and into a glorious life. Because ultimately, you and I were made for the glory of God. We were created for His pleasure. And our God is so beautiful, that when we please Him, we receive pleasure back. That's how true love works. It reciprocates.

Yes, God first loved us. We wouldn't have a chance if He hadn't come to Earth in the person of Jesus and gone to Calvary. That's why the cross is, and should always remain, at the center, in the crosshairs of our faith. It's the viewfinder to focus our spiritual eyes on the things unseen, to see beyond Christ's sacrifice to the victorious restoration of fallen man to God. The work of the cross was meant to bring people back into the purpose of their creation. We were created to worship, and Jesus's atoning work on the cross makes our worship acceptable. We could give our best, but it would never be good enough without the atoning blood. Ask Cain. He gave what he considered an acceptable offering, but it wasn't enough without blood, without life, without death. No "act" of worship—no matter how sacrificial, sincere, or excellent, is acceptable to God without the atoning work of the cross.

Love that Leads to Glory

When we look to the cross, ultimately, we see the love of God that was poured out and hung on a hinge, the fulcrum of the cross. Jesus opened the way to the kingdom of God, the peace of God, the glory of God, and fellowship with God. The cross reveals the love that leads us through sacrifice to glory.

When we keep the cross in view, we maintain our focus. The cross reminds us to look through the crosshairs of the beams of Calvary to God in Heaven—to see His glory, His holiness, and His beauty. When we look past the cross to the Everlasting Father, we look with eyes that behold the truth. God is sovereign. God is God. God alone is good. We must agree. We must say, "Yes, Lord, if You say this is good, it's good. If You say this is evil, it's evil." We must love what He loves and hate what He hates. We must measure good and evil by what He says.

The cross seems foolish to those who don't understand its significance. But it was the result of the wisdom of God creating a way to act in concert with His own righteousness. Through His love, He provided a sacrifice that satisfied the penalty for our sin. Through the cross, God made a way to recreate sinners into His image.

Because of Calvary, we can come boldly to the throne of God, but we come by the Via Delarosa, the way of the cross (see Hebrews 10:19–22)

Holiness

The cross represents the intersection of God's holiness and man's need for restoration. In this world we have access to the kingdom, while we're still tethered to humanity. As long as our souls are tied to Earth, we must continually bring our wills to the cross. If we fail to do so, we may be captured by the same temptation that caused Satan's demise. He lost his focus on God and focused only on the glory, and that led him to fall. The very atmosphere of Heaven God had allowed him to live in, made him proud. When God uses us, we need to make sure we never lose sight of the God who allows us to share in His glory.

In the shadow of the cross we can stand in the glory of God unashamed. At the fulcrum of the cross we measure our lives, focus, actions, thoughts, motives, and words. Are they Christlike? How do they balance on the fulcrum of His holiness and righteousness?

Hundreds of years ago, Isaac Watts wrote a beautiful hymn that has become a classic.

> *When I survey the wondrous cross*
> *On which the Prince of glory died,*
> *My richest gain I count but loss,*
> *And pour contempt on all my pride.*
> *Love so amazing, so divine,*
> *Demands my soul, my life, my all.*

Living life through the viewfinder of the cross keeps our sights centered on the kingdom of God. We can't look through the lens of our point of view, even when we have good intentions. When Peter rebuked Jesus about the necessity of His death, Jesus responded, "Get behind me, Satan; You are an offense to Me, for you are not mindful of the things of God, but the things of men" (Matthew 16:23, NKJV). Jesus immediately instructed His disciples to deny themselves, take up their crosses, and follow Him. The offense that trapped Peter can become a stumbling block for any who would choose their own way (which Jesus inferred was satanic) over God's way that requires sacrifice.

In response to the great gift we've received from God, we, in turn, give our own lives and wills away for the betterment of the kingdom. We don't just follow rituals and observe laws, we live out the present will of God as we walk with Him and serve others. Jesus broke the bread that symbolized His life and gave pieces of it to those near Him. He instructed His followers to do the same—in memory of Him (see Luke 22:18-20).

When we become conformed to Christ, our affections and lusts of the flesh are crucified (see Philippians 3:10, Galatians 5:24). We take what comes our way—enduring misfortune, calamity, evil, and affliction, and we inwardly afflict any ungovernable desires—our lusts and passions.

As we give ourselves away, we align our passions to God's. We will His will. We accept His will. And when we do, we walk pleasing to God in resurrection power.

David, the man who delighted God's heart, revealed his secret to pleasing the Lord. "I delight to do Your will, O my God, and Your law is within my heart" (Psalm 40:8, NKJV). We won't go wrong living sacrificially as we walk in His ways. When we delight to do God's will, we find strength and pleasure we could never know in this world apart from Him.

Acceptable Sacrifice

In the Old Testament, the people of God brought their sacrifices to the tabernacle gate. It was their key to accessing God and indicated their desire to be in relationship with Him. As much as I appreciate that believers today aren't required to offer animal sacrifices, we can't miss the connection between sacrifice, transformation, and access to God. When an animal was slain and burned on an altar, this act connected Heaven and Earth through a transformation process. Remember, God didn't eat the meat. He received the scent of the offering as a pleasing fragrance (see Leviticus 1:13). Some offerings were burnt entirely, but other sacrifices were shared. The priests and the person presenting an offering consumed the food in the physical realm, and God consumed the smoke in the supernatural. It makes me think of the incense of prayer rising before the throne.

Something happens at the threshold of Heaven when we desire to access a new dimension with God. Abraham, even when he was already in covenant with God, had to be willing to lay on the altar

> Sacrifices supernaturally moved people into God's presence.

what was most precious to him in all the world—the life of his son. Not only was Isaac Abraham's beloved miracle child, he was the progenitor he believed God had designated for the fulfillment of His promises. Sometimes sacrifice means letting go of how we think God is going to work in our lives.

The Old Testament illustrates the concept of sacrifices being offered at the door—the entry into God's presence. When we long for a new level, a new experience, or when we feel the Lord calling us to something new, to enter may require a sacrifice—one in which we burn off more "self." Sometimes we offer our passions, plans, and purposes; and other times we present our emotions. One level may involve a sacrifice of ego or pride, and another may call us to present God our feelings of inadequacy or unworthiness. To move forward may challenge us to offer our fears as a sacrifice to God—even fears of what others might think of us. We must will His will and sacrifice the right thing in the right way at the right time.

We may not know what lies behind the doors God leads us to walk through, but we can be certain that our offerings given in obedience and out of love draw us closer to Him. As we decrease and He increases, He takes us to new depths of relationship and perhaps to new dimensions of spiritual authority.

> "Binding and loosing is not the hard part of spiritual warfare. The hard part is crucifixion—the war within."
> —Vani Marshall

What we exalt is exalted in our lives, and when we are Spirit-filled and resist the leading of God, we experience frustration. Our wills agreeing with His will brings us into alignment, and instead of emotional friction, we experience wholeness, unity, and peace. With the fulcrum of the cross as our viewfinder, we refuse to allow our lower natures or reasoning to rule. In the times they attempt to exalt themselves, we cast them down and lift Jesus higher in our lives.

The true reflection of our devotion to God is revealed in our obedience to His Word and conformity to His will. In this section we've talked much about wholeness and oneness with Jesus—about Earth and Heaven being one. At its very core, these concepts boil down to one word: submission.

Submission may not be your favorite word. Perhaps you might prefer "agreement." We're talking about oneness, after all. Submission means choosing to subordinate our pursuits beneath His mission. His plan is exalted. His kingdom leads rather than our little kingdoms of self. Submission means choosing to agree with

God's words and directives, not just mentally, but with the words we speak and the actions we take. Submission means accepting the leadership of the peace of God and applying our hearts, souls, minds, and strength to the leading of His Spirit.

When we agree with God and the righteous ways of His kingdom of peace, we release ourselves from inner conflict. Surrendered to His benevolent, wise leadership, we gain the blessings of true freedom. Disagreement cuts off the flow of the Spirit and crimps our conduits. When we align ourselves with God, we experience a greater flow of His righteousness in and through us. In January 2018, I read Andrew Murray's classic book, *With Christ in the School of Prayer*. I remember one day I read something that pricked my heart so deeply I said out loud, "Lord, You're killing me." I was immediately impressed with the words, "That's what I've been try to do." I literally laughed out loud a long time and smiled even longer as I thanked the Lord for not giving up on me.

When we accept the crucifixion of our flesh, bringing ourselves into agreement with God's will, we know He's not seeking to injure us. He wants to teach us to break the power of the leading of our souls so we can truly walk in newness of life. Choice by choice, we put to death the old ways of doubt and the deeds of the flesh, and instead conform to God's will. The cross beckons believers in every generation to crucify our wills where they compete with God's and align with the kingdom. The resulting wholeness that comes when we surrender all and abide in Christ brings spiritual agreement and a dynamic flow from Heaven that manifests the glory of God in the Earth. We need more of Him because there's yet a great work to be done in this day—our day.

15

Distractions from Without and Within

*The thief cometh not, but for to steal, and to kill,
and to destroy: I am come that they might have life,
and that they might have it more abundantly.*
John 10:10

In the last chapter, we discussed willing God's will. I believe those reading this book desire to live in the dimension of power that comes through obeying the will of God. We must, however, recognize that we face a real enemy. Satan does everything in his power to rob, seduce, and sow discord. He oppresses, depresses, harasses, agitates, and misleads with designs of entrapping God's people to live in obsessions that paralyze our effectiveness and can lead us out of the kingdom itself.

The enemy never tires of attempting to keep us bound or render us anemic. Demonic possession is real, and we'll discuss ministering to those affected in Chapter 21. In this chapter, however, we'll discuss demonic distractions and tactics used by the enemy to disrupt the peace and flow of God in our temples. Those who fail to educate themselves on the enemy's tactics will be taken advantage of by their ignorance (see 2 Corinthians 2:11).

The devil's character clearly contrasts that of God. Jesus said Satan was "a murderer from the beginning, and does not stand in the truth, because there is no truth in him. When he speaks a lie, he speaks from his own resources, for he is a liar and the father of it" (John 8:44, NKJV).

> **Demonic lies and partial truths twist God's Word, but God's Word disarms Satan.**

 Perhaps the greatest truth that neutralizes Satan is a believer's knowledge of the authenticity of who they are in Christ.

Awareness in itself removes the fuses from Satan's devices. He lobs his lies, but they don't detonate. The Bible speaks metaphorically of the enemy's arrows and flaming darts, but these weapons aren't physical. Our weapons as believers aren't physical, either. Spiritual weapons are spiritual. Satan, intent on killing us, attacks our minds with lies, but we have mighty, divinely powerful weapons (see 2 Corinthians 10:4). God enables us to overthrow and destroy enemy strongholds. But if our weapons aren't physical, neither are the strongholds we battle against. Where are these strongholds found?

A stronghold is a place with a fortified position, and even though usually referred to with a negative connotation, a stronghold isn't necessarily bad. In our minds, a stronghold is a belief system (positive or negative). Our belief systems are inundated with the words we hear in our minds, injected by God, our enemy, or our own thoughts. As believers, we profess our desire for kingdom concepts to reign in our lives, but Satan incessantly drops twisted words in our minds that oppose God's plans. It's our responsibility to weed them out before they take root. God enables us to see and capture Satan's lies. We can demand any perversities concede to the truth by casting down imaginations and every high thing that exalts itself (see 2 Corinthians 10:5).

Satan is proficient and clever with his lies ensuring they sound as much like truth as possible. If he can convince us to accept a little untruth, he has an access point where he attempts to build demonic strongholds. He does this by finding areas of weakness or past struggles and reinforcing them in our thoughts. He casually hits the same weak spot over and again until we make a habit of believing his accusations and deceptions. This implicit agreement with the enemy cements a stronghold.

If we constantly struggle in certain areas, we must confront them. If we don't, we can actually give Satan access into our lives. In a sense, he sticks a flag in the ground at the point of entrance and builds a little fortress there. Then, when we read the Word, hear a message, or God directly speaks to us, the enemy attacks our minds from the fortified place. He attempts to persuade us that God's Word couldn't be true. He tries to convince us biblical principles are outdated and

> "The enemy knows what you lean on, and he will exploit it." —Tes Stewart

irrelevant. He can be very convincing, indeed, but we can keep him away by refusing to share any "common ground" with him.

 Jesus didn't share common ground with Satan, and therefore he had no claim upon Him. Jesus said Satan had "nothing in Him" (see John 14:30). Another translation expresses it this way, "He has nothing in common with Me; there is nothing in Me that belongs to him, and he has no power over Me" (AMPC). When we refuse to share common ground with the enemy, he also has no power over us.

Victory comes to us when we remember our place in God—a place far above our enemies. When we're "in Christ," we're in a position above the devil (see Colossians 3:3). He really is under our feet. Our enemy has no authority or power over us unless we allow him to displace us, and he will try, but believers are not to give place to the devil (see Ephesians 4:27). Metaphorically, this means we can't give him a station, position, or an opportunity to gain power.

Pulling Down Strongholds

You and I don't have to agree with every thought that comes our way. Satan's biggest lie is to convince us that we should believe him instead of believing God. He masquerades as an angel of light (Lucifer means "shining one") and his demons as "ministers of righteousness" (see 2 Corinthians 11:14-15). He is, in fact, a peddler of falsehood. That's why it's so important we know and use God's Word against him. Jesus exemplified this tactic. He fought the temptations Satan presented him with, "It is written," or "On the other hand." Satan offers partial truths and misuses Scripture, but when we respond with the whole counsel of God, it puts the devil in his place. Jesus lifted the Word of God to its position of rightful authority and silenced the enemy.

Every theory, argument, or reasoning that sets itself against the true knowledge of God originates with a satanic attempt to captivate our minds. We must filter the words we hear and determine their source: God, Satan, or self.

The Lord who spoke light and life into nothingness still speaks. His voice still vibrates in the atmosphere. Unfortunately, many don't realize the enemy also transmits messages using the same spiritual communication method. Continually

> It's vitally important to know the origins of our thoughts.

inundated with unseen "radio" waves to decode, our minds can affect our ability to receive and process what God is transmitting. Signals from the enemy's camp seek to lodge there to affect our spirits. We must constantly filter what comes to us. Purposefully, we reject negative spiritual interference or communications.

The Powers That Be

We've talked much about spiritual power available to believers. Let's look now at the type of power Satan has in our world today. We can deduce from Scripture that Satan doesn't have power to directly touch or harm believers. In the Old Testament we read of his encounter with Job, but note the devil had to get permission from God before he could engineer weather or elements or cause illness.

Surely, Satan would kill off every believer if he could, but he has no power to accomplish his murderous goals. Instead, he whispers and uses humans to influence each other, especially those in power. People become his agents and do his bidding, even those unaware. We see this exemplified in Ezekiel's address to the "King of Tyre" and the identification of the power working behind the man (see Ezekiel 28:13-17). We see how Satan attempts to position himself behind authority figures. From his hidden position, he then whispers instructions, and the leaders function as his pawns in the world. Many are completely oblivious to what's happening in the unseen realm.

Satan not only influences world leaders, he also lays snares to entrap the most devout among us (see 1 Timothy 3:7). He attempts to discourage or influence Christ followers, especially spiritual leaders, to entangle themselves with unbelief or to repeat former sins at his suggestion. He tirelessly promotes sinful manners, sinful mindsets, and sinful lifestyles in hopes that we'll turn back to our old sinful natures. The devil weaves his snare with attractive and alluring voices from the past, and then follows up with accusations if the believer should stumble. The devil endeavors to damage the effectiveness of our ministry by tricking us into compromising our reputation. The old fox loves to engage fear tactics and shame to frighten and dissuade us from exercising the power God gave us, but when we stay in tune with the Lord, we don't have to be afraid of the devil (see Zechariah 4:6-10, Psalm 27:1-6).

Ultimately, Satan wants to feed on God's people. Look at the language of Scripture. The Word describes him as a roaring lion aggressively pursuing to devour and setting snares like hunters who trap game for food (see 1 Peter 5:8, 2 Timothy 2:26). He seeks to consume our faith.

We're in a war. The battle lines have been drawn, but God's people already have the victory. We simply walk in truth and speak God's Word. When the devil accuses us, we turn to the Word that says, "If we confess our sin, he is faithful and just to forgive us our sin and cleanse us from all unrighteousness" (1 John 1:9). When we hear the whisper that we don't have what it takes to live for God, we combat that lie with "I can do all things through Christ who strengthens me" (Philippians 4:13). We cast our anxieties on God and remind ourselves that greater is He in us than he who is in the world (see 1 Peter 5:7, 1 John 4:4).

> We can't believe Satan's lies and God's truth simultaneously.

Delusions of Grandeur

Satan, the deceiver, invites us to join him on a spiritual snipe hunt where we seek to bag what doesn't even really exist: a self-governed "good life" lived without the constraints or blessings of the righteousness, peace, and joy of God's kingdom. His own delusion of grandeur contradicted his true identity and resulted in his fall. But still, he fans the fires of pride in our hearts to entice us to make the same mistake he did.

The apostle Paul wasn't ignorant of Satan's devices, and you and I should know our enemy, as well. We know his primary method is deception, but how does he do that specifically? One way is by misleading us. He uses false appearances or statements to coax people into wrong patterns of thinking so they will inevitably act on those thoughts. He deceives with false and empty promises. He brings to our minds complexities that confuse and cause us to question ourselves and God. We get trapped in thoughts of "what if this?" and "what about that?" and "if this happens, then what?" He plays word games with language to hide the realities of sin—for instance, reidentifying what God calls sin with new, contemporary labels. Murdering an unborn baby is "reproductive freedom." What God calls perverse, Satan calls an "alternative lifestyle" and even takes God's own rainbow as a symbol of pride flown as the banner of those who reject what is right, good, and proper. The Bible says, "Woe to those who call evil good, and good evil" (Isaiah 5:20). Sin, no matter the name, is still as wrong and wicked as God's Word says it is. Sin is transgressing the law of God, regardless of what we call it, and the wages of sin are still death (see 1 John 3:4, Romans 6:23).

Another enemy tactic includes information overload. In today's world we're constantly awash with information that requires great care to keep in check and balance. This same device can also divert our attention away from the most important things in life. We can become so absorbed in our cares, anxieties, and fears, we focus on things of lesser importance. Worse yet, sometimes these diversions cause division in the body of Christ. What first affects a person's inner peace, can eventually drive wedges of disagreement as individuals form camps supporting their opinions.

The devil also deceives by discouragement. Of course, we can feel discouraged without any demonic assistance, and there's always room for improvement, but we shouldn't live with a mindset of, "I can never measure up" or "I can never do enough." Not only does the enemy attack who we think we are and our abilities, he attacks our perception of who God is. If we listen to misinformation and accusations, our focus can flip from the kingdom of God and turn on ourselves. We become easily offended, and when our attention is trained on offences and issues, even demonically inspired feelings of inadequacy or shame, our effectiveness in the supernatural realm comes to a halt. We don't have the luxury to allow our feelings to diminish our capacity to build the kingdom.

> "The devil doesn't try to get you to give him your future—just your today."
> —J. H. Osborne

> "If you are going through intense training, God is positioning you for intense things." —Brandon McKenzie

Intimidation

The devil attempts to intimidate us. Not only so that we would be lost, but to keep us out of the field of God's harvest. You and I have no need to fear a vanquished foe. Yes, the enemy can be a pain in the neck. We need to make sure we have our armor on and resist the wiles of the devil, but we have a hedge that cannot be penetrated from the outside in. We can't be stopped unless we stop at the false direction of the enemy. We've already discussed Satan's devices, but consider this. Jesus destroyed the works of Satan. He came into the world for this purpose: "that He might destroy the works of the devil" (1 John 3:8). The blood of Jesus severed any claim Satan had on our lives. He still roars and seeks whom he can devour, but it's not going to be me, and it doesn't have to be you—or our children.

Satan's half-truths and intimidations are nothing more than a feathery veil suspended by the father of lies. With the diabolical intention of clouding our minds, he attempts to make us think our calling, destiny, and promises are out of reach. We don't have to stay behind Satan's shroud. We can sweep it aside. It has no power to keep us from what God has placed in our lives. But before we can sweep the veil aside, we have to recognize it for what it is—intimidation.

Why would people or demons use intimidation? Because they're trying to gain control, to influence, or to restrain. Intimidation is employed when reality—the truth of a situation—differs from what the enemy wants us to think. That's why he concocts the lies he whispers into our ears.

One day during my personal devotions, the Lord brought to mind an image of a scarecrow. A message began to form around the idea. A scarecrow is nothing more than a decoy propped in a field to frighten others away. As adults, you and I wouldn't be frightened from entering a field because of a powerless straw man.

The term "strawman" is one we usually hear in politics and other debates, meaning an intentionally misrepresented, exaggerated proposition set up because it's easier to defeat than an opponent's real argument. It's a form of argument that's based on a fallacy, as we see with the serpent's argument in the garden of Eden: "Did God really say. . . ?" This lie misrepresented God's words with the simple goal of making it easier to attack Adam and Eve. The devil has always used a strawman argument to lay a foundation to make his position seem to be the reasonable one. But a strawman argument is dishonest, and the enemy doesn't play fair. What he did in Eden, he still does today. He presented himself as more intelligent, having the better position, and Eve became persuaded the enemy made the best offer. We can't allow ourselves to get drawn into strawman debates with the devil, any demon, nor any demonically influenced member of his entourage.

A strawman attack isn't real. Those engaging the enemy's discourse may claim to have victory, but they base their rhetoric on a false position. In reality, a strawman argument reveals weakness, not strength. Take heart. Our God is mighty. He's able. And He's undefeated. The earth is His, and the fullness thereof.

In our world today, we usually think of scarecrows along with hay bales and pumpkins displayed in the fall, but farmers plant scarecrows in the fields at springtime with their seed to protect it until the harvest is brought in.

Our enemy is standing guard over the unregenerate souls in the world's harvest field, but the Word of God says the fields are ready for reaping. The scarecrow's job is to run off unwanted visitors. His goal is to scare

> Scarecrows are guardians of the harvest.

us away, to frighten us. The only weapons he has in his arsenal are his words, and so he uses them to intimidate.

Intimidation is a word made of three parts: *in-* means "to enclose;" *timid* means "lacking in self-assurance or courage, fearful or shy;" and *-ation* indicates an "action, state, or condition." Put it all together and you get in-timid-ation:

- Being enclosed in a condition of a lack of self-assurance or courage.
- Being confined in a state of fear or shyness.
- Being restrained by forces that dominate—forces from without and forces from within.

At some time in our lives we'll face intimidation. Elijah (one of God's boldest prophets) ran for his life when Jezebel threatened him after a great victory (see 1 Kings 19:2-3). Sanballat and Tobiah mocked and intimidated Nehemiah when the Lord sent him to rebuild the walls of Jerusalem (see Nehemiah 4:3). The Lord called Gideon a mighty man of valor, but Gideon's focus on his low situation filled his mind with doubts and questions (see Judges 6:12-16). The apostle Paul acknowledged his personal struggle with intimidation when he said, "And I was with you in weakness, and in fear, and in much trembling" (1 Corinthians 2:3).

The root of intimidation is fear, and when people are afraid, their focus turns to themselves. But God's Word tells us, "Perfect love casts out fear" (see 1 John 4:18). When our love is perfect toward God, it refocuses our attention, and compels us to lay down our lives and our fears for the kingdom. In fact, our relationship with God is what empowers us to resist Satan (see James 4:7).

Order in the Church

Satan, "the ruler of this world," is also called "the prince of the power of the air" and the "god of this world" (see John 12:32, Ephesians 2:2, 2 Corinthians 4:4). But in what sense does Satan truly "rule" the world?

"World" refers to several things in the Word. It speaks of the moral world and the people who are indifferent or hostile to God. In this sense, "the world" refers to corruption and evil—to the ungodly. It's not referring to the church. God's redeemed live in the world, but we're not of it (see 1 John 4:4-6). When the Bible speaks of Satan ruling over the world, it's clarifying his limited authority over a realm of sin—only among those who live in willful opposition to God. The enemy leads the rebellion against God, but he has no power over you and me unless God gives it to him. We don't find in Scripture many instances of that happening. Job was the exception, not the rule.

Unreckoned, un-dealt-with intimidation, can keep us from functioning in our calls. It can cause the gifts of God within us to go dormant. The devil knows this, and so he continues implementing his time-tested tactics. Intimidation may scream or whisper, but its message is the same. "You aren't good enough. Who do you think you are? You can't do that. What will people think of you? You're going to fall flat on your face. You better sit down—back off."

We touched on this concept earlier, but I want to give you a specific strategy for dealing with intimidation: what I call word-immersion therapy. We must immerse ourselves in the Word. Rehearse who we are in Christ and revel in the joy of being not only free from sin, but free from shame. When God looks at us, He doesn't see past failures. He sees something beautiful—a beloved child cleansed from all unrighteousness (see 1 John 1:9).

Peter failed the Lord. He denied him, but the Lord filled him with boldness to speak before a great assembly on the day of Pentecost and used him to help found the New Testament church. Like Peter, we can dust ourselves off from failure and move forward with boldness. Amelia Earhart called fear "paper tigers" that keep people from making decisions toward action. The church of the living God shouldn't let paper tigers hold us back from accomplishing God's purposes in the earth.

Someone once said, "A brave man dies but once, a coward dies a thousand times." If we don't want to die a thousand times, we have to knock down fear with faith. We recover our courage and regain strength when we remember that Jesus died once and for all. When we (and our fears) are crucified with Christ, we truly live (see Galatians 2:20). And when you and I act bravely, we can open doors that were closed. We can rescue people previously held hostage by the enemy's lies.

Hannah Hurnard, author of the book *Hinds Feet on High Places*, once struggled terribly with fear. I read her story in the April 6, 1995, entry of *The Daily Bread* devotional. In the article, she said she heard a sermon on scarecrows that challenged her to turn her fears to faith. She said the preacher's message went like this, "A wise bird knows that a scarecrow is simply an advertisement. It announces that some very juicy and delicious fruit is to be had for the picking. There are scarecrows in all the best gardens. . . .

"If I am wise, I too shall treat the scarecrow as though it were an invitation. Every giant in the way which makes me feel like a grasshopper is only a scarecrow beckoning me to God's richest blessings."

The preacher Hannah was listening to concluded his message with this: "Faith is a bird which loves to perch on scarecrows. All our fears are groundless." She testified that this humble parable encouraged her to walk along some frightening but fruitful pathways more times than she could number.

What is your scarecrow today? Difficult circumstances? Personal inadequacy? Uncertainty? The enemy of your soul wants to keep you away from the place of God's blessing, but you are authorized to settle on that scarecrow by faith. Start singing like a bird on a perch and expect an abundant feast! The Word of God says, "Cast not away therefore your confidence, which hath great recompence of reward" (Hebrews 10:35). The harvest is great.

It's time to silence the strawman, to close our ears to his twisting words and ways. To be confident and walk out and do what God has called us to do—today, this week, this month, tomorrow at the grocery store, wherever and whatever. We must refuse to let the enemy's roars of intimidation stop us.

Before the actual writing of *Kingdom Come*, I spent months gathering my notes and doing research that I broke into chapters. The day I began the work of composing this chapter, freakish things began happening in our home. A closet door wouldn't open, and when I gave it a hard tug, a very heavy vintage ironing board fell down and hit me hard on the head. The pointed end slammed into my forehead. Thankfully no goose egg formed, and I didn't even bruise until a couple of days later (revealing the depth of the injury). For three days, pain remained and even traveled down to affect my vision. At the same time, a financial issue surfaced that required hours of frustrating research. All the effort was for nothing, and we ended up owing thousands of dollars we thought we wouldn't have to pay. While busy with the paperwork, out of the blue, the water stopped working in the house. The well pump had an issue that demanded attention at 10 p.m. at night. Thankfully my husband was able to fix it, but it was only temporary, and became a major issue with our well.

> "The lion's roar is meant to intimidate—create pandemonium and fear for miles. Just because you hear the roar doesn't mean you are in danger." —Tes Stewart

It seemed the enemy was coming in like a flood, situation after situation, wave crashing upon wave. Two requests for interviews surfaced and a request for an article—all within three days. And I won't mention the concerns that arose with people dear to my heart. Honestly, I was super frustrated with the timing. I felt hijacked and struggled to keep peace in my temple. Even the content of this chapter challenged me as I attempted to reconcile all I'd studied and written with what I was experiencing in the moment—that seemed like a curtain of fire from the enemy's camp.

Chapter 15: Distractions from Without and Within

I needed clarification on just what kind of power the enemy has in a believer's life, because Hell seemed to be breaking loose in my house. As I set about getting the coffee pot ready for the morning, the Lord gave me some understanding. What I'd written wasn't wrong, just incomplete. The enemy had sent his floods, but God raised up a standard—He brought a refreshing word that drove away the overwhelming feelings I was experiencing.

The enemy has no power in our lives to make us sin. There's nothing any demon could do that could separate us from the love of God or break our relationship with Him. His power is limited to the things of this world. We aren't of this world, but ironing boards and water pumps and bills are. So while we know God keeps the eternal part of us, in this world, the enemy does have influence. He lies to us. He manipulates others to do evil or even just become distractions. Perhaps he has the ability to affect some of the physical things around us in this world. My recent experience reminded me of the importance of praying for God's protection and blessings as well as holding loosely to the things of this world. Even people.

We must remain suited up in the armor of God. I understand the positive impact "praying on the armor" has had for many, and I'd never advise anyone to stop doing that, but I want to make the point that this armor is spiritual. It's not something we visibly attach to our bodies in the morning when we dress. God's truth unceasingly protects us from being victimized by Satan's lies. Our righteousness is as a breastplate that continually guards our hearts from evil. We stand firm in the good news of the gospel even when we're barefoot. We don't step out of our gospel shoes when we step in the front door of our homes or when we go to bed at night. The shield of faith ever helps us deflect the fiery darts Satan throws our way. God knows we need the helmet of salvation on our heads at all times to keep our minds focused and aware so the enemy won't gain any strongholds in our thoughts.

Consider this: when soldiers are out in the field doing operations or engaging in battle, they may not be able to take their uniforms off for days and must keep their weapons close at hand. In the military, troops are rotated out of this environment to recharge and relax, but when they're in the combat zone, they must be ready at all times. You and I serve in a spiritual military combat zone. God gives us seasons of spiritual rest, but we're always on call to battle and always a target for the enemy.

So yes, believers "put on" spiritual armor, but we don't willfully step out of it and expose ourselves to our enemy because he is ruthlessly seeking whom he may devour. Our words are not what matter as much as the reality of what we live. Truth, righteousness, faith, peace, salvation, God's Word and Spirit must remain active in our lives. This way, we can be prepared at all times to live in spiritual victory.

"And do this, knowing the time, that now it is high time to awake out of sleep; for now our salvation is nearer than when we first believed. The night is far spent, the day is at hand. Therefore let us cast off the works of darkness, and let us put on the armor of light. Let us walk properly, as in the day, not in revelry and drunkenness, not in lewdness and lust, not in strife and envy. But put on the Lord Jesus Christ, and make no provision for the flesh to fulfill its lusts" (Romans 13:11–14).

> The more truth we walk in, the more power we have over Satan.

Distractions from Within

In addition to activity from Satan's realm attempting to influence our lives, sometimes distractions come from within. People struggle with inner distractions such as anxiety, doubt, fear, pride, and jealousy that interfere with their focus. Understanding the origin of internal distractions will help us address them effectively.

Sometimes distractions stem from spiritual transformation issues. Other times they're enemy provoked as we have discussed at length. Still, other times they're simply human tendencies that must be brought into agreement with God's Word. In addition to the traits mentioned above, we need to evaluate our personal contributions to distraction. Perhaps our own unrealistic expectations of others and self can cause inner turmoil. This goes hand-in-hand with a tendency toward all-or-nothing thinking that can cause anyone to swing like a pendulum between feeling like a failure or the king of the mountain.

When we face internal distractions, we need to hit the pause button on the thoughts that replay like video clips looping over and over in our minds. We stop the procession, evaluate our thoughts against the light of truth, deal with what is, and move on. It's also beneficial to remember we don't have to accept every negative thought that comes our way. Put them on the witness stand and cross-examine them with the Word of God. Where did it come from? Is it true?

Sometimes we make ourselves too busy or fall victim to the many gadgets and notifications that beg for our attention. Our focus can be derailed by watching what others are doing and wishing for more opportunities for ourselves. At the end of the day, each of us must focus on what God has called us to do. If we fail to keep our thoughts in agreement with His, we may find ourselves discouraged or driving off-road as we stare in the wrong direction.

Chapter 15: Distractions from Without and Within

 Remember that every interruption isn't necessarily a distraction meant to defeat us.

Jesus allowed Himself to be interrupted, and sometimes God allows our days to be interrupted by divine appointments. At times He calls us to turn aside and be with Him or stop what we're doing to minister to others.

Satan will never stop attacking, and our brains are going to keep whirling, so we must be attentive, aware, and prepared to face the distractions of life. We can overcome distress and disorder by defeating the works of Satan and his domain of darkness. God's truth breaks his power and sets us free (see John 3:8). When we walk in the light of truth, God's Spirit exposes the darkness and His light pushes darkness out of hiding. The enemy may send a lion to destroy you, but you're powerful through Christ that is within you. Pick up your sword and slay it—and you just may find honey in its carcass. Honey you didn't make, but that you can eat and press to the lips of others who need strength and deliverance.

16

Secret Weapons

His divine power has given to us all things that pertain to life and godliness.
2 Peter 1:3

God, in His grace, has positioned and privileged us with all we need to live a life pleasing to Him and function in His kingdom. He equips us by divine power and works in us to mature our faith. In this chapter we'll look at what I'm calling "secret weapons." The enemy knows their power, but the church needs to recognize the power at her disposal.

Worship

No one understands the power of worship like Lucifer. He knows that when people worship, a shift happens in the spirit world. This is the very reason he tempted Jesus to worship him. Worship is a powerful weapon—one that can reverse the current trend of events and pave the way for victory.

Worship enthrones the Lord in our hearts, and God hears those who worship Him (see John 9:31). When we worship, chains break. As we worship God, what the enemy sent to restrain us backfires from Heaven and binds the power of the enemy. Psalm 149, a psalm of praise, speaks of singing, rejoicing, dancing, and playing instruments before the Lord—and not just at church. Worship can take place anytime and anywhere, even on our beds at home. The high praise of God in our mouths executes "vengeance upon the heathen, and punishments upon the people; To bind their kings with chains, and their nobles with fetters of iron" (Psalm 149:7–8).

Our worship grants to us the power to execute judgment. Not simply reserved for the elite, this privilege is available to every saint. Yes, to every believer (see v 9). The enemy has attempted to bind the hands of our families and our churches, but when we praise, those chains open and fall to the ground. Loosed from the shackles that were meant to place us into the servitude of the enemy, we instead tether our adversary with fetters of iron.

Imprisoned in Philippi, Paul and Silas could have worried, but that wouldn't have changed their circumstances. Worship, on the other hand, brought Heaven to Earth. The shackles and bands that had restrained the men suddenly fell to the ground when they prayed and sang praises to God (see Acts 16:25). The two ministers weren't the only ones set free. Other prisoners found themselves loosed, and even the prison guard was freed from the most powerful restraints of all, the shackles and bonds of sin.

Praise so many times precedes victory. It's also a mighty weapon (see 2 Chronicles 20:22, Joshua 6:20).

Both Old Testament and New Testament illustrations reveal the power of praising God—in the good times and the bad. I know at times life pushes so hard against us we can't express our petitions in words. But I also know that no matter our circumstances, we can always express love and praise to the Lord. I found in my own life that when my heart was broken and I didn't know what or how to pray, I could still find within me the words to say, "I love You, Jesus. I trust You. I worship and honor You." I believe these simple words are among the highest forms of praise.

When we praise God, even though our situations see no improvement, we can still live in victory. How? Because the atmosphere changes. God's presence joins us. The enemy isn't going to hang around in the atmosphere that forms when we worship the Lord.

The highest praise comes from the lowest places.

While meditating in my place of prayer one day, I was considering how God responds to the praises of His people. He shows up. I thought of how in an earthly kingdom, royalty never travels alone, and so it is in the heavenly kingdom. When He enters a place, He brings an angelic host with Him—an entourage from the court of Heaven. An image kept coming to mind of the Lord of Hosts entering a room surrounded by royal attendants lined up and waiting for their assignments. I imagined people worshipping. The delight that worship brought to the Lord's heart activated His intervention on their behalf. See Him delighting in your worship and dispatching angels, "You, go take care of that need for My son, My daughter."

I believe in prayer, but I also believe that we sometimes forget the power of our worship. God assigns ministering spirits and warring angels to move on behalf of those who entertain His presence. Perhaps we wouldn't have to fight with darkness quite as often if we would simply entertain the presence of the Lord and let the Lord fight our battles instead. If we want to experience more angelic and spiritual demonstration among us, we can create an atmosphere with our praise and worship.

Words of praise spoken into the supernatural realm open the prophetic, because praise ushers in the presence of God. David knew the power of worship. He also knew he couldn't let what others thought of his exuberant praise hinder him from giving his all to God. His wife, Michal, openly despised David's uninhibited worship, and for her mockery, she ended up isolated, barren, unfruitful, and miserable. When David worshiped, not only was he blessed, but the borders of Israel expanded, and the nation prospered as never before. What would Michal's life have become if she had rejoiced with her husband? What would God release into our lives if we would truly abandon ourselves in worship to Him?

> "The more you worship, the less you warfare." —Billy Cole

A Word from Bill

I share the following testimony with my husband's permission.

The Lord had been speaking to me about prayer and praising—instructing me and encouraging me. One day, a revelation about the delivering power of worship opened to my mind. I let loose and danced through my house, shouting, worshipping, and declaring the name of Jesus over people's lives. I remember standing on the carpet in our prayer room and singing, "Take the shackles off my feet so I can dance."

The very next day, my husband Bill joined me in our prayer room, which also serves as a guest room. I sat in the rocking chair reading and he "lay before the Lord" on the bed. I didn't know until later that he'd been peeking at me behind closed eyes and asking the Lord, "Why am I so tired? I know Lori's tired, but she's not sleeping all the time."

I left the room for about ten minutes, and when I came back, Bill was standing with his arms stretched out and an unusual look on his face.

"What's going on?" I asked.

As he lay beneath the wall art that said, "With God all things are possible," the Lord impressed him with the words, "You've been struggling with depression."

A light bulb came on. Originally blaming his feelings on fatigue, it had never crossed his mind that his tiredness could be connected to depression. He was now convinced it was more than simply a physical cause.

He asked the Lord, "What do I do?"

The Lord answered, "Worship me."

Bill sprang to his feet and began singing, "Take the shackles off my feet so I can dance." He was shaking his wrists and dancing until I burst in on him and asked, "What's going on?"

After he explained what had happened, we rejoiced together: deliverance had manifested. God-fearing, God-loving, people all over the world may be struggling with things they can't even identify or describe. Our praise can change the atmosphere in such a way that the Lord brings issues to our attention. He still delivers those who worship Him.

There was victory and deliverance in the Wagner house that day, and it came after I responded to what the Lord had shown me about worship. Worship breaks our chains and sends them back to bind the enemy that sent them. And the atmosphere, now saturated with the presence and power of God, liberates others. There's strength in worship—even an intercessory force. Have you ever considered the power of "intercessory worship?" If God's people will truly worship the Lord in the beauty of holiness, who knows what will break free.

The devil hates our worship because when we worship the Lord, we are taking his place (see Ezekiel 28:13). We partake of the glory he lost forever. He knows the power of the manifestation that happens in the flow of the Spirit. Worship strengthens God's people and releases a flow from Heaven to Earth. He strives to diminish this. He doesn't want you to experience it for yourself or use it as a weapon against his evil agenda.

When we're free in worship, the sound of our footfalls can release a spiritual reverberation that sends enemies running in the opposite direction.

Like the Lord amplified the steps of the lepers outside Samaria and brought a great victory, God uses the foolish things of this world to confound the wise (see 2 Kings 7:3-20). Our weapons of war aren't only those mentioned by Paul to the Ephesians—a shield of faith, a sword of the Spirit, and so on. We also have shouts of joy, clapping hands, and dancing feet. We strike the ground in victory with every step and inflict damage on the kingdom of darkness—liberating others, creating unity, and activating supernatural activity. When we fill our houses with praise, He fills them with His glory. And where His glory is, there is power, freedom, victory, love, and miracles.

> "Praise is God's address—an invitation to Him to show up and do the supernatural."
> —Jimmy Toney

Spiritual Awareness

Spiritual awareness is another secret weapon in our arsenals. Discerning of spirits is a spiritual gift, but the broader topic of spiritual awareness includes supernatural knowledge and insight available to every believer. God imparts revelation. He gives clarity and direction. At times we may see an image, receive a word in our minds, or an impression in our spirits. These help us recognize and break free from distractions that compete for our attention, our service, even our devotion.

Spiritual awareness is sharpened or dulled according to our spiritual condition. Are we connected with God and ready to receive at any time? Or are we thinking and acting carnally? Discernment operates to a higher degree among those who are sensitive to the spiritual atmosphere around them. They see and sense things others don't, such as visions and dreams that make them aware of the supernatural realm. Sometimes it's as simple as "sensing"—or a feeling of unrest. Other times it's an ability to intuitively "know more" than the information being presented or to experience a hyper-awareness of the conditions in a situation or environment.

While spiritual awareness is something every believer can develop, the Lord also at times operates in the church through the spiritual gift called "discernment of spirits." Out of the blue, a person operating in this gift can perceive information needed to warn others in times of danger, keep them from being led astray, and also encourage obedience in the right direction (see 1 Corinthians 12:10). As a gift of the Spirit, discernment is granted as the Lord determines, and may manifest at any time that God deems it beneficial for the common good (see 1 Corinthians 12:7). This God-given ability to distinguish whether a source is divine, human, or demonic, is helpful in knowing how to minister to others.

Jesus operated with discernment. He said and did only what He saw and heard, and when we see and hear, then we'll also know what to speak and do. When God opens our eyes to a gift or calling in someone's life, this spiritual understanding enables us to confidently pray the will of the Father for and even with them. Armed with accurate information, we partner with God to release His vision. We become channels of Heaven to Earth.

The gift of discernment can reveal to us another person's pure intentions, their human desires, or even demonic influence. When we receive insight from God, we should stay especially attuned to the Spirit, yielded to the things He reveals. Sometimes it means walking away from a situation, other times it means pressing in, regardless, we hone in on the voice of the Spirit and persevere in prayer until we see an answer or a burden lifts. God equips us with spiritual awareness so we can minister to others and also so we can power through distractions that break the peace in our temples. God reveals to us where the enemy attempts to infiltrate our communications lines and lets us know the origins of any disruptive signals.

When we walk with discernment, our comprehension deepens past what we can see in the natural, and delves into the spiritual nature of a matter. We are informed by the kingdom how to operate with wisdom and laser-focus. Spiritual discernment provides the insight we need to function creatively, maneuver as necessary, and face the enemy head-on. Following the leading of His Spirit is a mark of the maturity of our faith and our kingdom usability.

Prayer and Fasting

Prayer and fasting also helps us develop spiritual insight. As we focus our attention on God, we curtail mental and spiritual clutter to become more sensitive to hearing His voice. The book of Job speaks of fasting, but the first fast mentioned in the Bible isn't recorded until the time of David's reign (see 2 Samuel 12:21). Joel proclaimed a fast (see Joel 1:14, 2:15), Esther called a three-day fast, and Nineveh's fast saved the nation from destruction (see Esther 4:16, Jonah 3:5). In the Old Testament, fasts were called in response to calamities or impending doom. They demonstrated humility and repentance, which seem to be the primary reasons believers today would fast as well. The New Testament reveals Jesus's fasting and His teaching on how to fast properly (see Luke 4:1-4, Matthew 6:16-18). The early church fasted and prayed before sending out missionaries, but Scripture doesn't specify any mandated fasts by the church at large (see Acts 13:1-3). What we should note is that in the Word, there are special times of fasting called, and fasting always intends to demonstrate humility, seek divine intervention, and acknowledge His sovereignty.

Fasting and prayer seem to work together to humble our souls, increase our faith, deepen our spiritual sensitivity, and improve our ability to keep our carnal appetites under control—all of which impart a greater dimension of power (see Psalm 35:13, Matthew 17:20-21). Simply going without food might not seem a power-enhancing activity, but the result of fasting with a right motivation is yoke-breaking power and anointing that sets captives free.

Dr. David K. Bernard said on the subject of prayer and fasting, "When Jesus said 'this comes not out but by prayer and fasting,' He meant that they needed supernatural resources to draw from, a depth of relationship that is enhanced through prayer and fasting, rather than attempting to take authority by using simply a human command."

Jesus expects His followers to fast, but He gave only the most basic instructions. "When you fast . . . anoint your head and wash your face" (see Matthew 6:16-18). In other words, we don't make a public show, but we fast in secret. God, who sees our secret actions, openly rewards.

> "Fasting is spiritual concentration. Concentrating your mind, body, and soul to know God and to know His will." —David Nasser

Fasting can affect health—for the positive or for the negative. For this reason, individuals must know their own bodies, potential health issues, and be led by the Lord before engaging in a fast of any length. In the New Testament, to fast means to entirely abstain from food or drink for religious reasons. The length of a fast was usually a day but was at times longer. The primary idea behind fasting was keeping the mouth shut, which speaks to more than just not eating. When we fast, we close our mouths and forgo unnecessary talking. We close our mouths and open our ears and hearts to see and hear what God has to say. Today, the concept behind fasting could also include abstaining from certain activities of entertainment, enjoyment, or social involvement. Although not technically a biblical fast, shutting out activities that normally consume our time in the spirit of a fast (to see and hear from God), can help us focus on His voice.

We do need to be aware that fasting is not a means of earning blessings, neither do we fast to punish our flesh. As a general practice, fasting helps us keep our priorities straight, and at times, focus on specific needs. Fasting and prayer can, in a sense, affect God to move on behalf of His people. He responds to those with contrite hearts—those who change their attitudes and seek Him.

Some might say Jesus rebuked the Pharisees for fasting, but His rebuke was more about their attitude regarding the practice. They fasted as a religious tradition and to gain public honor because of their reputation in the practice. There's always a human tendency for fasting to slip into becoming a duty or mere discipline. If that happens, we turn our hearts to again approach fasting from a biblical perspective. Anna the prophetess offers a beautiful example of one who willingly gave herself to prayer and fasting (see Luke 2:37). God blessed her consecration and sacrifice by allowing her to be one of the very first to see Jesus and recognize His role in the redemption of Jerusalem.

> Biblical fasting offers what we would consume to another.

God desires to bring great revival, and I believe prayer and fasting are important components to seeing the kingdom activated in the Earth. But we must not forget God's correction of those who, while seemingly eager to know His ways, fasted food, but forsook His commands. They didn't eat, but they spent their days in quarreling and strife. God said He wouldn't answer their prayers or reward their fast unless they fasted acceptably, lived righteously, and lived with hands extended to others. That included doing away with criticism and malicious talk and instead spending themselves on behalf of the hungry and helping the oppressed (see Isaiah 58).

> What food does for the body, fasting does for the soul.

Fasting means nothing to God when our conduct lifts a stench to His nostrils. But for those who seek to demonstrate the nature of God with pure motives, it prepares and positions them for spiritual breakthrough. With increased power, anointing, and revelation, we're led less and less by our carnal nature. Fasting and prayer prime the pump and draw us closer to God. They keep our conduits clean from obstacles that would block the flow of the Spirit.

The Helper

The Lord said He was Israel's Help. This word translated from the Hebrew word *ezer*, is the very same word used to describe Eve, the one made to be Adam's helper. *Ezer* means "aid" and "help." It comes from a root word focused on girding, surrounding, and subsequently, defending. When God is our helper, He's a strength, a military ally, and a shield about His people.

As we seek to walk closely with the Lord, He's promised to help us. We need only to look up (see Psalm 121:1). I will close out this chapter with a personal story to share that God not only promised to help, He wants to help, and He does help.

Chapter 16: Secret Weapons

In 2018, I was ministering in Newport News, Virginia, when I learned of the passing of a precious lady, Joy Scott. I met Joy in St. Louis while doing research for a book I was writing, a biography on the life and ministry of evangelist Willie Johnson. I felt compelled by the Spirit to forfeit my return air ticket, and instead rent a car and drive the five and a half hours to Marmat, West Virginia. I'd never heard of Marmat, but that was the place where Joy Scott would be laid to rest, and I felt I should be there for her funeral.

It was going to cost several hundred dollars to rent a car and get a hotel, so I prayed and asked the Lord for confirmation. While I was still thinking about it, I received an email from the Pentecostal Publishing House ordering enough copies of Willie Johnson's biography to more than cover the price of the trip.

I suddenly had such peace about going. I spoke to my husband and asked for his input. He's not usually quick about making decisions, and so I was surprised when he immediately said, "I think you should go." I made the arrangements to drive to Marmat, and as I looked at the directions, I saw the little town was nine minutes from Charleston, West Virginia, where Willie Johnson had lived and based her ministry for decades. It was also the place of her burial. I knew with certainty that God, once again, had set me on this path for a specific purpose. After picking up the rental car, I drove the winding roads from Virginia to West Virginia. I had no trouble finding the cemetery, but I had no idea how I was going to find Willie's gravesite.

On the day of my visit, Sunset Memorial Park served as the final resting place for the remains of 13,156 people. It was raining, and I drove around clueless where to begin. I turned a corner and saw a building at the back of the graveyard. I thought perhaps it was an office or might provide a map, but it was a mausoleum.

I stepped back inside the car and prayed. "Lord, You brought me here. You directed me to this place and made a way for me to come. If you want me to find her, show me where she is."

I drove just a short way around a curve in the road and put the car in park. I felt impressed to stop and get out. It was raining, the ground was wet, and I was wearing open shoes. But there, among thousands of gravesites, I exited the car, circled around the back, and immediately saw her marker. I went to the site and did a little dip in amazement. With joy I cried out to God, "You did it! You did it!" I confess, I even jumped a couple of times.

I know I shouldn't have been surprised, but I was just so delighted. I cleaned off the grave marker and had a time of prayer. Although some things are too personal to share, I can say it was a miraculous day. After the cemetery, I was also able to find her house, which I recently learned was demolished not long after my visit.

I share this story with you as a testimony to our God who is our help. Over the years I've heard stories of missionaries who miraculously crossed guarded borders and almost unbelievable accounts of angelic protection and provision. But in this one moment, God helped me. He set me on an assignment. He took me right to Willie Johnson's gravesite. He provided for the trip. God still leads. He still guides. He still provides. Our help is in Him. Perhaps He used an angel to guide me. I don't know what it all meant, but I know I felt a presence with me. And I feel to urge you to take on whatever calling God has assigned—to not only continue the great work of the church of days gone by, but to go beyond it.

We have access to our all-powerful God every moment. Isaiah said the government of the entire world was on one of His shoulders. That means He still has one arm free to help, to uphold, to defend, to provide, and to comfort. We'll see God's kingdom thrive when we engage our secret weapons. If we'll consecrate ourselves to God through prayer and fasting, worship the Lord in the beauty of holiness, and create an atmosphere for revival, our help, the King of Glory, will break through with healing and joy (see Psalm 126:1–3).

17

Life Waves

In the day of prosperity be joyful, But in the day of adversity consider that God has made the one as well as the other.
Ecclesiastes 7:14, AMP

Our lives are composed of days of prosperity and days of adversity, times of pleasure and times of pain. People often quote the words of Job, "The Lord gave, and the Lord hath taken away; blessed be the name of the Lord" (Job 1:21). Job was right in worshipping even in the worst moment of his life. In reality, God gave to Job, and Satan took things away from him. I don't know all the reasons God allowed Job's trial, but I do trust that He knows what is best for my life and yours. Perhaps the proper way to approach the ups and downs of life—what I call "life waves"—is to remember a key biblical principle: rain falls on the just as well as the unjust (see Matthew 5:45).

While saints and sinners both experience blessings and hardships as part of life, an increase in a person's spiritual development or kingdom activities can result in a rise of opposing demonic activity. In the course of life, there's a rhythm, a pulse we must learn to navigate. To be effective conduits for the kingdom of God, we can't allow natural or supernatural pushes and pulls to manipulate us or hinder our walk.

People often tend to look at life one dimensionally like a timeline or a graph. We picture the ups and downs like roller coaster tracks. But I want to remind you today, that life is far more than one-dimensional. Life is multifaceted. It's more than what we're going through right now. As our times, seasons, and experiences move up and down, they propel us onward in the same way the action of the currents surge the seas forward.

Multifaceted You and Your Multifaceted Life

We discussed the multifaceted nature of God in Chapter 1. In this chapter, we'll look at the facets God shapes in us as we navigate the seas of life. Returning to the diamond metaphor, there's much to consider spiritually; but the primary point I want to focus on is that even with all its little planes, its little faces, a diamond is one gemstone.

In the same way there is one multifaceted God, you and I are multifaceted people living multifaceted lives. We touched on this subject in our previous discussions of transformation and dealing with distractions. But let's now bring these elements together so we can better learn how to keep our cool when life gets hot, keep our balance when the path is rocky, keep our integrity when we reach a pinnacle, and keep our minds uplifted in the valleys.

Diamonds in the raw look like any other stone, but even in a rough condition, a diamond has value if it's in the right hands. You and I are in good hands with God. He's our master diamond cutter working to carve away the roughness of the outer us and reveal the beauty He already sees within. With each facet, we increase the shine of His glory in the Earth. On January 11, 2015, I journaled, "Today I thanked God for the trials that cut the facets in my life so I could minister to others—connect with them—so they could see a different aspect of God."

Scripture tells us that God considers His people a peculiar treasure. The Lord spoke of His work among His people as making up His jewels (see Malachi 3:17). The New Testament identifies God's people as living stones. Even now, you and I are being fashioned in the quarry of life where we're cut, shaped, and polished for God's spiritual house (see 1 Peter 2:1-5). Through faith we come to the "living stone" (Jesus), and we're being fashioned into His image.

This isn't a new project. Isaiah wrote to the Israelites, "Listen to me, you who pursue righteousness and who seek the Lord: Look to the rock from which you were cut and to the quarry from which you were hewn" (Isaiah 51:1, NIV). This Old Testament passage refers to looking back to Abraham and Sarah—the founders of the faith who believed themselves in the promise of the Messiah (see Genesis 22:18, Galatians 3:8). As New Testament believers, when we look to the rock from which we were hewn, we aren't focusing on the past, but recognizing where we came from as we turn our attention to what we're becoming.

Each of us comes from the same quarry of faith. The Rock from which you and I were hewn is Jesus Christ, and we're being polished to the brilliance of His image (see Romans 8:29). Looking ahead, Scripture portrays Christ's bride as the holy city adorned with the glory of God whose "light was like unto a stone most precious, even like a jasper stone, clear as crystal" (see Revelation 21:11). You and I are members of God's household, built on the foundation of the apostles and prophets, with Jesus Himself as the chief cornerstone (see Ephesians 2:19-22).

When we face life's challenges, we look to the Rock from which we were hewn. As the Lord reveals different facets of Himself through our experiences, we not only know Him better, we behold what we're to become.

> **Embrace the face God reveals.**

A couple of years ago while in California, I shared this "little faces" concept with some ladies over lunch. The next morning, I woke with three words in mind before I ever opened my eyes. I knew God was specifically telling me that I needed to embrace what He was going to reveal to me. I couldn't have been more surprised how the next few hours unfolded. That very day I was called onto the platform at the annual Landmark Conference in Stockton, and before I knew it, I was on my knees in prayer, getting a direct word from the Lord that I never expected. God called me to embrace another facet, another plane, another purpose of my life and of His ministry. He had prepared me that morning with the words, "Embrace the face," and made me ready to receive an impartation and new responsibility in ministry—a new facet He was cutting and polishing in me. Although God revealed something unexpected in a moment, I'd already said yes. If in our devotions we say "yes" to His will and ways in advance, even when He surprises us, we're ready to accept the unexpected. Sometimes the "facet" He makes known is an assignment. Sometimes He reveals a new aspect of Himself. When He does, He expects us to say "Oh, that's what I'm supposed to be becoming."

When we reach new heights in our spiritual experiences, we view new dimensions of God. When we walk through trials and testings, we experience God in new ways as our provider, counselor, and strength. As grief befalls us, we learn to know Him as our comforter. Each experience brings an understanding of His nature and forms it more clearly in us.

We're talking about the pulse of life, and certainly on this outpost for the kingdom of God, we see high-highs and low-lows. The apostle Peter offered some advice to a church that endured hardship. When he addressed their pain, his words to them included joy and heaviness in the same sentence (see 1 Peter 1:6–7). He told God's people that even though they faced manifold, (many-faced or many kinds of) temptations, they should be truly glad. There's wonderful joy ahead, even when times are rough here. The experiences and seasons of life, even the heavy ones, have purpose. Not every lump of carbon becomes a diamond, but those of us born again of the water and Spirit are living stones destined to become God's jewels!

 The addition of each member in the body of Christ adds depth and dimension to the composite which is a greater reflection of His glory on the earth.

If you're like me, you would prefer to become a diamond without the trials and temptations, heat and pressure. But they're part of life, part of the whole. We must learn to accept the things God allows in ways that preserve our wholeness and peace. Nothing can unseat our King, and nothing should steal our praise.

It's ok to embrace the face of grief when we experience seasons of loss or great trials. God understands. Grief is one of His facets. The Lord knows what it feels like to be despised and rejected. He intentionally acquainted Himself with our grief and sorrows and bore them on our behalf (see Isaiah 53:4). Allow yourself to express your pain, but then refuse to live beneath it for too long.

> "You are only as mature as the level of your praise in the midst of your tribulation." —Mickey Bonner

John Piper said it's ok to "occasionally weep deeply over the life you hoped would be. Grieve your losses. Then wash your face. Trust God. And embrace the life you have." I've been there. I've wept many times over the life I'd hoped would be but never saw come to fruition. It's also worth mentioning that we don't have to hide our pain in order to appear more "spiritual," but pain is part of life. We need to shed our tears. Life is hard. Grieve your losses. Even Jesus wept.

Faces of Favor

The face of God represents His favor as well as one of His most comforting aspects—His nearness. God blesses His people. He keeps us and makes His face shine upon us. He's gracious when He looks upon us with love and grants us His peace on our best days and on our worst (see Numbers 6:24–26). Embracing God's purpose in our peaks and valleys doesn't mean simply accepting things as they are without trying to make them better or without praying. There's a difference between being complacent and content. We know that along with contentment comes power (see 1 Timothy 6:6). That power allows us to accept our circumstances and face our challenges, griefs, and trials. The Lord promised to keep us when we walk through valleys and fires and high waters (see Psalm 23:4, Isaiah 43:2). We actually find God waiting there, in the midst of our hardest situations. Yes, like Him, we suffer for a little while, but we also partake of His glory.

Whatever the Lord gives us, even what's not in our plans, we receive it as His ordained portion. Sometimes the mountains are beautiful, and we climb them with gladness; but other "valley experiences" we would prefer to reject. God asks us to embrace life's waves with all their ups and downs—to understand the roles both joy and sadness play in our lives. The highs strengthen and encourage, but sadness teaches us we can trust our God who is always present to comfort, heal, and restore our souls. Life teaches us in the times we cry, laugh, grieve, and dance (see Ecclesiastes 3:4). So often in Scripture God presents joy and sadness together, walking side by side. We learn victory through our struggles and rejoicing in times of anguish and searching (see Psalm 116:1-6, 61:1-8). Some losses that may seem painful at the time result in net gains (see Philippians 3:7). So even when it seems next to impossible, because we have the Lord, we can be happy in our faith as we continue in prayer and give thanks in every situation. This is what God expects from those who belong to Jesus (see 1 Thessalonians 5:16-18).

A minister visited Pete during what would become his final hospital stay. I remember the man's dear face as he said, "Even when things aren't working out the way you think they should, or on your time table, you still have to trust in God, even if He's not meeting your expectations, because our expectations may not be what God wants to do." Sometimes life doesn't give us what we expected, what we hoped for, or what we thought we signed up for. But that's when we need to step back and see the big picture.

I've known the thrill of ministering on a platform before over 16,000 people, and I will never forget the way I felt when an experience of deep pain drove me to the floor in a crumpled mess. Each of those experiences is part of the composite of my life. And each played a role in fashioning me into who I am.

In the ups and downs, God works to offer us new perspectives. He invites us to examine a facet of our character or an area we need to improve. Sometimes He brings "sandpaper people" into our spheres of relationships, and other times He opens our understanding through suffering or success.

As we lean on Him to accept each day for what it brings, and as we walk and live in His will and presence, He helps us keep our focus. His brilliant, beautiful light leads the way, and although we walk through the shadow of the valley of death itself, there's no shadow or darkness in Him.

A Diamond of the First Water

Life waves create brilliance. An English idiom, "a diamond of the first water," refers to a technical term from the 1600s for grading diamonds. It describes a diamond of exceptional beauty, brilliance, flawless clarity and luster—pure and transparent—like water. This categorization system utilizes three designations: first, second, and third. They represent the level of quality or the extent of conformity of the gem.

When God fills us with His Spirit, His deposit works from the inside out to conform us to His perfect design. The Lord, who *is* the perfect diamond, begins cutting facets in us that reflect Him. He improves our ability to reflect light as we display a pleasing balance of internal reflection (brilliance), strong and colorful dispersion (fire), and brightly colored flashes of reflected light (scintillation). I know this may seem abstract or random, but please think back with me to the kingdom components. Consider Heaven and its wondrous display of God's internal brilliance, fire from the throne, and colorful flashes of light.

Diamonds form under extreme heat and pressure far below the earth's mantle and are transported to the surface by volcanic eruptions. The book of Revelation tells us we'll see a fire before the marriage supper of the Lamb. Jesus said He came to cast fire on the earth—a fire that will complete the release of His jewel—His bride.

Life waves ebb and flow from high to low, and dark to light. Darkness has never been God's enemy. His work often begins in the dark. When we walk in dark places, especially in the most challenging times—when God is silent—we can have confidence that He knows what He's doing. Rather than despair at our circumstances, we worship and look for the treasure—the knowledge communicated by God to train and instruct us.

As the highest praise comes from the lowest places, so great treasures come from the deepest places of obscurity. God said, "I will give you the treasures of darkness And hidden riches of secret places, That you may know that I, the Lord, Who call you by your name, Am the God of Israel" (Isaiah 45:3, NKJV). What forms within us in the dark places can bring us to a greater level of revelation that will shift us to a new place with God. God calls His people to arise and shine in the dark.

> *Arise, shine;*
> *For your light has come!*
> *And the glory of the Lord is risen upon you.*
> *For behold, the darkness shall cover the earth,*
> *And deep darkness the people;*

Chapter 17: Life Waves

> *But the Lord will arise over you,*
> *And His glory will be seen upon you.*
> Isaiah 60:1-2, NKJV

Riding the Waves

When life ebbs and flows, we ride atop its waves like a surfer. We refuse to be dragged underneath, instead we keep our footing as waves break all around us with their opportunities and challenges. Ocean waters are never still, but consider this: waves transfer energy, not water. Think of a crowd in a stadium doing "the wave." The people don't move, but energy fills the room. With life waves, God releases energy to accomplish His purposes.

God prepares elevations for His people—in local churches and even positions of great authority and power. To walk in the realms He wants to deliver into our hands requires a greater level of submission on our parts. We must accept God's sovereignty in every wave of our lives—at the peak and at the trough. He gives us chances. He calls us to humble ourselves before Him and grants us opportunities to submit ourselves to His will. As we reach and cross over new thresholds by submitting to His lordship in greater measure, He brings increased anointing. God has given His people the power to trample on serpents and scorpions and to overcome every power of the evil one. He's looking to see who He can trust to deliver His power to.

When life bottoms out, we still choose to celebrate the good. We can't wait for every duck to line up and every checkbox on our list to be marked with a big X before we rejoice in God or allow ourselves to serve others. Hope in God. Trust in God. Wake up in the morning and say, "This is the day that the Lord has made! I will rejoice and be glad in it!" We must let go of trying to figure God out, and simply trust Him instead. For *when* we walk through the fire, the flood, the valley, He is with us. Filter every situation through His Word and keep a heavenly perspective.

When Pete was in the hospital, I learned an important concept. God impressed me that I wasn't to ask Him *why?* But that I should instead ask, "What am I supposed to be learning from this? How am I supposed to be responding?" At that time, I knew I could never see all of God's purposes, and I'm sure that I still don't, but as I walked through that season, He told me that trusting Him is enough. Someday we might understand the "why," but when we get to that place, it probably won't even matter anymore. Until then, it's encouraging to remember that although Satan

> "Hope believes that God is not done."
> —Sam Crabtree

considered the crucifixion a great victory, it was, in fact, his undoing. In every trial we can trust the Lord who makes all things work together for good.

Suffering

In life's ups and downs, there's nothing more important than knowing we have God's approval and favor. God's beautiful world has been deteriorating since the Fall. Yes, we've made great technological and medical strides, but as we see clearly in recent history, there's been an increase in diseases, disorders, viruses, and bug-born killers. Stronger and new strains of infectious diseases and pathogens are coming on the scene. E-Coli, H1N1, West Nile virus, Zika virus, and of course, the Coronavirus. Sickness and death are part of the human experience.

We've spoken about the cross in detail. Another aspect to consider is how the cross not only represented submission and the offering of Christ's life for ours, it was also a cross of persecution. Jesus endured affliction that came from without.

Our lives are not without external problems and persecutions, but through pain, sicknesses of the body or soul, Jesus invites us to pray for healing. He heals diseases of the body, mind, and spirit. At times, suffering could serve a higher purpose. Whether or not God chooses to heal us or deliver us from our trials, we should respond with grace. God may allow a sickness, and we shouldn't consider it a punishment. Instead we can choose to see our circumstances as opportunities to learn or experience something new—and perhaps to reach to someone who might not have been reachable by other means.

When my pastor's wife fell in China while on a missions trip, it certainly looked like a demonic attack. She suffered greatly, but as a result, the therapist who treated her upon her return and throughout her recovery came to know the Lord. She was baptized in Jesus's name and filled with the Spirit of God. No one wants to suffer, and it pained us all to watch, but what joy we felt when this Hindu woman came to know Jesus and receive salvation.

Paul taught the church to rejoice always, pray without ceasing, and give thanks in everything (see 1 Thessalonians 5:16–18). Don't be confused. This passage isn't telling us to rejoice *because* we suffer from sickness or weakness, but it does let us know we should be prepared to suffer persecutions for the sake of the gospel (see 2 Corinthians 11:23–29). The apostle Paul never identified the "thorn"

> "Suffering is a mystery that all of us have had to wrestle with."
> —Francis MacNutt

Chapter 17: Life Waves

in his flesh. Given that he mentioned it following the long list of maltreatments and imprisonments he suffered for his faith could indicate it was a persecution rather than a physical problem. The fact Scripture refers to Israel's enemies as thorns also seems to support this idea (see Numbers 33:55, Joshua 23:13, Judges 2:3). Jesus said we're blessed and should rejoice when we are persecuted for His sake. So even though we don't rejoice in pain, we celebrate because we will one day receive a great reward in Heaven (see Matthew 5:11-12).

With a renewed outlook, we can accept the crashing waves with confidence in the comfort of God's Spirit. A kingdom perspective includes understanding that the trials and tests God allows are for our betterment—even for our advancement. Satan tempts to bind us, but God tests to free us to walk in greater authority and power (see Hebrews 5:8-9).

The Suffering and the Glory

Throughout Jesus's earthly ministry, He not only fulfilled the Old Testament Scripture, He quoted it. Isaiah held a special significance for Him and was third in line as His most quoted volume. The book's overall theme is set forth in Isaiah 12:2, "Behold, God is my salvation; I will trust, and not be afraid: for the Lord Jehovah is my strength and my song; he also is become my salvation." Another major topic covered by Isaiah was the suffering and glory of the coming Messiah (see Isaiah 53:4-12). Both aspects pertained to Christ's earthly ministry. As a disciple of Christ, we will experience great highs and lows, but through it all, God gives both the strength to endure and a song for our hearts.

This brings to mind Willie Johnson, the granddaughter of a slave, rejected by her father, sold by her mother, and abused by her husband. Willie Johnson rose above violent mistreatment, social stigma, and cultural limitations to minister with powerful anointing and confidence in pulpits all across America. Her ministry intermingled song, Scripture, and a unique demonstration of spiritual gifts that were unusual in her day. But her story wasn't always one of positive affirmation and strength.

Before her conversion, feeling hopeless and desperate, she walked toward a bridge to end her life of physical and verbal domestic abuse. On the way, music from a revival meeting in a storefront church caught her attention. The sound drew her in, and she momentarily paused to listen. When she stepped inside the building, the love of God ministered to her soul. She received the Holy Ghost, and along with God's Spirit she was filled with an overwhelming joy.

She returned home. No, nothing had changed there, but something had transformed inside her. God's power enabled her to endure her hardships in an overcoming way. In fact, she began ministering to others. Everywhere she went, she was beloved and highly esteemed. As Willie sang and spoke, people were healed of illnesses, delivered of bondages, and filled with God's Spirit. It was a different world in the 1930s when Willie first received the Holy Ghost, and I share her story not to encourage victims of abuse to stay in harm's way. The point I want to emphasize is that even in the harshest and most desperate of circumstances, God can bring joy. And He will use people of no reputation or background—even in miraculous ways.

I learned many things writing Willie Johnson's biography—some of the points are shared elsewhere in this book. One of the greatest was how the power of her faith-filled worship brought the presence of God into the room with her. His Spirit ministered through her to the people. Even while delivering a message, if she needed to reconnect with Him, she would stop and just start singing a song. She knew the power of His presence. She also correlated the depth of her ministry with the depth of her suffering. She held loosely to the things of this world and accepted life as it came. She suffered hunger, even during ministry trips, and yet she entered the sanctuary with her cape flying behind her, joy on her countenance, compassion in her heart, and a deep river of living water flowing out of the core of her being.

Willie accepted life with no pretense—with its joys and its sufferings and in the power of the resurrection. She experienced God as her strength and song—the God who gave her the victory even as she endured painful circumstances. She achieved great success on the battleground of "self," the war within our inner persons between flesh and spirit. She lived in a continual state of connectivity with God and served as a powerful conduit for the kingdom in her world.

This brings to mind a famous monk, Brother Lawrence. Of course, most of us can't sequester ourselves away from life. The lessons Brother Lawrence taught continue to serve those who live beyond monastery walls. This man, while known for his gentleness and servant's heart, had a supernatural encounter with God that set him afire. At times he would leap and cry out and sing with ecstasy. Even as he worked in the kitchen, he learned to maintain the presence of God in his heart. He willfully rejected any thought that would break his continual conversation with the Lord. Perhaps an absolute contrast to Willie Johnson, Lawrence portrayed the joy of living a simple life of service. He said, "It is not necessary to have great things to do. I turn over my little omelet in the frying pan for the love of God."

When finished preparing food for others, he would prostrate himself on the ground and worship God, as "content as a king." The collection of Brother Lawrence's writings assembled by Joseph de Beaufort, included the compiler's comments: "Sometimes a crowd of unruly thoughts would violently shove out his thoughts of

God. He would then simply push them gently aside in order to return to his normal conversation with God." De Beaufort said, "His perseverance was rewarded with a continual remembrance of God." What we learn from Brother Lawrence about prayer in his private devotion and during his work was that whether distractions come from internal or external sources, we can keep control of our thoughts and emotions and purposefully reconnect with God in prayer.

Sister Willie and Brother Lawrence both seemed to reach a place where they could have one ear open to the world and another open to the Spirit. The circumstances swirling around them didn't agitate them internally. They learned to take the pulses of life in stride and walk in the Spirit. They learned to practice the presence of God.

Whether in a pulpit or in a kitchen, you and I can learn to live in a place where our outer persons are able to function in the world around us while we remain internally in constant fellowship with God. We can learn to obtain a habitual sense of God's presence through silent, secret conversation. When we give our all for God's all, even in times of difficulty, we develop an intimacy with Him that opens the way for asking and receiving and enables us to minister the love of God to others.

If we can learn to keep Jesus at the center of everything, the winds and waves won't take us off course. We can become "perpetual prayers" even as we live and move and work in our world. We can get to a place where we really do pray without ceasing—because prayer is communion with God, not just an encounter on our knees in the morning. We can live with contentment while we wait on the Lord and at the same time constantly seek more of Him. Always able to intentionally descend to our spirits within, we can pray in our consciousness by our own thoughts or in the Spirit regardless of what we're doing.

There is a pulse to life, to prayer, and to worship. Life's waves would take us up, and then down, but God calls us to be steadfast and unmovable, always excelling in the work of the Lord, knowing that our labor is not in vain (see 1 Corinthians 15:58).

> "There was a period when I chose a time and place for prayer ... but now I seek that constant prayer, an inward stillness." —Madame Guyon

When I was meditating one day on the peaks and valleys of life, a picture of a slinky came to mind. The metal toy springs and moves, stretches and contracts. I wanted to use one as an illustration, so on my way to service, I stopped at a store and bought one. When I stretched the slinky across the pulpit, it was easy to see the tops and bottoms of the spiral coil—and also to note the continuity of the one strip of steel wire. The simple toy provided a visual demonstration that no matter where we are in our timeline, whether high or low, it's all part of one life—and it's a good life.

Rest

Part of the process of living above the effects of life's waves includes allowing for what Wayne Muller calls "a rhythm of rest in our overly busy lives." There seems to be a principle in God's Word that is proudly neglected by some Christians—and that is rest. Exhaustion is worn by some as a badge of honor, but God designed humans to require a time of refreshing. Every night we must sleep, and every week should include a restful sabbath. Rest fuels our future endeavors.

With my schedule, and especially when ministering out on weekends, my Sundays are certainly not days of leisure. I confess my struggle with writing margin time into my calendar. I'm not good at relaxing (except on a cruise), but I'm very faithful to carve out hours of spiritual rest. It's during times of rest we receive renewing for our bodies and minds, spiritual refreshing, and treasures from God. What we receive then flows through our conduits and blesses the world around us, hopefully beginning with those in our own homes. If we fail to get proper rest, the people nearest and dearest to us pay the price of our irritability, distraction, and unrelieved stress.

The concept of rest intermingles with wholeness and peace—sabbath and shalom. It's more than setting aside work, but it includes fellowshipping with God and God's people. During sabbath rest, we take time to enjoy the company of loved ones and fellow believers. Jesus said the sabbath was a gift from God for our benefit. Rest is not a duty, but a blessing. When we "sabbath," we unplug from the busyness of our days and take time to plug in to the most important relationships in our lives.

Biblical sabbaths weren't days of inactivity, but rather God's people spent time on spiritual observances, reading the Torah, praying, visiting family, and resting. There are many elements of the sabbath celebration that would be worth studying, but for this brief look, I'd like to focus on the kiddush cup. *Kiddush* means holy, sanctified, set apart—and that's what sabbath is, what rest is. It's holy, sanctified, set apart and consecrated.

The kiddush cup is unique. Traditionally, it's silver and has a matching saucer. What's the saucer for? To catch the overflow. It's a common practice for the person leading the sabbath meal to overflow the cup on purpose. Spilling during the pouring out of the wine symbolizes having an abundance, having an overflow. It represents the blessings and joy of the Lord that can't be contained. As believers, when we "keep the sabbath," what we receive from our time of refreshing overflows into the world around us. This is the life Jesus desires for us. He said, "I came that they may have and enjoy life, and have it in abundance [to the full, till it overflows]" (John 10:10, AMP).

I heard somewhere once that *sabbath* means "stop," but when I looked up the word in the lexicon, I discovered it came from a word that means "intermission." An intermission is the space of time between two activities. One writer said that Sabbath is a "tabernacle in time." The Hebrew word *mishkan,* often translated in English as "tabernacle," can also be translated "to rest." It's related to the Hebrew word that means to dwell, rest, or live in reference to the indwelling presence of God.

The Lord invites us to set aside our work and routine and enjoy time "tabernacling" in His presence. Sabbath is a gift of time. The concepts of prayer, rest, and dwelling with God are all related. Think of it in musical terms. What

> **Sabbath is a tabernacle in time in which God invites us to dwell and rest with Him.**

would a song be like if there were never any rests, or if the music just played on and on with no pauses? Rests in music are just as important as the notes in a composition because the rests allow the musical notes to take shape—to rise and fall between them. Without rest, our lives are chaotic, and we miss out on some of the beauty God intended for us to enjoy.

We shouldn't think we can hurry through life and neglect our bodies, minds, or spirits. Nonstop activity causes stress and we end up functioning less than optimally. We must build in recovery time, write in some margin—even some time for fun, because a merry heart is good like a medicine (see Proverbs 17:22). When we're properly rested, life's waves don't agitate as much, and life's interruptions don't make us as irritable as when we find ourselves running low. When we rest, we allow ourselves time to think and ponder and wonder—to meditate on the things of God. We hear from the Lord the words that not only rejuvenate our souls, but that guide our steps in our lives and ministry to others.

A lack of proper rest affects our souls. Even if we feel we're getting nothing productive done as we rest, our living agreement with God's divine order brings a greater dimension of peace and power. There's power when we live out the principles of God's Word.

When we rest, we follow Jesus's example. He often withdrew from the crowds and even His own disciples (see Luke 5:16). Jesus exemplified a rhythm of life:

> **The pulse of life demands a rhythm of rest.**

engage, engage, engage, withdraw (repeat). He taught His disciples to rest (see Mark 6:30-32). When we rest, we follow God's example set at the very foundation of the world. On the seventh day of creation, He rested and enjoyed the work He'd completed in the previous six days. God designed labor to be balanced with rest. We're expected to relax and enjoy the fruits of our labor (see Ecclesiastes 2:24).

Resting reveals our trusting. We don't have to work nonstop, because we're not worried about what we eat and drink. Our focus is on our relationship with God, and everything else flows from that. Resting reveals our appreciation, our agreement with God's sovereignty and His kingdom principles. It also testifies to the level of His lordship in our lives.

Romans 8:28 offers such comfort to the people of God. We see the Lord's good intention for us running like a thread through every aspect of our days. In every moment, He is with us. Where we are, God is. He is our refuge and strength, and a very present help in trouble. Therefore, we won't fear life's ups and downs. We can make time to be still and know that He is God, and He will be exalted in the earth (see Psalm 46:1-2, 10-11).

18

The Dynamic Duo

*Look at the proud one, His soul is not right within him,
But the righteous will live by his faith [in the true God].*
Habakkuk 2:4

As we continue to discuss peace in the temple, the subject of wholeness comes to the forefront again as we turn our thoughts toward two elements that are critical to our spiritual health—faith and humility. The principle of wholeness mandates this balance. God's Word tells us as believers we can do all things through Christ (see Philippians 4:13). It also tells us that apart from Christ, we can do nothing (see John 15:5). There's a relational aspect between faith and humility, and that's why I call them the dynamic duo.

We've discussed elements of faith in reference to our belief in God including hope, grace, and an aspect of personal surrender (see John 1:12). It's our faith that gives us victory. It's by faith that we ask and receive (see Matthew 21:22). By faith we access the grace to sustain our right relationship with God (see Romans 5:2, Ephesians 2:8). As new creatures in Christ, we know who we are because of our faith in God's Word (see Galatians 2:20). We're alive in Christ because the Spirit of God, who is greater than the enemy in the world, lives within us (see Ephesians 2:5, 1 John 4:4). We have the power of God to do miracles and take authority over our enemies (see Mark 16:17-18, Luke 10:17-19). We are chosen, spiritually transformed, and set apart for God's purpose (see 1 Peter 2:9, 1:23). We are joint heirs with Christ and more than conquerors (see Romans 8:17, 37). All that is true! God imparts authority, dignity, and power to His people.

On the other side of the spectrum, humility beckons us to remember who we are in comparison to God. The root of the word translated humility and human is the same—a Latin word, *humus,* which refers to earth and ground. We should note the connection—humanity and humility ground us to our origins, the dust of the earth (Genesis 2:7, 3:19). As humans, we came from the earth, and being humble relates to the soil of the earth.

In Scripture, the word *humble* refers to a lowliness or humility of the mind. Humility means being without pride or arrogance. God formed humanity from the dirt, and we ought never to lose sight of that. The same God who empowers us also resists the proud, and so we must clothe ourselves in humility (see 1 Peter 5:5, Colossians 3:12).

When we lift up the Lord, He exalts us. When we lift ourselves higher than we ought, we put ourselves in dangerous positions. "For all those who exalt themselves will be humbled, and those who humble themselves will be exalted" (Luke 14:11). We've discussed God's plan for mankind as referenced in Psalm 8. We were made a little lower than the angels and yet given authority and dominion. God wants us to know who we are, but He also requires that we never forget who we are in relation to who He is. Flattery corrupts (from others or self), but those who are spiritually mature and know their God shall be strong and carry out great exploits (see Daniel 11:32).

The dynamic duo of faith and humility births the miraculous and exalts Jesus. This shows us the beauty of their interrelationship.

Some things just go together—like peanut butter and jelly—like love and marriage. As the old song says, "try to separate them, it's an illusion." Because at its core, faith is a form of humility.

Without faith, we can't attain the humility required.

> **Faith is a form of humility before God.**

He has shown you, O man, what is good;
And what does the Lord require of you
But to do justly,
To love mercy,
And to walk humbly with your God?
Micah 6:8, NKJV

Even people with incredibly low self-esteem aren't truly humble until they walk in humility with the Lord. Low self-esteem isn't humility. It's actually a form of self-pity—a preoccupation with self which is a manifestation of pride. Pride is a hot topic. Some Christians, for conscience's sake, won't even say "I'm proud of you" for fear they're instilling or feeding arrogance that could lead to a fall (see Proverbs 16:18). Pride in a job well done or having an accurate estimation of a person's God-given abilities isn't the "bad" kind of pride that tells us we don't need God. This takes us back to the issue of self-government (which lacks both faith and humility) that lies at the root of demonic and human downfall.

The book of Proverbs lists seven things God considers abominations, and the very first one is a proud look (see Proverbs 6:16–17). A proud look reveals a haughty heart—one filled with scorn for others or an overestimation of one's own self-worth. The things God hates, we should hate as well, even when we see them in ourselves. God hates pride. Pride brings disgrace, but God gives grace to the humble (see Proverbs 3:34, 1 Peter 5:5). Grace implies benefits, bounty, favor, and liberality. When we walk with God in humility, we gain the opportunity to grow in grace, experience greater blessings, and fulfill God's purposes for our lives (see 2 Peter 3:18). Humility also protects us from reacting compulsively based on our emotions. The partnership of faith and humility creates a synergistic effect to produce a greater flow of God's Spirit through a believer.

Biblical Humility

Biblical humility means living with a clear perspective of God. We choose to "self-forget" and focus our attention on knowing God, knowing our place in His big picture, and fulfilling the service He desires. Biblical humility recognizes a person's identity, worth, and purpose in relation to both God and man. Biblical humility puts the interests of others before our own. Biblical humility doesn't discount anyone's worth, instead it appreciates every life given by God and recognizes each individual's value as His child.

Paul said it was on the basis of the grace he received that he was able to tell other believers not to have exaggerated opinions of their own importance. Instead, every believer should use good judgment about the degree of faith God apportioned to them and their God-designed purpose for serving (see Romans 12:3). God has given gifts, powerful gifts, to His church, and He promised to guide and teach His ways to those who are humble (see Psalm 25:9).

The dynamic duo of faith and humility not only blesses our lives, but walking with a right balance of the two enables us to effectively impact others for the kingdom. International evangelist

> **Humility empowers, and the Lord crowns the humble with victory (see Psalm 149:4).**

Doug Klinedinst understands the balance required between having boldness in our hearts while being dependent on the Lord. He said, "You have to be bold to be heard, and humble to be received." What's true for clergy is true for any Christian desiring to be used by the Lord.

Moses

Is it possible to be humble and know it? Or would that be considered pride? When we look at biblical humility, perhaps it's not as hard to comprehend. Moses is attributed to writing his own proclamation that he was not only a very humble man, but that he was more humble than anyone else on the face of the earth (see Numbers 12:3). Could Moses possibly *be* humble and write those words? Could Moses have been truly humble when he stood before Pharaoh making demands on behalf of God?

Perhaps looking at Moses's background will provide some insight. Moses was raised as a prince, educated in all the wisdom of the Egyptians, and was powerful in his speech and actions (see Acts 7:22). Moses also knew his lineage as a Hebrew slave (see Exodus 2:11). After his failure and run to the backside of the desert, Moses's view of himself and his abilities changed (see Exodus 4:10). In his youth, when he served as a prince in Egypt, humility didn't seem to be his most notable character trait. He murdered an Egyptian and was publicly humiliated as a result. He became a refugee as God prepared his heart for the work He knew needed to be done.

Moses's humiliation changed the way he thought about himself. He no longer considered himself qualified or even able to speak to the same people he had previously ruled alongside. At the same time, at the burning bush, Moses recognized God's sovereignty and yielded to what he knew the Lord had called him to do (see Exodus 3:11, 4:20). Moses's example shows us that the greatest aspects of humility include submitting to God, facing our fears with courage, and serving others. Even with past failures and current doubts—our feelings of "I'm not enough" contradict who we are in God. Our faith must override any feelings that present themselves as contrary to our call or identity in Christ. True humility accepts God's sovereignty and God's assignments—even when we, like Moses, might prefer that God chose someone else for the task (see Exodus 4:13). When God calls us, we must keep the right balance between humility and faith. When we do, the dynamic duo work together in acts of obedience followed by divine confirmation and demonstration.

Moses exemplified both humility and faith as he bravely stood face-to-face in the court of Pharaoh, the most powerful man in the world. Through Moses, God released miracles and deliverance for His oppressed people. But before

Moses stood before Pharaoh, he humbled himself in the court of the most high—standing barefoot in the desert before a burning bush (see Acts 7:30-33). Yes, he acknowledged his inadequacies, but then he stepped out in faith and fulfilled what God called him to do.

God allowed Moses 40 years between his exit from and re-entry into Egypt. This delay was in God's will and included a transformation process that required specific timing. God isn't in a hurry. As Willie Johnson said, He "spends years with those He expects to use greatly."

Humility may be confused with lacking in self-assurance or being apprehensive, but biblical humility is not bashful, ashamed, or hesitant. Neither is it arrogant or pushy. Biblical humility means knowing who we are in Christ and acting within that knowledge.

> Humility is "the soul's attitude before God."
> —P. T. Forsyth

Great, Unshakeable Faith

A humble believer, when obeying God, can move mountains. Abraham, the father of our faith, was given a divine promise. He trusted the Lord to keep His word even though he was being asked to offer his son back to God. Abraham had an unshakeable faith. He walked before God and remained humble and surrendered to God's will no matter how emotionally difficult it was.

Jesus spoke of great faith twice in Scripture and both were in response to the humility exhibited by non-Jews: the centurion and the mother of the demon possessed girl (see Matthew 8:10, 15:28). He gave accolades to gentiles and called His own disciples men of little faith (see Matthew 8:26). His closest followers competed and jockeyed with one another for what seemed to be favor with Jesus, and He told them directly their behavior was not in line with the way of the kingdom of Heaven. The greatest in the kingdom is the servant. The first is the last.

> Faith motivates believers to face difficulty and danger even when their natural man harbors fear.

Perhaps we err in the church, even with good intentions, when we focus on faith alone for miracles, healings, and deliverance. Maybe at times we fail to see how a lack of humility affects our ability to release God's Spirit in the earth. We can't seek to exalt ourselves, even in service in the kingdom. Jesus humbled himself. Humility was His path to glory. When we seek God's glory rather than our own, humility purifies our motives.

Jesus was born in humility—His first bed was a manger. The child of a less-than-well-to-do couple, He apparently had no home of His own in His ministry years (Matthew 8:20). We note His life of service and humility in the Word (see Philippians 2:5-11, Mark 10:45, 2 Corinthians 8:9). He confronted pride in religiosity and among His own followers (see Luke 11:37-54, 9:46-48). He was meek and lowly of heart (see Matthew 11:29). He washed His disciples' feet and humbled Himself by becoming obedient to the point of death, even death on a cross (see John 13:3-7, Philippians 2:8). In contrast to religious leaders of the day, much of Jesus's ministry caused keen irritation to those who proudly displayed their positions, their rationale, and their religious observations. He blessed the poor in Spirit and the meek who had nothing to give or promote.

Why would the Mighty God choose to enter the world as a humble servant? Because He came to undo what was done by pride. He came to repair what had broken His relationship with humanity and severed people from His plan that they should have dominion on the earth. Jesus revealed the path to power—the laying down of His will on the way to the cross (see Matthew 26:39). Jesus came to reverse the consequences of the Fall. At Calvary He "bought" boldness for you and me who access Him through faith (see Ephesians 3:12). When we see the greatness of His plan, we bow before Him and receive strength and mighty power in our inner persons (see v 14, 16). We live with humility and unselfishness and receive gifts to equip us for ministry (see Ephesians 4:2, 11). We imitate God, walking in love and giving ourselves for others as Christ gave Himself for us making the most of the time we have (see Ephesians 5:1-2, 16). We put on the armor of God, pray, and serve as ambassadors for the kingdom of God (see v 11-20). Hidden in Him, we lower ourselves to gain, we humble ourselves to receive. Jesus lowered Himself and received great victory for you and me.

Sink into greater glory.

All for the Glory of God

Jesus revealed what it takes to defeat Satan. He submitted to the will of God. He didn't seek glory for Himself, but gave Himself. Jesus "amened" God's Sovereignty. The word *amen* is, for the most part, a universal word. From Albanian to Yiddish, a form of the word amen derives from the Hebrew word *emuna*, meaning faith or trust. It has a wide variety of meanings including: let it be, yes, may it come to pass, and praise the Lord. When one person says, "amen," they're confirming the words of another.

The same word, also translated "verily," was often used by Jesus at the beginning of important teachings. When the Lord said "verily" or "truly I say unto you," He introduced concepts He expected His followers to "amen"—to agree with. In fact, the original language of Scripture calls God, the Lord of Amen (see Isaiah 65:16, "amen" is translated "truth") and "the Amen" (see Revelation 3:14). When we say amen to a teaching or following a prayer, we indicate our agreement with what was spoken and our desire to take the substance of the words as our own.

When Jesus spoke, He often began by saying, "Truly I say to you." He expects His people to respond, "Truly, as You said, let it be. Yes, may it come to pass, and praise the Lord." We say amen to the glory of God (see 2 Corinthians 1:20). In Heaven, angels bookend their blessings and honor and thanks to God with the word "amen" (see Revelation 7:12). So it is in Heaven, so it will ever be. The elders and angels together bow before God saying, "Amen! Hallelujah!" (see Revelation 19:4). From the Old Testament through Revelation, "amens" ring in unbroken connection of the sovereignty of God and the response of His creation. What Jesus "amens," we should "amen." And we should be careful to let Jesus say "amen" first. When we "amen" what He "amens," that's another dynamic duo.

> "Our prayers are hinged on two things: a knowledge of His Word and a dependence upon His Spirit."
> —Charles Mahaney

With Christ in the School of Humility

We spoke in the last chapter about life's waves. God reveals to us in His Word the significance of remembering all the ways He's led His people in the past. He specified His intentions: to humble and prove them (see Deuteronomy 8:2, 16). God miraculously provided, even in the wilderness, so that after the humbling and testing were complete, His people would benefit in the end by changing an important part of them. Sometimes we have to endure what I call a "Holy Ghost shakedown." God uses these to reveal what's in us—faith or fear; humility or pride. That's why we shouldn't despise the afflictions or calamities we endure. God intends them to keep us humble—leaning on Him and trusting in Him rather than on our own thoughts and desires.

Paul told the Corinthians that their faith could not rest in the wisdom of men (even their own wisdom or human philosophies), but that godly faith rests in the power of God (see 1 Corinthians 2:5). When we elevate ourselves, we dampen our ability to understand the things of God. The truths of God are taught by the Spirit, which requires humility (see 1 Corinthians 2:13-14). Exalting human wisdom brings us into a soul-led realm, not a Spirit-led realm, and can set us on an erroneous path where intellectual or emotional strongholds develop. Any wisdom man might possess could never exceed the wisdom of God. Through humility, we enter the Lord's classroom—the place where truth is learned, and abundant life is experienced. We learn the truth about God and His plan for our lives (see Ephesians 2:10).

The Teeter Totter

Balance in the temple looks something like a teeter totter. Remaining poised with a right equilibrium of faith and humility helps us maintain a principled walk between asceticism and fleshiness. Asceticism is the practice dedicated to pursuing spiritual ideals. Typically, ascetics abstain from pleasure for the purpose of purification and transformation. Think of monks and hermits who lived exceedingly strict, austere lives for religious reasons—even some that were masochistic in nature. Colossians warns the church against the imbalance between fleshly indulgence and asceticism (see Colossians 2:20-23).

While asceticism offers some positives, such as putting away things that could influence a person toward sin, it can also lead toward legalism and Gnosticism. Legalism attempts to achieve spirituality through physical means, and Gnosticism similarly takes the heretical view that flesh is evil and therefore, spiritual blessings could be attained by causing the flesh to suffer. Asceticism embraces the loveliness of faith but can lean toward laziness when it comes to practical matters of life. For instance, an ascetic may think their prayer time is more sacred than taking a meal to a family who just lost a loved one. Jesus implied that giving a cup of cool water in His name was a holy ministry. Too often we think we must choose this or that when God's desire is this *and* that.

An ascetic pursues the spiritual at the expense of living in true community in fellowship with the body of Christ. Consider the ancient pillar dwellers who believed mortification of their bodies would ensure their salvation and so they lived atop pillars. One man named Simeon Stylites, climbed a pillar in Syria in the 5th century and remained on it until he died 37 years later. Simeon practiced physical self-deprivation, but he missed out on the true beauty God offers.

On the other side of the teeter totter, some who preach grace lean toward fleshiness or "carnal Christianity." Fleshiness seeks to satisfy our lower natures and impulses rather than please God and uses grace as an excuse. Of course, every believer has areas still "in process," but a carnal Christian excuses what God's Word calls sin. Fleshy believers are dominated by a manner of thinking that pursues pleasure and are unwilling to present themselves as living sacrifices (see Romans 12:2). Fleshy Christians want to survive on milk rather than mature in their faith (see 1 Corinthians 3:2). Fleshy Christians are critical, competitive, and self-seeking. Paul addressed this concern, "What shall we say then? Shall we continue in sin, that grace may abound? God forbid!" (see Romans 6:1). One of the lovely aspects of grace is that it's meant to be our teacher. "For the grace of God that bringeth salvation hath appeared to all men, Teaching us that, denying ungodliness and worldly lusts, we should live soberly, righteously, and godly, in this present world" (Titus 2:11-12).

As Christians, we're called to live a life in which our spirits dominate our souls and our flesh. God's Spirit controls our thoughts and desires bringing them into agreement with the example lived out by Jesus.

At the same time, we must balance the call to a high spiritual life in Christ with the necessary elements of day-to-day living and reaching out to others. As believers, we're called to practice self-control, and consider others better than ourselves. We seek to grow spiritually and, at the same time, selflessly love our fellow believers. We can't do that when we live on top of invisible spiritual pillars that separate and isolate us from the people God called us to love and minister to—one to another.

Finding Equilibrium

The key to finding the equilibrium that helps us to live in a right balance between asceticism and fleshiness, or humility and faith, is a constant diet of God's Spirit. We put off the old man led by flesh and put on what we've learned from Christ (see Ephesians 4:20). Instead of being led by our flesh, God transforms our nature as we choose to constantly renew our minds (see v 22-23). In other words, we become who God says we are, and when we live it out, we can truly demonstrate His desires.

We can't pursue extremes and expect to be balanced. Some would live out their faith through social justice and charitable deeds at the expense of truth and consecration to God. Others tow a tight doctrinal

> A lack of humility erects barriers on God's intended paths for our lives.

line but too often keep their hands in their pockets rather than serve others. Martin Luther said, "Never are men more unfit than when they think themselves most fit, and best prepared for their duty; never more fit, than when most humbled and shamed under a sense of their unfitness."

At church one day, pacing and praying in the altar before service. I was saying, "Be exalted, oh, God. Be exalted." It came to mind that I can't make God higher, but I can lift more praise to Him. As we carve out more of us, we become lower, and He becomes higher. It's a purposeful displacement of self. When we say, "Less of me, more of You," we make room for more of His Spirit in our lives.

Humility seeks to build the body to the glory of God. Humility knows it's more blessed to give than to receive (see Acts 20:35). And humility is faith's partner. They balance each other and hang together. In concert, the dynamic duo allows God to work through us in more powerful ways than if only one or the other was present.

> **Humility lives for love—the love of God and the love of humanity.**

We've not yet completed our journey. God is still giving grace for grace (see John 1:16). Upon our original reception of grace as a free gift of God for salvation, we have access now to a continuing supply of even greater power. God's grace is constantly flowing, and the more we step into the flow and use what He's given us, the more increase we'll see. Jesus wants us to experience an ever-growing fullness. As in the parable of the wineskins, we can't put new wine in old bottles, but this grace for supernatural ministry implies a substitution—one grace for a greater grace.

God only pours into our lives what we can handle, but as we grow, He measures out more and more privileges and advantages. Grace receives and grace extends—over and above what we've already been given. Faith and humility are the means God uses. To him who has, more will be given. Jesus told Nathaniel that he would see greater things, Heaven open, and the angels of God ascending and descending. God always has more for His people to experience. Every grace you've received has a capacity for a higher level of divine favor and power. As we learn to live this balanced life, grace exchanges with grace like a junction of highways with an interchange that allows one vehicle to pass from one stream of traffic into another.

19

Pursue

Forgetting those things which are behind, and reaching forth unto those things which are before, I press toward the mark for the prize of the high calling of God in Christ Jesus.
Philippians 3:13–14

Jeff Arnold said, "You'll never possess what you don't pursue, and you'll not pursue what you're not persuaded about." He boldly added, "If He promised, I believe it. I'm going after it." Today is our opportunity to walk in our God-given authority. I believe God is sending a restoration of apostolic power and authority among His people. There's a greater dimension that so many of us have longed for but have not yet walked in.

In Chapter 18, we discussed two aspects of grace, in this chapter we'll look at two aspects of pursuit: pursuing our enemies and pursuing the kingdom of God. We'll begin by looking at the enemies that are "in our land." In Numbers 33:51–55, the Lord instructed Moses that the children of Israel were to drive out the inhabitants of the land before them. They were to destroy all their idols and high places, and if they failed to do so, those they allowed to remain would become barbs in their eyes, thorns in their sides, and give them trouble.

God gave His people a land. He said it was theirs, and that it was a good land, but it came with conditions. God's given us our "land"—our "dwelling place"—the place where His Spirit abides with us. He wants us to live in our land with peace and prosperity, but that doesn't just happen. The Israelites were delivered from the bonds of Egypt, but they didn't walk right into the Promised Land, did they? There was a God-ordained process that had to happen to prepare them to possess the land and all God's promises. When it was time, after the desert season, the Israelites first had to cross the Jordan River. The Jordan River represents a place of transition and new beginnings. It was also a boundary line.

As we walk with God, He often leads us from one place to another, one boundary line to another, precept upon precept, line upon line. In this ongoing walk, we continue to face transitions, and as long as we live in the flesh, we'll continue to deal with some "enemies" or "beasts" that must be conquered.

When it was time for the Israelites to take the Promised Land, God gave a specific order in which they would face each enemy nation. These nations were greater and stronger than the Israelites, but God said He would deliver the enemies in front of His people. When He did, they would smite and destroy them as well as their altars and idols (see Deuteronomy 7:1-5). I present this to you as a spiritual analogy building on concepts we've previously covered.

You and I are land, and God's Word tells us there's more than one enemy to conquer. There are many, and God purposely delivered them to His people one at a time. It would be nice, in my opinion, if we could just get all the battling done and move on, but the Lord said He was going to put those nations in front of His people "little by little." A process of time was required. Why? Deuteronomy 7:22 tells us God moved them incrementally through the land so that the beasts of the field wouldn't increase upon them. I did some research to get insight, and it means just what it says. Without a strategy that took segments of the land in pieces, the beasts would increase to become a threat to God's people.

This is the work of sanctification, and it's a process. If the Lord had allowed them to immediately conquer every nation, they would likely have fallen to an even more insidious foe: pride. Secure in their self-sufficiency, enemies more dangerous than wild animals would've increased upon them. Today, we face this same adversary, and without the help of the Lord, it may increase in our lives, too.

> In the same way God drove the enemies from the land a little at a time, He drives corruption from our lives little by little.

God could have crushed the beasts in one tremendous act, but He chose to bless His people in a different way—a way that allowed them to partner with Him. It required several organized efforts, but by degrees, and through the battles, I believe it was God's desire that His people learn through personal experience to put their trust only in Him. When we walk with God, sometimes we experience divine delays, even when He's made us direct promises. Often, the delays are there for our good.

God knew what we would face. He also knows how our minds work. He said, "If thou shalt say in thine heart, These nations are more than I; how can I dispossess them? Thou shalt not be afraid of them: but shalt well remember what the Lord thy God did unto Pharaoh, and unto all Egypt" (Deuteronomy 7:17-18). What God did in the past—deliverance, miracles, parting seas, light in Goshen, protection from plagues, and more—He still does today.

 As God presents before us the "giants in our land," He invites us to take the sword of His Word and slay them. If we don't advance, we'll lose ground. The world will chip away at the progress we've made. Wherever we stopped, we must revisit that place, find the courage to face the enemy that held us back, and determine to move forward.

God's given us the weapons we need, but remember, His presence is our greatest weapon of all. Worship the Lord and experience chains breaking, heavens opening, strongholds being demolished. Hold to His Word and refuse to back down. God has promised the victory—so sing. Those seven nations were greater and mightier than God's people, but they weren't fighting alone, and neither do we.

Pursuing the Heavenly

Perhaps one of the most popular verses on pursuing God is the one chosen as this chapter's theme. I once spent some time studying this passage, and I share here with you my version of Philippians 3:13-14:

"Fellow believers, I don't consider myself to have attained full understanding, but this one thing I do understand: I forget, I purposefully no longer care for (truly, certainly) the things that happened in my past; and in addition to that, on top of that, I press myself forward to the things that are already in sight ahead. I eagerly pursue and run toward the goal I see for the heavenly reward that is higher—a divine calling and vocation from God in Jesus, the anointed Messiah. Close your memory to things that happened in the past and stretch yourself to a higher purpose."

My last ministry trip before the Covid-19 shut-in began, I attended a World Network of Prayer event in Minnesota. The power of God was present, and I feverishly wrote notes as the minister, evangelist Lee Stoneking, spoke. He said people are "sick of the games and the politics, sick of all the nonsense, and they've decided we're going to have the real thing or nothing at all."

I was sitting near the front, and he turned and looked me in the eyes. I know he was speaking to everyone, but he was burning a hole in me when he said, "I'm talking to you here today because you're that generation that has set fire to that particular thinking that is what shook the Roman Empire. You understand me when I tell you that twelve ignorant, unlearned fishermen for the most part destroyed the Roman Empire because the fire couldn't burn it, the walls couldn't hold it, the lions couldn't eat it. There was nothing that could control it. It was like a forest fire out of control. That thing is trying to get ahold of our world right now in this hour. You don't need to apologize to anybody. You've got it, and God has called you to the kingdom for such a time as this. So do what you've never done before. Get in there and go at it like you've never gone at it before. You've got nothing to lose."

We live in a day when we need to be courageous and stand against the enemy. Stand up and be a voice for the kingdom rather than sitting quietly while demonic influence prevails. But we have to want it *and* pursue it. We can't allow ourselves to be satisfied with less than God intends for us to have. And know, my fellow traveler, that God wants us to succeed.

> It is never too late to have a positive spiritual influence.

What a Difference a Door Makes

There are times when God's people stand at thresholds and they aren't even aware of the opportunities before them. When Paul presented the Ephesians with the fuller truth of baptism in Jesus's name and infilling of God's Spirit, he opened a door. They immediately responded (see Acts 19:1–6). They wanted all God had for them, so they chose to pursue a deeper experience.

The opportunity to walk through a new door doesn't always mean we're leaving something awful behind. Arless Glass said, "When a greater truth is revealed it does not nullify the previous truth. It strengthens it." You and I are progressing. God has declared the end from the beginning, and He's working in us what needs to take place, so His purposes are achieved. We're building on what we know as our previous experience. God is flinging open doors. He's inviting each of us beyond the threshold of our current spiritual residence into a new place.

Paul stayed in Ephesus for two years. People came to the Lord. God did extraordinary miracles through him. Handkerchiefs and aprons that had touched Paul were taken to the sick and illnesses were cured. Evil spirits left. There was a Jewish priest in Ephesus named Sceva. His seven sons wanted to perform the same miracles God was working through Paul. Now, don't get me wrong, God will work through any Christian, but these men wanted the gift without a true relationship with the Lord.

Chapter 19: Pursue

These seven men entered the house of a possessed man and attempted to cast out the demon (see Acts 19:11-16). The wanna-be-exorcists devised a formula—an incantation—to say over a person needing deliverance. (That's what the Ephesians did. They were really into incantations.) The men decided on the words, "I command you by the Jesus preached by Paul," but it didn't work. The name of Jesus is powerful, but one cannot simply speak the name of Jesus like a magic formula. Just saying His name without being in spiritual alignment with Him doesn't work, especially for profit (see Acts 8:9-25).

The evil spirit spoke through the possessed man and said, "I know Jesus and I've heard of Paul, but who are you?" and then he went berserk. He jumped on them, beat them up, and tore off their clothes. Naked and bloody, they ran out the door and got away as best they could. I'd like to believe these men had good intentions. They may truly have desired to see the tormented man delivered, but they had no business going through that door unprepared, unauthorized, and unknown by the very God they were calling on.

Good-intentioned people have walked through doors—maybe even the "right" doors, but at the wrong time. Believers walk through ministry doors excited and full of expectation only to come running out, bruised, bloodied, and beaten. They're stripped, but not of their clothing. They lose their dignity and drop their dreams. It may not have been a bad door. Their motives may have been pure, but it wasn't the right door at the right time. If they're God's dreams, they will come to pass. So when we experience this type of disappointment, it doesn't mean we should give up.

In Ephesus there was a great tension between believers and pagans. Even some of the believers were carnal and practiced paganism. Jewish involvement in magic during the New Testament era is documented in various historical writings from Josephus, the apocrypha, and others. After this encounter in Ephesus with the seven sons of Sceva, word spread like wildfire among the Jews and the Greeks. A solemn fear fell on the entire city, and the name of the Lord was honored. Imagine the effect of a scenario like the sons of Sceva—or Ananias and Sapphira—happened in the church today. If we had contemporary demonstrations like Uzzah and the ark, Nadab and Abihu, we might have a revival of the fear of the Lord—and what a difference that could make in our world.

In Ephesus, the fear of God did fall, and many of the believers were so convicted they came out and made a full public confession of wrongdoing, including those in the church who practiced witchcraft (see v 18-19). Have you ever wondered why God despises witchcraft and idolatry so much? Consider the spiritual aspect. These types of activities are man's attempt to gain supernatural power for themselves—so they can feel they are in control. When people participate in witchcraft, they mock and mimic the true prophetic work of God.

In Ephesus, Jews, pagans, and Christian converts had books and charms they used in their attempts at foretelling or influencing the future, but when the people heard the truth, those who opened the door of their hearts to God repented and then took action. They brought the paraphernalia from their homes and threw it, one item after another, on a pile that burned in the sight of everyone. There was real repentance, real conviction. Believers who had harbored wrong practices confessed and thoroughly exposed them.

The Ephesian believers saw their books, formulas, spells, and horoscopes for what they truly were. With this new perspective, what they'd paid dearly for in the past, now held no value. They realized its origin was demonic, heathen, and selfish. The value of all that was burned was counted at 50,000 pieces of silver.

> "Conviction is the voice of love that says, 'You're better than that.'"
> —Jeff Arnold

Spiritual Access Points

Everyone has their own spiritual access points—both negative and positive. In Ephesus, those negatives were idolatry and witchcraft. It helps to know our access points—the places we're vulnerable. If you don't know yours, I'm praying God opens your eyes to see them and then gives you the desire and strength to shut the door on them once and for all.

As I was thinking about spiritual access points, a song kept playing through my spirit—a calypso song.

> *Shut de do*
> *Keep out de devil*
> *Shut de do*
> *Keep de devil in de night*
> *Shut de do*
> *Keep out de devil*
> *Light de candle*
> *Everything's alright*
> *Light de candle*
> *Everything's alright*

This is a playful song, a lighthearted presentation of a heavy message, but we can't play around with its intent. Think back on the sons of Sceva. There are real demons out there, fallen angels. And when they influence people, they can cause injury.

There's a real Heaven, and there's a real Hell. We have to be careful that we don't give access to the enemy and inadvertently open a door to demonic influences. Each of us faces doors throughout our lives—doors of blessing, doors of opportunity, and doors of temptation that ultimately lead to destruction. What a difference a door makes.

Resisting the enemy is about more than standing strong for ourselves, it means opposing what opposes God! The church must stand in the gap for those in bondage. Our intervention can bring deliverance from the influences of evil and the bondage of sin that separates others from God.

Deliverance ministry requires an authentic walk with God that includes access to kingdom power. We can't be effective with one foot in the church and one in the world—one foot in one door, and one foot in another. It's time to pursue God's kingdom with everything we have.

As believers, filled with God's Spirit, you and I are His temple. As His dwelling place we must not allow any altar to a false idol in our lives. We must shut the door and leave the devil outside in his darkness. Allow the Holy Ghost to shine His candle within us. When our candle is lit by the fire of God's Spirit, He works in our lives. We couldn't possibly clean up enough to "get Jesus." We get Jesus, and He cleans us up.

Jesus is in the life-changing business, and His candle lights the corners of our hearts, minds, and spirits to what He considers to be sinful or what we've elevated to a wrongful position.

If we want to see miracles—if we want to see Jesus honored and exalted like He was in Ephesus—we must remove anything that could poison our hearts. Anything that could keep us separated from His manifest presence has to go. Anything that might close us off from His blessings must be cut out. It doesn't matter how much time or the cost of the resources we've invested in the past. We have to be willing to bring anything God points out to us out of hiding and throw it on the fire.

When the Bible talks about "curious arts" it refers to more than just magic. Most people reading this book don't spend their weekends on mountains performing pagan rituals or secreted away with Ouija boards. In addition to magic, "curious arts" also means to be "busy about trifles" and to be "neglectful of important matters." In 1 Timothy 5:13, the apostle Paul was writing to Timothy who pastored in Ephesus after the church was established. Paul was familiar with the culture. He mentioned women who were wandering from house to house—not only wasting time but gossiping and being busybodies—speaking things which they ought not. This refers to telling the tales of Diana and practicing "curious arts."

These women were corrected and silenced because they were engaged in spreading false teachings, but also because they were spending their time on things that had little value. They dedicated themselves and spent their resources on lesser vain and empty things, while they neglected more important matters. These women were walking through the wrong doors at the wrong time with the wrong message. God is calling us today to consider the doors we're walking through—to consider our ways. How are we spending our time? Our resources?

Of course, we have to live, function in the world, take care of our health, homes, and families; but is there anything that has lifted itself to a higher importance in our lives than our relationship with Jesus? Is there anything we're hiding, something keeping us from giving ourselves without restraint or hindering us in some way? Today is the day to throw it on the fire, shut the door on the devil, and walk through the open door before you.

The world might think we're crazy to give up or burn things it considers valuable, but when God says, "Get rid of that thing you love more than Me," we should listen. We must clean up our temples and clean up our houses. This is how we shut the door on the devil, our past, and the words of our own minds so we can walk through open doors and enjoy free access to God and all He wants for us.

We must keep the door of our hearts closed to the whispers of the enemy and the desires of the flesh that tempt and twist God's Word. God wants to do something amazing in our lives—to break us free from functioning *around* the influence of the enemy. We can know, from this day forward, we don't have to be scared of failing. In fact, once we know who we are and the power we have access to in the spiritual realm, we can make the devil scared of us.

Why would a demon be scared of you or me? He isn't! He's scared of the God in us! That's why He tries to diminish our power, pollute our temples, cause leaks in our spiritual conduits. As the source from which we gain authority and dominion, our connection with God must be our top priority.

> **There is an invisible world that sometimes makes itself known so we can reach for more.**

On February 8, 2020, I had an intimate experience with God.

Chapter 19: Pursue

There was something going on in the spiritual realm. Flashes of light in the room confirmed that although none of my family were home, I wasn't alone.

I asked God, "Do you have a message for me?" and something happened. He told me private, sacred things. A few hours later, the Lord brought an issue to my attention that needed change. It was difficult. I didn't even realize this "thing" was ingrained in my life to the extent that it would hinder me. It wasn't evil. It wasn't wicked. I wouldn't lose my ministry credentials over it, but there was something dulling me emotionally, mentally, and possibly spiritually. God wanted me to shut the door.

In this spiritual season, we need to be keen and connected to the Holy Ghost. I didn't tell you my "issue" because I want you to see your own. One thing is certain. The enemy doesn't want you alert and aware of his devices because when your eyes are open, you threaten to expose everything the kingdom of darkness has been building. He pushes from without, trying to create chaos around you. But the truth is, he's not really that powerful. It's time to push back—from the inside out. Let the Holy Ghost flow in a greater dimension of liberty and power.

Something happened that day. I'm not the same. When I obeyed His voice, one door slammed shut and another opened. God is beckoning. Beckoning me and beckoning you. Is there some habit, some mindset, some wound from your past? Perhaps even a secret sin God is bringing to your mind to deal with? If so, I believe God is presenting that information to you because He wants you free. He wants you liberated once and for all.

It doesn't matter how much we invested in the past. God is telling His people today to bring our "books," our "charms," our "habits," our "mindsets," our "victimhood," our "coping mechanisms" to the altar and throw them on the fire. Even things that seem harmless, can crack open a door. Quit trying to be in control. Stop being controlled by the past. Surrender everything to God. If we're going to see the full demonstration of the Spirit, like Paul saw in Ephesus, we have to let go of what's holding us back.

You're reading this book because you have faith in God. I expect the words on this page to mix with the faith in your heart to activate positive change. This means saying yes to Jesus when He knocks on your door to focus on and handle things that haven't been addressed. It can mean saying no to yourself, someone else, or a way of life. It includes an absolute openness of soul when God exposes what's been hidden—intentionally or otherwise.

God wants to help you shut any wrong doors, and when you do, you can walk through a new one into a broad place of freedom and authority. You can't open this door for yourself. The Waymaker makes the way, but once you cross the threshold, you'll be changed. There you'll find deliverance from the darkness that quietly crept into your life or has harbored for years in the shadows of a lifetime.

Jesus is knocking. He's at the door. He's inviting you to experience deliverance from distractions, restoration in your mind, and healing for your hidden wounds. Even purification in your private inner world of imaginations.

As I prayed about this subject, I saw an open door. An arm, open palm extended, reached toward me—inviting, welcoming. I don't believe the vision was just for me. Some people know when they're unraveling. They experience panic attacks, doubts, or fears, but others wouldn't consider themselves "broken" at all. The truth is, though some of us have achieved a certain level of success, in the end, it doesn't matter what we do or what acclaim we may enjoy. No amount of public praise or affection will ever heal internal issues or faulty integrity.

> **Cross the threshold. Enter His presence. Experience a greater wholeness and increased flow of the supernatural in your life.**

It's time to make this personal. Today is the day to shut the door on what's oppressing you. Sever the influence of a mocking spirit, rejection, molestation, a spirit of fear, or a spirit of loss. Cut off the fear of mental illness, resentment, and addictions. Let go of longing for what you haven't been allowed to do or lust for things that aren't yours to have. It's time to part ways with pride, vain ambition, low self-esteem, unworthiness, and a desire for fame or renown. When we're complete in Him, He provides the wholeness required to be conduits for His kingdom.

> **Today is the day to confront the voices, reject the lies, and sever negative influences.**

God has set you on a path to an open door. Press in. Pursue. He didn't pick the wrong person when He picked you. But there may be something that needs to happen to move forward. The voices in our heads can be the most powerful voices. Invite God to disrupt the dialogue, interrupt the lies, and turn what was meant for evil to good.

I believe you want to be a tool in God's hand. I do, too. God asked me a hard question as I was writing this, "Are you willing to go first?" I've attempted to do that, to go first and point you to a beautiful door of liberty, a place of true fulfilment in Him. God wants to change us, to help us let baggage go. To make us whole and free to love, live, and serve.

Chapter 19: Pursue

Have confidence in God. Pursue His presence. Don't resist. Don't shrink back. Today is the day. We no longer accept the status quo, but we answer the call that inspired us to begin this journey. As we work together, our many streams of living water converge into one dynamic flow of the Spirit. The kingdom of God is here, and the Lord's asking us to be ready and in position to manifest the power of God in our world.

End of Section 2

SECTION 3

Joy to the World

20

Kingdom Ambassadors

Fear not: for, behold, I bring you good tidings of great joy, which shall be to all people.
Luke 2:10

The kingdom of Heaven is righteousness, peace, and joy. Ask any of my children what their mom's favorite verse is, and they'll tell you 3 John 4, "I have no greater joy than to hear that my children walk in truth." The greatest joy is seeing those you love desire to know and walk with Jesus themselves. Experiencing the joy of seeing others come to the Lord is the focus of this section. A key insight on true joy can be found in a simple children's song. Where is joy located? According to the song, down in our hearts.

We tend to think about joy as a mindset. People talk about thinking themselves happy, but how does this apply in the kingdom? Kingdom joy far surpasses any externally triggered happiness. More than being rooted in happenstance, true joy is a fruit of the Spirit. Joy is a product of internal peace. Joy celebrates relationships. Though it may cost us something, joy celebrates the pleasure we find in doing good for God and others. We see the perfect example in Jesus. For the joy that was set before Him, He endured the suffering of the cross.

As I contemplated the topic, a thought came to me:

> **Joy and righteousness are roommates in a place called peace.**

The greatest joy is the joy of our own salvation. It's joy unspeakable and full of glory, and our joy brings joy to all of Heaven as well (see 1 Peter 1:8, Luke 15:10). God rejoices over His people with singing and shouts of joy (see Zephaniah 3:17). And some day, we'll enter permanently into the joy of the Lord (see Matthew 25:21–23).

The joy of the Lord strengthens God's people. Those who receive His Spirit share in Christ's mission of helping the grieving exchange their mourning for joy (see Nehemiah 8:10, Isaiah 61:3). With God on our side, our assurance of victory means we can have joy regardless of the obstacles or challenges we face (see 1 Corinthians 15:57–58). As God's righteous children, we have a promise from Him that we will go out with joy, even from exile (see Isaiah 55:12). We hold to His pledge with assurance of victory and rejoice now. Our joy is the result of abiding in the kingdom of peace rather than plotting and scheming to gather possessions to ourselves. Joy fills the hearts of those who plan for good (see Proverbs 12:20).

All this peace and joy sounds wonderful. Of course, not everyone reading this book feels blissful and delighted about their current circumstances, but we can look ahead to joy that's coming in the morning (see Psalm 30:5, 2 Corinthians 4:17). Nights filled with tears will give way to a joy-filled morning. But until that time, God's sure word shines like a lamp, breaking the doom and gloom of our dark places (see 2 Peter 1:19).

Pete and I first became aware of the severity of his condition when he picked up our ten-month old son and fell to the ground. I wasn't home at the time, and since this occurred in the era before cell phones, I was unreachable. My five-year-old daughter did her best to care for her daddy and baby brother until I returned and walked into a moment that changed our lives forever. We discovered Pete's back pain and subsequent fall were the result of holes eaten in his bones that caused his spinal column to collapse. After checking him into the hospital, his doctors prescribed morphine to be administered around the clock. Pete stayed on morphine for the next year—as cancer advanced, shingles broke out, and through two extremely agonizing bone marrow aspirations. The pain was so intense Pete couldn't move, and the big man who once took care of me, could no longer walk or care for himself. There were hard days, but during that time of suffering, we also experienced beauty and victories.

Pete was a wonderful man—such a giver and a servant. He gave his best in everything he did, and yet, he had areas he struggled. He believed that in his illness God was helping him fight and defeat strongholds that he self-identified as pride, selfishness and self-control. In his own words, he said, "Amazingly, God broke down the walls one by one. Each day I was drawing closer to Him. He gave me a true liberty in the Holy Ghost (speaking in tongues), and probably the most exciting thing was when He gave me joy. My brother Eddie and I were singing and laughing in the

Holy Ghost once for almost two hours even though I was in tremendous pain at the time. These were things I had dreamt about having for almost twenty years!"

I remember that day well. I'd run away from home for a few hours just to escape the heaviness. When I came back, there was such a joy—a joy that overrode our circumstances, a joy that can only come from the presence of God. It was a great miracle; one I will never forget.

When I say life isn't always easy, but God is always good, it isn't a trite expression or some proverb I memorized. I know through experience that when we have Jesus, we can have joy. He told His followers He was giving them His own joy to remain in them and that their joy would be complete and overflowing (see John 15:11). We have joy now. We don't have to wait. Mary rejoiced in God her Savior *before* she conceived the promise (see Luke 1:47). The wise men rejoiced with exceeding great joy when they'd only seen the star (see Matthew 2:10). If God has given you a word—you can rejoice in that now. If He's made you a promise—rejoice!

Kingdom Ambassadors

In the Old Testament and the New, God called those who kept His covenant a treasured possession, His kings and priests (see Exodus 19:5-6, 1 Peter 2:9). When the Lord reconciled us to Himself, He called us to join with Him as ambassadors in His ministry of reconciliation (see 2 Corinthians 5:17-20). He expects us to be zealous in doing good for others (see Titus 2:14).

Peter said, "But ye are a chosen generation, a royal priesthood, an holy nation, a peculiar people" (1 Peter 2:9). The KJV uses the word *peculiar* in reference to God's people. Most of us would prefer words like *passionate* or *purposeful* over *peculiar*, but peculiar doesn't mean being weird. It means having a different character or nature than the world around us. We're not peculiar because we're odd. We're peculiar because we're His. We're "peculiar to Jesus," which means we belong to Him and to His service.

This verse tells us we're different for a specific purpose: to show forth praises to God. How do we do that? We accept that we're chosen by Him, to serve as His ambassadors. We "show forth God's praises" when we spread the joy of the kingdom.

In secular government, an ambassador is a high-ranking diplomatic official sent on behalf of a sovereign as a resident representative authorized to contract business on behalf of the one he or she represents. Being an ambassador for Christ is an honor, but it's also an incredible responsibility. God calls us to minister to those who are spiritually blinded by the spirit of the world. He calls you and me to shine the light of the gospel upon them (see 2 Corinthians 4:3-4).

Called and Empowered

We learn from many sources: pastors and teachers, experience, and our own study. But we have one superior teacher ever present to instruct and guide our way. Jesus said His Spirit shall teach you all things (see John 14:26). God Himself conducts one-on-one ambassador training. He leads and guides us through discernment. He's willing to walk and talk with us.

Sometimes the Lord impresses us to take a certain action, but too often we brush it off. We think *someone else can do that. I'm already busy.* But as He prompts us, we must recognize His voice, stop and listen, and then accept the will of God to minister to the broken around us. We read the Lord's charge to His people to make disciples of all nations in the Great Commission, but Jesus provided the details of His own mission when He picked up the Isaiah scroll at the beginning of His ministry. As He read the prophet's words, He outlined His plan (see Luke 4:18-19). And now He anoints us, His Spirit-filled believers, with power to touch others on His behalf.

I distinctly remember a time the Lord dealt with me on the subject of giving myself more fully to the kingdom. It was after a service, and everyone in the congregation had gathered around the altar. We were singing the song: "I give myself away, I give myself away so you can use me." Standing there, eyes closed, singing with all sincerity, I received a strong impression, "How much 'self' are you talking about?"

> "His calling is his enabling."
> —Myrtle Beall

With this probing question, the Lord hijacked my worship. I knew what He was asking. "Self" means more than our time, talents, and treasure. It is who we are—our identities. God was asking me if I was willing to trade my visions, dreams, and plans for my life for the ones He had for me. That's what giving "self" away means, including any lack of confidence or overestimations of who I think I am.

This giving away of self is an ongoing work, but when we trade our dreams for His, we can have confidence that we're in His perfect will. Our confidence isn't in our abilities, but His. By grace and the power of His Spirit, we have the liberty to step beyond "self" and do great things!

I've said many times to many people that to be who God has called us to be, we have to get our "stupid selfs" out of the way. I don't usually use the word stupid in

Chapter 20: Kingdom Ambassadors

reference to people, but honestly, God's calling isn't about "self" at all. It never has been. It's all about Him. Anything else is—well, stupid. As we consecrate ourselves, any ministry God calls us to is already in His hands. We can confidently move forward in His will.

Poured Out

As Christians, we pour the living water we received from God out to others. It flows from God to us to them. In the book *Heaven on Earth,* author Francis J. Connelly wrote, "If you believe in Jesus you will influence all those you come into contact with, saturating them with faith, love, and hope. The greater your love for Jesus, the greater will be the outpouring." When we sacrifice ourselves for others, the supernatural follows, because unlike our human nature that seeks to fulfill its own desires, sacrifice intends to bless others. Paul said, "Even if I am being poured out as a drink offering on the sacrifice and service of your faith [for preaching the message of salvation], still I rejoice and share my joy with you all" (Philippians 2:17, AMP).

True love offers more than caring, it gives of self for someone else. True love endeavors to live and minister sacrificially. A sensitive conduit follows the leading of the Spirit to bless people in need. We become His vessels of hope and comfort (see Psalm 86:17).

As kingdom ambassadors, we order our lives to prevent distractions that endanger our connectivity with Jesus. We intentionally abide in Christ, and He reveals things to us we can't see with our natural eyes alone. He grants us spiritual discernment and strategies as well as vision to see the needs of others, minister to them, and release the miraculous.

Jesus served others. F. B. Meyer said, "He rose from the throne; laid aside the garments of light which He had worn as His vesture; took up the poor towel of humanity and wrapped it about His Glorious person; poured His own Blood into the basin of the Cross; and set Himself to wash away the foul stains of human depravity and guilt."

The true test of our faith lies in our ability to apply our beliefs and see results. Jesus didn't come to merely deliver words or establish doctrines. When Jesus came, the kingdom of God materialized—it became "at hand," and God set things in motion. He called out forces of evil at work in the world and addressed sin in human hearts. He invited "whosoever will" to cast their cares upon Him, do the will of the Father, and serve. This is the path to true greatness.

God cares about people—and about our every need. When Jesus healed the sick, He proved His power to perform miracles, but that wasn't His most significant accomplishment. At the same time that He healed their bodies, He also freed the people from their sin (see John 5:36, 10:25).

Love and healing are part of God's nature. Francis McNutt said, "Jesus did not heal people to prove that He was God; He healed them because He was God." And Jesus passed to His followers His own power and authority over devils and diseases. He sent His disciples out to continue to preach the kingdom of God and to heal the sick (see Luke 9:1-2). He empowered them to liberate those suffering from all sorts of demonic influence, including oppression and disease. He gave this power to His followers at the same time He commissioned them to preach the gospel. As His ambassadors, we, too, are called to shine in our generation (see Matthew 5:16).

> Healing people was part of Jesus's day-to-day life. It was part of His "normal."

The power Jesus imparted wasn't limited to twelve select men. God delegated the same power to the church at large. Scripture mentions individuals by name like Stephen who did great wonders and miracles, and Paul who did unusual miracles (see Acts 6:8, Acts 19:11). In the Book of Acts, the power of God that fell in the Upper Room and upon all them that came to receive God's Spirit, was the Spirit of Jesus. And that same Spirit continues to do His works through His people. This is how the church is able to do "greater" works than Jesus did, by multiplying His mission in every generation until He comes again.

Early Christians knew the Source of their power. They knew it was God's hand at work. They prayed, "Stretch out your hand of power through us to heal, and to move in signs and wonders by the name of your holy Son, Jesus!" (Acts 4:30, TPT).

The early church prayed with authority. Knowing they'd been appointed to continue the work of Jesus and were praying in the will of God. Their words revealed their expectation. They said what He said, "Arise. Stand. Take up thy bed and walk."

A City of Refuge

As ambassadors for the kingdom, we, in a sense, fulfill similar roles to that of the Old Testament Levites (see Revelation 1:6). When the Israelites took possession of the Promised Land, God established cities of refuge that were given to the Levites as part of their inheritance. You and I, New Testament priests, are to inhabit spiritual "cities of refuge." We are the ones who open the gates to those running for shelter, for sanctuary, and for safety.

Who is this sanctuary intended to serve? First, it's for God's people—the ones who made mistakes and seek refuge. Think about that. Jesus's offer of reconciliation to the world reached first to His own people. There are those who've stumbled on their walks with God. Some harder than others. The church has a responsibility to offer restoration to all regardless of how far they've come from. We have no right to snub our noses, even though we've been faithful to the Father. But Jesus said if a person hates someone, they've committed murder in their hearts. We aren't all murderers, but we've all been guilty of shooting daggers at a brother or sister from time to time. Everyone needs grace. Let's open wide the city gates and welcome those running home.

When God established cities of refuge, He included specifications for the roads leading to these safe havens. The path was twice the width of a regular road and marked with signposts. They were made especially smooth and even, so that even if a person was running, they would have the best chance possible to make it. The Israelites prepared the way to these cities, and I feel the Lord is asking us today to prepare the way in our land for backsliders, for those who have stumbled and need mercy and restoration. We need to be easy to approach so everyone feels safe and welcome in the Father's house. This is part of our ministry as ambassadors for God's kingdom.

> We are His priests, waiting at the gate to receive those running for help.

Can't Stop!

Our faith in our calling must be greater than any fear we face. We represent our Lord and Savior without fearing the cost, the unknown, or rejection. God is greater than anything that sparks fear in our hearts. The Lord goes before us, and we never walk alone. He empowers and equips His kingdom ambassadors to be victorious in the world we live in. God taught His prophet how to prophesy, and instructed him not to fear people, as He promised to put His words in his mouth (see Jeremiah 1). As we represent God, He will lead us by His Spirit.

As Christians, one of our greatest pleasures is found in living lives filled with purpose. And we bring joy to the Father's heart when we dedicate ourselves to His pleasure.

The Song of the Redeemed

*My lips shall greatly rejoice when I sing unto thee;
and my soul, which thou hast redeemed.*
Psalm 71:23

The Bible is the story of redemption. It's an epic narrative of the unfolding plan of God over the course of the history of the world. It tells of those who've been redeemed—delivered from evil, from death, hell, and the grave by the blood of the Lamb and by their obedience to the gospel (see Acts 2:38). The redeemed know what God has done for them and that God Himself has put a new song, a hymn of praise in their hearts.

God created people for His glory to worship Him in all of life (see Psalm 66:4, 150:6, 1 Corinthians 10:31). He created us for communion with Him—to love Him with all our hearts, souls, and might (see Deuteronomy 6:5). In Pentecostal churches we often hear messages about worshipping the Lord in the beauty of holiness. I believe that is a part of our calling as God's chosen people, and that worshipping in the beauty of holiness includes each of us singing a new song unto the Lord (Psalm 149:1, Isaiah 42:10). But what is the new song of the redeemed (see Revelation 14:3)? Is it a composition we write with words and melody and sing with our mouths, or is it something more than music?

I present for your consideration that the song of the redeemed is the "song" of our holy lives. We tap out its rhythm with our feet as we walk in love with Him and minister to others. We conduct the music with our hands extended in worship and service. We sing the words in our hearts with the breath of God and share His love with the world around us. This is a very holy hymn and the most beautiful song we could ever offer to God.

In 1988, Christian music artist, Cynthia Clawson, recorded a project titled *Hymnsinger*. Words from one of the songs have resonated in my spirit since that time:

> "Let the essence of my life be a song others will want to sing."

The substance of our lives contains characteristics and properties of God that affect the way we live and compose the songs of our lives—songs meant to be beautiful, harmonious, peaceful, pleasant, and inspiring. We live out the beauty of God with our words and ways that reverberate into the atmosphere and touch lives around us.

We've discussed the delivering power of praise and that worship is warfare. We've looked at our demonstration of worship through singing, dancing, and playing instruments before the Lord and how that brings strength, joy, and victory to our lives. But worship is more than an offering of praise alone or some act performed in a worship service. We must live right to worship right. The Living Bible translates the familiar psalm of David, "Worship the Lord with the beauty of holy lives" (Psalm 96:9, TLB). A holy life is required to bring a holy offering. Worshipping the Lord in the beauty of holiness means to worship in the honor of holiness. And when we worship, we join with Heaven where angels are crying out "holy, holy, holy" and the glory of the Lord radiates from the throne of God.

A Song of Serving

We've been blessed to be a blessing. While it's unlikely one of us could impact the whole world for the kingdom of God, it's also true that every person affects the lives of those near them. This is where we sing our song. The song of a holy, redeemed life is a song of serving. We've discussed how ministry and the gifts of the Spirit are given to profit everyone, but let's turn our attention for a few minutes to gifts of serving.

Paul taught on these gifts in Romans 12—the same chapter that opens with a plea to believers to present themselves before God as living sacrifices—holy—the kind He can accept.

This writing to the church in Rome teaches us to use the faculties, talents, and gifts God has given us by His grace. Those He calls to prophesy should speak out His word. Those with

> Whatever your gift might be— use it with sincerity

gifts of practical service, should give themselves to serving. Those called to teach, should teach.

Our song of serving requires that we keep our passion burning, be hospitable, and be blessings even to those who curse us. We rejoice with those who rejoice and weep with those who weep, living in harmony with one another. This is the servant's song. When we sing this song, we show evidence of the Spirit in us and bring God glory in pure worship. It's the giving of self for the profit of all, which in turn, blesses the body.

Paul said, the manifestation of the Spirit is given to every man to profit all (see 1 Corinthians 12:7). The original language of this verse tells us that when we manifest God's Spirit, it results in *symphero*, the Greek root of the word symphony. This type of loving service creates a beautiful song; a new, joyful song in the spirit of holiness.

Your Measure

The song of the redeemed, your song and mine, has a measure (from the Greek word *metron*). Every song includes measure. They require a rhythm—a pace and a place. As we use the term here, a "measure" means "a determined extent, portion measured off, measure or limit." As we noted above, the Bible speaks of the measure of faith given to each person. God has measured something and deposited it inside each of us. As we step out in faith, our measure includes a certain sphere of authority and influence. What I find so encouraging is that both our inner faith and outer spheres of authority and influence can grow. Our individual, little melodies can develop into symphonic masterpieces. When we sing our songs to the best of our ability, God brings kingdom increase in us and through us.

We've talked about the pulse of life, and the concept continues as we join together in a beautiful symphony. We score the notes when we pick up the ringing phone and give ourselves to a person in need, even at times when we feel spent. We create the melody when we purposely make time to serve, teach, and bless—even when our schedules get interrupted. A richness fills out our song when we *don't* do what we want to do, but instead do as the Holy Ghost teacher in our spirits leads. Our symphony is made beautiful when we "hold our peace" and don't speak from our own minds, but instead offer Jesus.

When we speak of personal measures or *metrons,* that doesn't necessarily refer to a certain geographic region. It could refer to a group of people with common interests or circumstances like widows, victims of abuse, professionals, a cultural group, or the people at your child's school. Remember, wherever your *metron* is, God hasn't stopped drawing it. When we're faithful in small things, He enlarges our influence.

A person's *metron* is based on a God-given call and God-given gifts, but its effectiveness and borders are influenced by character, humility, obedience, and teachability. A lack of integrity, moral impurity, or compliance to God's will can shrink a person's *metron*. Just as people can respond differently to the same song, you and I may not be effective in reaching every person with the same style or approach. That's why it's so important we allow the Lord to lead as we serve as His conduits. The Apostle Paul understood this principle. He knew his assignment. In his letter to the Corinthian church, he said, "We will not boast of things beyond our measure, but according to the measure of the rule which God hath distributed to us, a measure to reach even unto you" (2 Corinthians 10:13).

Paul was not like the people who had made wild claims and written their own testimonials. But he and his companions rejoiced in the work God had given them to do. That work took place within the lines God had marked out for them. Paul wasn't interested in going beyond what God had called him to, but he was certainly faithful and diligent to His assignment.

Sing with Joy

If we release our song with joy and confidence, we might be surprised to see who turns to listen. If someone rejects your song, it won't do any good to try to force them to listen. Jesus spoke and taught to the masses but recognized there were those who would never choose to join in the kingdom. Wherever God put us, that's today's assignment, and so we should act like it by exercising the dynamic duo of faith and humility. We have confidence knowing He supplies what we need for every appointment.

No matter how big or wide our spheres of influence, if we try to operate outside of the limits God set

Humility and teachability can grow your sphere of influence.

for us, we can cause problems for ourselves and others. I've seen the demonstration and power of the Lord in many places where I was invited to minister. God showed up and touched the people. If I took the same action in places I hadn't been called or authorized, I couldn't expect the same positive results.

When I'm ministering at my home church, I'm not the guest evangelist—I'm just Sister Lori, fellow member for the past 30+ years. The expectation level isn't the same as when I'm invited to speak at a state-wide conference. I've found, however, when attending conferences where I'm not on the platform, I most always have a place of ministry in the altar. We don't have to be the one speaking to minister. The altar is often a place to sing our redemption songs, touching and serving others.

If we attempt to sing a song out of our range or abilities, we won't create a pleasant sound, but disharmony that is far from symphonic. But when we find that song that is in our range—that fits our tone and our personality—and we start singing it in our *metrons*, our songs are beautiful. They will be graceful and powerful, and the favor of God will be evident—the favor that anointing brings and takes us places giftedness alone cannot.

How do we know the starts and stops of our musical *metrons* in our unique, individual songs? God speaks to us through His Word. He reveals to us His general will, and He also speaks to us personally. Scripture seems to light up on the pages as we read it and it becomes alive within us.

We've spoken about developing our gifts, and that certainly plays an important role here. We develop as we serve. We exercise what we've been given. And we listen to spiritually-minded people around us—especially our leadership. The people who know us best may see us in ways we might not see ourselves. They might see gifts and potential unnoticed by us, and they also may have a better understanding of our spiritual maturity and readiness to move forward. Our spiritual leaders should know if we've developed enough to carry the weight of what we feel called to do or if we need to be trained before we can carry it out.

When we're asked to do something that causes us to stretch, we should pray about it. I never wanted to be a leader in prayer ministry. In fact, the first year I was approached about taking the position as the local National Day of Prayer leader, I said no without even praying about it. I knew it wasn't for me. A year later, the same lady came to me and said, "I've been praying for a year, and your name is the only one that comes to me. Will you pray about it?"

I didn't want to pray about it. But I did. God directed me to serve, and as I gave myself to the work, my role expanded from a city event coordinator to county coordinator, then tri-county coordinator and eventually State Coordinator. I felt out of my area of expertise, but God pushed me, and as I grew in service, He expanded my reach.

When it comes to growth, we need to recognize that when we receive a gift, that doesn't mean it comes fully developed in us. A singer's first efforts won't sound like Mahalia Jackson at her peak with a mature depth and range. We submit ourselves to practice, to training and teaching. But at the same time, we shouldn't discount the purity and value of our songs right now. Some of the sweetest concerts ever given were those of children who sang off-key, but who thoroughly delighted their audiences (their *metrons*).

While we sing and serve, we continue to search out new ways to invest our time and talent. It can be helpful in these times to consider what moves us most. What causes us to respond with the deepest emotion? What makes us cry? What makes us mad? What brings us the greatest joy? Do we feel drawn to a particular type of person or ministry activity? What have we overcome in our lives that could help us minister to others in similar situations? Who do we feel most compelled to pray for? To encourage? The answers to these questions might determine a new area of service.

> **Learn from others. Be in contact with people who are like you.**

Redeem the Time

Paul wrote in Ephesians that because we are redeemed, we should redeem the time we have here on Earth. We should make the best use of our time—every opportunity we have. The whole of Ephesians 5 talks about how believers are to live holy lives and share the gospel with others. Someday this temporal life will come to an end and each of us will stand before God's throne. Meanwhile, how are we, the disciples of Jesus, supposed to live while we're redeeming the time? Paul provided the answer. Be wise and understand the will of the Lord. Don't be drunk on the pleasures of the world but filled with God's Spirit. We should speak to ourselves in spiritual songs and thanksgiving and submit ourselves one to another out of respect for the Lord (see Ephesians 5:16–21).

Giving-Living

Like scoring out music, our redemption song requires an ordering of our days, priorities, and resources. We prepare ourselves for lives of service in a paradigm I call "giving-living." As we become the kind of people God uses to release His blessings into the world, we must "live" and "give" in concert.

Giving-living means being a generous, noble, self-sacrificing, and benevolent person. It means being liberal in loving and giving—which have always been part of God's plan. What we've been given, we're instructed to freely give others, but reality and giving-living sometimes butt heads. We get tired of life's demands, tired of serving, tired of giving, entertaining, funerals, visits, phone calls. Sometimes we freely give ourselves to certain areas, but withhold in others we should also invest in.

Yes, there are boundaries in relationships and giving, but all of you and all of me belong to all of God. Sometimes God asks us to sacrifice something we haven't before. He might ask us to give up sleep to sit with someone in an emergency, to change our plans, or to spend our time doing for someone else instead of doing what we want. This is giving-living, and it's truly a key to abundant life and bodily health. Nate Larken said, "When we make another man's progress our concern, giving him a listening ear, a caring heart and opening ourselves as a conduit for God's grace, we find our own walk propelled to a whole new level. We are truly helped by helping, taught by teaching, and encouraged by encouraging."

"There is the one who [generously scatters [abroad], and yet increases all the more; And there is the one who withholds what is justly due, but it results only in want and poverty" (Proverbs 11:24, AMP). What we hold tightly to keep for ourselves, we lose. When we intentionally invest in others, the Bible promises an increase.

The word *invest* actually comes from the term putting on vestments—the priestly garments. We have established our call to God's royal priesthood, and so we should suit up. This may seem a bit of a tangent, but as I considered the subject of giving-living, the five "love languages" written about by Gary Chapman came to mind. People thrive when they receive what they need of these five "languages": words of affirmation, acts of service, receiving gifts, quality time, and physical touch. We should give to others, especially those closest to us, what is "justly due." And we should give expressions of love also to the people we serve with and minister to, even those who aren't yet part of the family of God.

If we selfishly withhold words of affirmation, for instance, instead of giving them to the ones who need them to thrive, the result is want and poverty. The end result is needy people.

As I read Chapman's "love languages," I found the corollaries fascinating between them and the acts of service outlined by Paul to the Romans. The apostle said believers should speak to encourage, perform acts of service, give generously, lead diligently, and care for others with cheerfulness (see Romans 12:6-8). God is telling His church to express love in these five languages. In fact, we are commanded to love our brothers and sisters (see 1 John 4:21). Love is more than a feeling. God so loved He gave.

Greedy people make needy people.

Each of us has something to offer someone else. We give and serve in our departments. We do our "God things"—sing in the choir, teach a class, mow the yard, or clean the kitchen; but as we serve, let us be in tune with the people around us. We need to evaluate ourselves. Are we connecting with the sick and the lonely? Are we giving generously of ourselves, our time? And this is a big one: Are we sharing our lives with others?

When we give of ourselves, we get back joy. That's the way our God works. Giving is a holy activity and an important aspect of discipleship. Even the smallest things we do carry divine import as we offer ourselves as God's instruments. I remember some precious cards I received with only $2 in them, but the little message inside and the thoughts behind them still warm my heart. We must believe what we're doing makes a difference. If we believed and really understood that we aren't saved *by* good works, but *for* good works, perhaps we would be less complacent. God desires that we would continually flourish in His work. He promised that by His grace that overflows toward us, we would have everything we need to abound in every good work (see 2 Corinthians 9:8).

Whatever our offering—whether it's prayer, teaching, outreach, a potpie for a neighbor—we give with thanks. God loves a cheerful giver, and our joyful service contributes to covering the earth with His glory.

Serve the Lord with gladness!

 We exemplify Jesus when we serve one another.

John Wesley said, "Do all the good you can, by all the means you can, in all the ways you can, in all the places you can, at all the times you can, to all the people you can, as long as ever you can." God so loved the world He gave—not money, but love—His own flesh and blood, an investment of time, energy, and prayer for others.

In Paul's final charge to Timothy he said, "Command them to do good, to be rich in good deeds and to be generous and willing to share. In this way they will lay up treasure for themselves as a firm foundation for the coming age, so that they may take hold of the life that is truly life" (1 Timothy 6:18-19).

Intercession

The song of the redeemed carries others to the throne of God through intercession. We see those in need of light and life, and we have compassion on them. We intercede for the lost and hurting and try to bring broken things back together through prayer. Jesus's compassion, rooted in love, motivated Him. He interceded for sinners, and the cross became a channel for His love.

The Lord is looking for intercessors—those who would be conduits for His Spirit to pray through. Jesus ever intercedes when we partner with Him. The Lord expressed disappointment to Isaiah when "he wondered that there was no intercessor" (Isaiah 59:16). A wooden plaque in my cabin on the church campground was signed by a woman renowned for her fervent intercession. She wrote, "Share my burden—Vesta Layne Mangun." I read that, and I thought Jesus might say the same, "Share My burden." To carry God's burden is an honor, but one that requires a level of brokenness.

True intercession requires a willingness to carry someone else's need to the throne of grace. Deep intercession costs. It's a strenuous activity that can at times cause physical pain to those who battle in prayer.

> To be "broken" in intercession means sharing Jesus's burden—reaching for others through prayer.

Throughout history, intercession has sparked great revivals. Two elderly women united in prayer for their community and ignited the infamous Hebrides revival. Evangelist Charles Finney depended on the support of his personal intercessor, Daniel Nash. Nash targeted areas for revival and prayed for up to several weeks until he felt the community was prepared, and then would send for Finney. His prayer continued throughout his revival meetings. As these people yielded themselves to lives of servanthood through intercessory prayer, new life was born. Our intercession is powerful. God uses our prayers to form Christ in others (see Galatians 4:19). Intercessory prayer is an act of pure love.

Those who strive to live in connectivity to God often receive specific information that informs their prayers. They're able to intercede powerfully because they believe they are, in fact, kingdom conduits praying for what God wants to happen in the earth. Even when we don't have a specific direction, we can pray kingdom principles. We pray for the release of spiritual understanding in the minds of the unsaved. We pray for faith to arise and for relational healing in the church and out. We pray for fresh anointing and a demonstration of the gifts that flows more freely out of intercessory prayer. We pray for liberty and power for others. And when we don't know what to pray in English, we can always pray in the Spirit. As T. W. Barnes used to say, "Pray until it flows."

In 2017 while on a World Network of Prayer conference call in which we were praying for the harvest, I saw an image of a large irrigation machine in a field. The thought came to me that intercessors provide the irrigation for the seed that's been planted in the ground. The life within the seed is activated when moisture enters its interior. The spiritual environment in our world today is dry, and intercessory prayer waters both the ground and seed. As we break through the soil to plant the seed of the living Word, we pray the Lord of the harvest causes life to spring up.

> "Don't pray the problem, pray the solution, Jesus!"
> —Vani Marshall

While an intercessory burden often drives us to our knees, at times it leads us to strategic warfare prayer that inspires action. When my husband enters strategic warfare prayer, he stands to his feet and starts pointing his fingers in all directions, moving about with boldness and speaking with authority. I don't know what he's saying as he prays in the Spirit, but I know he's pulling down strongholds and pushing back darkness. In prayer, he forcefully and aggressively advances on enemy territory.

The prayer of strategic warfare addresses the need from God's perspective—taking dominion and demanding surrender. We pray revelation is loosed in the church. We pray believers engage in the work of the kingdom. We speak the Word of faith and proclaim the name of Jesus. We declare His kingdom to be manifest in the earth. Prayer connects us with the heavens and establishes God's will around us. When we call on the Lord and sing our redemption songs, He does great and mighty things. "Therefore the redeemed of the Lord shall return, and come with singing unto Zion; and everlasting joy shall be upon their head: they shall obtain gladness and joy; and sorrow and mourning shall flee away" (Isaiah 51:11).

22

The Divine-Human Partnership

For we are labourers together with God.
1 Corinthians 3:9

In the task of sharing God's kingdom, no one works alone. We partner with God Himself, and work in harmony with other believers. As God's dear children and heirs to the kingdom, we serve, but not merely as servants. We minister through our covenant relationship with God armed with His promise to provide the knowledge and revelation necessary to defeat our enemies. God graciously helps us accomplish His purposes by giving us wisdom and understanding of the times (see 1 Chronicles 12:32, Daniel 2:21). Through our connectivity with Him, God downloads to us the information we need through dreams, discernment, and other gifts of the Spirit.

When the Lord appeared to King Solomon in a dream and invited him to make a request of Him, Solomon asked for an understanding heart and discernment (see 1 Kings 3:9). Solomon first gained God's attention with lavish offerings, but I believe His prayer was answered because it was offered with a sincere heart to know how to lead God's people. What God granted Solomon, He desires to impart to the "kings and priests" in His New Testament church. It's amazing that an infinite God would link His divine power with frail, finite humans, but He does. His Spirit is in motion even now. He reveals strategies and tactics and empowers those who unite themselves with His kingdom purposes.

As we've discussed throughout *Kingdom Come,* men and women were never meant to function independently from God, and that certainly holds true in ministering on His behalf. This is one arena we must be diligent about forsaking self-government, abandoning our desires to please self, and acting in complete cooperation with the leading of the Spirit. We labor together with God, and that means taking direction when and how He gives it—even when we don't understand why He's asking us to do a certain thing. Nathaniel Haney once spoke of the great need for preachers to know who they are. I believe his words apply to every child of God because each of us is called at one time or another to be an oracle of God—sharing God's wisdom through prophetic words or spiritual advice. Haney said,

> In the same way the Wright Brothers celebrated the completion of their first flight at Kitty Hawk, you and I can celebrate our spiritual progress even while knowing there's still much to learn.

"We've got to understand our partnership with the invisible world." I agree.

When we're filled with God's Spirit, we don't become spiritual puppets. We choose, of our own free wills, to engage in ministering to the world around us rather than stubbornly overriding His call.

It's our intentional determination to partner with God that invites the Lord to be active through us as we seek to build His kingdom. This is another way a believer pleases the Lord and demonstrates a will conformed to His (see Romans 12:1–2).

In His Name

When we're in relationship with God, in covenant, we utilize the terms of the agreement. We align our thoughts and words with His. We don't beg. As Jesus instructed, we go boldly to the throne of God through faith in His name. Prayers prayed in the name of Jesus are power-packed because His name isn't simply a word to identify a certain person. Praying in Jesus's name means praying on His behalf, praying as He would pray, and doing what He would do. When we minister in His name, we see people and their needs as He would. We extend our hands to touch the people He would touch with healing, liberty, peace, joy, and restoration. We do it all in His name—not just reciting a formula—but praying with authority.

> Praying in the name of Jesus invokes all the power of Heaven to move on our behalf.

Power

In Chapter 5 we looked extensively at Psalm 8 and how David underscored the power of unwavering trust and pure, childlike faith. In the divine-human partnership, our faith isn't in our faith, but in our God who gives what we need to do His work. A childlike faith asks, seeks, and knocks with confidence because it knows a loving father would never give a snake or a stone to a child who asked for fish or bread (see Luke 11:10-13).

When God speaks to our hearts, He gives us perception beyond our visible circumstances, either for our benefit or the benefit of others—which serves to benefit the kingdom of God. When working together with God, we're free to step out in faith on His Word. Charles Mahaney wrote about the "satanic power of doubt" and how the enemy uses doubt to interrupt our faith. We have no cause to doubt the direction or promises of God (see Romans 4:20).

In the natural world, scientists have learned to harness the nuclear power God placed inside atoms. They use the energy to create electricity that lights up towns. As Spirit-filled believers, we have access to a force more vast and grand than this world's greatest natural source of power, one that's able to change lives for eternity.

Empowering the Body of Christ

The church is more than a building or the people assembled within a building. It's a supernatural body fashioned, framed, and joined together by God for His pleasure and purposes. In order that the body might function well, God grants spiritual gifts to His church. In this section, as we examine gifts endowed to believers by God, the foundational concept to keep in mind is that spiritual gifts are just that—spiritual.

Jesus said, "Lo, I am with you always . . ." Brian DeVries, a missionary minister who works primarily in South Africa and is the principle of a theological university there, expressed his thoughts on the importance of gifts and growing the church this way. He said, "Since the Holy Spirit works through believers to build up the body of Christ, advocates of biblical church growth should seek to employ His means to motivate spiritual giftedness in the church."

> God is constantly pulsing a stream of gifts into the church to be utilized to fulfill the work of the Great Commission.

The operation of God's spiritual gifts releases the tactics, intelligence, and power of Almighty God to His "boots on the ground" troops. What does this mean to you and me? If we want God's kingdom to grow, we must allow His Spirit to grow it. In other words, what we're talking about at its very core, is "spiritual life." At conversion, God bestows spiritual life (*pneuma*) to every believer. According to the Word, the demonstration of His Spirit through His people doesn't come and go. His "moving" is a manifestation of His supernatural presence and power that is always with us. Jeff Arnold said, "God only exists in two forms—manifested and unmanifested. The purpose of worship is to move us from the unmanifested presence to the manifested." When God manifests His presence through the operation of spiritual gifts, He does so for the advantage and bringing together of all. Paul wrote, "Now to each one, the manifestation of the Spirit is given for the common good" (1 Corinthians 12:7 NIV).

In effect, God (who is a Spirit) parcels Himself to a believer as He chooses. He divides Himself and gives differing aspects of His divine nature and resources to men, women, young people, and even children to equip them to minister at His direction on His behalf. "All these are the work of one and the same Spirit, and he distributes them to each one, just as he determines" (1 Corinthians 12:11, NIV).

The singular work of the Spirit is the mission of God to reach the people of Earth. I consider the operation of spiritual gifts in the church to be an "organic process." In this process, everything originates from God, our Source.

Similar to a composite light that splits when it hits a raindrop, the Lord reveals Himself as living light and divides various aspects of His own nature out into the world like the colors of the rainbow. This draws attention back to Section 1, where we describe Ezekiel's vision of God as a rainbow-colored, dazzling gem, surrounded by clear, shining splendor. From one source comes many streams of light. This is how spiritual gifts enter our world.

Again, God is the source. We are His "drops" created to reveal and reflect Him in the church, in our world, or in whatever He's giving to us to do in any given moment. God knows what's needed, and He gives it. The process is organic because it's derived from a living source. God is a living, moving spirit. He chooses how and when He wants to work in our world.

So, while we can't manufacture the supernatural into the natural, we can prepare ourselves, and we can encourage, educate, and equip others to learn how to "catch" what God is "pouring out." To move with Him, and to act comfortably on His behalf at His direction.

Within the church body are distinct ministries in two basic categories: Governing ministries (*diakonia*) are the apostles, prophets, evangelists, pastors, and teachers mentioned in Ephesians 4:11. These include offices, or positions of service in the church. Another avenue in which the Spirit ministers is through the release of spiritual endowments given to believers by the operation of the Spirit (*charisms*). Most teaching on spiritual gifts is based on 1 Corinthians 12 and covers nine gifts in three categories: revelation gifts: words of wisdom, words of knowledge, and discerning of spirits; power gifts: faith, healing, and working miracles; and oral gifts: tongues, interpretation, and prophecy.

We consider both the *diakonia* and *charisms* to be gifts to the church, and each "gift" offers service to the body. Governing ministries and spiritual endowments work uniquely one from another, but also with one another. God designed them to intertwine and integrate for the health of the body. A biblical understanding of the New Testament promotes the principles and practices of first-century Christianity, including the active function of *charisms*. But a lack of empowerment to the members in local churches to function in the gifts can impede the health of the body of Christ. This, in turn, hamstrings our ability to demonstrate the kingdom of Heaven on the Earth.

Peter said, "God has given each of you some special abilities; be sure to use them to help each other, passing on to others God's many kinds of blessings" (1 Peter 4:10, TLB). Knowing God offers opportunities for service to each of us, understanding the function and exercising of gifts (*charisms*) helps believers and church leaders work in community to complement each other, complete each other, and fulfill the mission of the church. Each of us is only responsible for that which we've been entrusted with, but each of us should also be open and willing to develop and train others.

The mission of the church takes many forms, and so the Spirit ministers to and through the body in many ways. Every service provided is valuable—complementing and completing the overall health of the body.

Spirit-led Serving

The serving works of *charisms* and *diakonia* provide the means in which the church ministers both internally and externally. Internally, these gifts aid the church in achieving a greater wholeness such as Jesus taught and manifested. Spirit-led serving through the operation of the gifts also provides an evangelistic function (see 1 Corinthians 14:24–25). David K. Bernard said, "Supernatural spiritual gifts strengthen believers and confirm the gospel to unbelievers." When Jesus gave the Great Commission, He promised His followers that His power would accompany those who proclaimed the gospel. The Lord makes His gifts available to the church in every generation and expects His people to function in these gifts until the end of the age.

Vine's Expository Dictionary defines *charisma* as "His endowments upon believers by the operation of the Holy Spirit in the churches." This definition leads us to consider spiritual gifts as spiritual "graces" given by God to perform a certain operation as directed by His Spirit. It's your job and mine to embrace God's graces and flow with what He's doing, giving, and speaking.

Paul began his teaching in 1 Corinthians 12:1 saying, "Now concerning spiritual gifts, brethren, I would not have you ignorant." The word "gifts" in the KJV is presented in italics, which indicates it was added by translators. The word that *is* in the original manuscript is *pneumatikos* (translated "spiritual"). In the Greek texts, the words of Paul to the Corinthians could translate literally, "Now concerning the spiritual . . . ." We could say, "Concerning this spiritual life. . . ." The same word is also used to reference the whole company of believers as a "spiritual house" (see 1 Peter 2:5). Scripture speaks of the church as an organic spiritual life in a lively spiritual house lived out by Spirit-led Christians who are members of the family of God.

> God empowers His graces in the church through the operation of His Spirit.

Charisms, for the most part, are understood as ministry roles, some of which require miraculous abilities, and some which do not. All of which, I propose, are spiritual in nature and operation. It's my conviction that every ministry gift and endowment gift is God-inspired. Some confusion perhaps comes from an overlap of terms. But consider the words of Peter, "As every man hath received the gift (*charisma*), even so minister (*diakoneo*) the same one to another" (see 1 Peter 4:10). Peter went on to say, "This is how we display the manifold grace of God." Manifold means various sorts, like the various, variegated colors of the rainbow.

A healthy church understands that spiritual gifts are more than oral or other highly visible gifts. Gifts of serving, helping, hospitality, giving, and administration are equally spiritual.

His Instrument

In the era in which we live, Scripture supports the position that God must have an instrument, a vessel, to work through. This requires our participation in the divine-human partnership. We bring our faith into agreement with His will and offer something vibrant and powerful to the world. Paul Mooney said, "There is a hunger in our world for something true." The church needs to provide that "something true."

Chapter 22: The Divine-Human Partnership

We owe it to ourselves and others to defy the skepticism of the world, step out in faith, and demonstrate the supernatural. What do we have to lose?

The Lord can teach us to better hear His voice and speak His words with confidence. We previously discussed the training of Jeremiah, but he isn't the only person the Lord helped in this way. Isaiah said, "The Lord God hath given me the tongue of the learned, that I should know how to speak a word in season to him that is weary: he wakeneth morning by morning, he wakeneth mine ear to hear as the learned" (Isaiah 50:4, NKJV). Of course, not everyone serves in the office of a prophet, but regardless of our individual gifts and callings, all believers can learn to flow with God's Spirit in divine-human interactions. As we learn to hear God's voice, we recognize that He speaks in different ways to different people. I know one missionary who feels a puff of air before a word comes from the Lord. She learned the method God used when He spoke to her. The method He used with one person He may not use with anyone else. As we begin to notice the patterns in the ways He speaks, we can begin to move with more confidence in what we're hearing or seeing. To become more sensitive to hearing His voice, we must follow through with the last words He impressed upon us. Our cooperation hones the hearing of His voice more distinctly. Our obedience causes growth that cultivates a greater demonstration of the gifts of God.

> "If you want to see something you've never seen before, do something you've never done before."
> —Lee Stoneking

Overcoming Fear

It's normal to be nervous and perhaps even full throttle scared when we first step out to minister in some new way. But our obedience to God's leading is the most important component to seeing the kingdom released on the earth. Faith alone doesn't do the work. A need alone doesn't inspire a miracle. Our compliant response to minister at God's direction to an expressed need releases the miraculous.

As believers, we never claim to *be* God or attempt to *play* God. We simply act in faith on His Word. We may feel inadequate, but when God moves us to pray for a person or need, we obey and trust the Lord to do what's best.

At some point, God may reveal to a praying person the identity of someone He intends to heal or deliver. When He does, we know exactly how to pray authoritatively with expectancy. In the times that we don't have a specific word for a person, we can always share God's love and affirm His ability to heal. God moves often without revealing His plan in advance, and sometimes He chooses not to heal. We demonstrate our faith in God whether we pray with or without knowing the outcome of our prayers in advance.

As we seek to move in the supernatural, it might be tempting to follow the "template" of someone else's ministry or endeavor to move in a gift we want rather than one God gives us. God made each of us uniquely and each of us should minister according to our God-given temperaments, personalities, and gifts. Lee Stoneking said, "God stocks man along the emotional, spiritual and intellectual trails he walks."

While God may endow any person with any gift at any time, He often uses people in areas of primary giftings. For instance, one person might operate more in physical healings than any other gifts, and another person might be used primarily for interpretation. As we seek to grow and develop as conduits for God's gifts, we purpose in ourselves to be open to whatever He imparts. At the same time, we realize that not every gift is a right fit for every believer. Consider this, even Jesus changed His tactics from one person to the next. In the case of one blind man, He simply spoke a word, and for another, He made mud from spit (see John 9:6–7, Mark 10:52). Wisdom dictates we should refrain from making a case that one method or technique works over another in a global application. Neither should we criticize how God uses someone else.

Always be authentic.

Pray and minister in the methods and manners that feel right to you, and as you progress in following the leading of the Lord, you will develop your own style of ministry. Some people pray loud, authoritative prayers and lay hands on people they pray for. Others never raise their voices but speak with confidence as the love of God flows through them with power. Still others, declare bold words of faith into entire crowds and God releases His Spirit and miracles. The volume and delivery of our prayers aren't nearly as important as praying with confidence and authority. We pray, God hears, and then, in His own way, He answers.

Often healings are associated with warm sensations. The person we pray for might feel a warmth flowing through them or growing from a specific area. Tingling can also occur. Myrtle Beall, often used in gifts of healing, reported that it came along with a burning sensation in her hand. At times I've felt both heat and tingling in my hands as I prayed for others.

As much as we would prefer that in our divine-human partnership we could never make a mistake, the truth is, we're human. Humans make mistakes. Someone once said, "God factors in our failures." It's good to know God is bigger than any of our errors. When we make mistakes, we should take inventory, but we shouldn't give up. We own our errors, dust ourselves off, and try again. If it's appropriate, we may need to apologize to a person or an entire congregation. When in doubt, get counsel from someone more experienced. Like a child beginning to walk, we may stumble in the learning process, but God isn't disappointed with us. He knows our motives and our human frailty, and He enables us to move on from missteps and mistakes. As Lee Stoneking said, "Anything divine in the hands of man is subject to error and misuse. So God gives mercy."

As many leaders have expressed, in the same way we can't take the credit when God heals, neither can we take the responsibility when He chooses not to heal. Sometimes God heals right away; sometimes people experience a delay rather than an immediate answer; and at times, the Lord chooses not to grant a request for physical healing. These variables demand that we be careful neither to overcomplicate nor oversimplify the gifts of the Spirit. God's sovereignty always bears into each individual situation. When prayer for healing seems to go unanswered, it can cause guilt or emotional wounding, even give fuel to skeptics. Without a divine revelation, we simply can't say God did or did not heal for a specific reason.

Discernment is a key to effective one-on-one ministry. As we minister, we should seek the Lord about each person's needs.

People deal with emotional, physical, and spiritual issues. One person's issue could have a demonic origin, but another person might deal with a similar concern as a result of past pain or chemical imbalances. Take care in assigning demonic origins to things that could well be rooted in purely physical conditions. We can't expect healing to come by casting out a demon that isn't there. We don't want anyone receiving prayer to leave feeling worse than they came—especially those already suffering from emotional issues. When we pray for people, everyone at the very least should feel God's love and peace as together we trust their situation into His hands.

Any word given to another in the name of the Lord must originate from the Lord—not our desire to see something happen. Unless we're directed by the Holy Spirit, we can't make claims of victory or healing, or individuals will become discouraged or lose faith when our words don't come to pass. This can create a future lack in their own faith, as well. Sometimes the things God wants to heal go deeper than physical needs. Jesus offers more than physical fixes. He affords spiritual healing, strength, peace, and joy. And so, as we pray, we trust that God is working in the ways that He chooses are best for each person. He sees the greatest needs and works according to His sovereign wisdom. As His ambassadors, we have nothing to prove, we simply represent His kingdom. We offer compassion and ask God to bless those who seek Him.

By Love

Remember, all the gifts work by love, and you and I minister on behalf of God. The work isn't ours, it's His. We're simply the conduits He uses. The people we pray for should not sense faith alone, but also feel the love of God in us as we pray for their needs. Perhaps one of the best strategies we can utilize in praying for others is creating an atmosphere where the love of God helps people feel safe and expectant. In writing Willie Johnson's biography, I heard many testimonies of people who were healed while worshipping. The Spirit of God invited in sincere worship, moved without even a prayer for healing being offered. People were saved, delivered, and changed forever.

The flow of love requires a repentant heart. Both the praying person and the person being prayed for should make sure their hearts are right with God before asking for inner healing, physical healing, or deliverance. Some ministers lead congregations in mass prayers of repentance in preparation of healing and deliverance ministry—asking forgiveness from God and forgiving those who have hurt them (see Mark 11:25). Letting go of bitterness and resentment that blocks the flow of God facilitates the inner healing that needs to happen before a physical healing can manifest.

Every Spirit-filled believer is qualified to pray for any need, but not everyone is called or experienced to function in every area. For instance, sometimes people need deliverance from demonic influence. If you feel uncomfortable, it's not a bad idea to call for back-up. It's not weakness, it's strength to know when we need support or when we should refer someone to a person with more experience. This is another reason why discernment is so important—even when deferring to counselors or other medical professionals.

Chapter 22: The Divine-Human Partnership

Prophetic Workings

The gift of prophecy, different from the office of prophet, is available to every Spirit-filled believer. Through prophecy, God allows us to see and hear His intentions. At times, God chooses to give us information for our benefit, or sometimes the benefit of others. When a word is received, and we're not sure how to respond, we can ask the same Spirit who gave it to us to reveal how or if we are to share it. On some occasions, the moment we receive it is the moment it should be shared. It's like a fire in our bones and we have to let it out! However, I've been in many services when I've received something from the Lord, but I didn't feel free to share it at that moment as a public declaration. At times I've gone to the pastor and shared after the service. The word was right on, but if I had spoken it out at that moment I had received it, it would have interrupted the flow of what God was doing.

Some words aren't for the whole church, they should be shared privately. We have to go back to the principle of being governed by peace. When we feel at liberty, and that He has given us the method and timing to share the information, we deliver it with an authority that stems from the peace resonating in our spirits. When the green flag waves, go forward. When the yellow flag waves, use caution. Ask the Lord for wisdom. When a red flag waves, put on the brakes! Sometimes the information is just for you to be warned or to know how to pray.

If you're just stepping out in the prophetic realm, and you feel God is giving you words or visions, before making public proclamations, run what you believe God has given you by your spiritual leadership. They can help you. If you're beginning to feel the Lord calling you into this type of ministry, your pastoral leadership will be a resource and a fence about you as you learn how to hear God's voice more clearly. They will advise, correct, and pray with you. They may be able to connect you with people of like giftings who can help you develop and grow.

Not long ago I forgot something I needed to remember. I asked the Lord to bring the thought back to me. He did, but the memory didn't come to my mind. It came from somewhere deeper, suddenly appearing in a still, quiet way, I simply became aware of it. Throughout the years, God has given me words, pictures, visions, or just a sense of knowing something I couldn't know on my own. Many inspired messages but all of them gave me helpful ministry information.

God's presence isn't static. It's like a flowing river that doesn't pool in one place. It constantly moves. When His living water moves among us, we should move with Him. Wayne Huntly once preached a message, "Stretch for the Supernatural." In it he said, "God put in the church everything we would ever need—every spiritual component" (see 2 Timothy 3:17, 2 Peter 1:3, Colossians

2:10). He said, "The secret source of the supernatural was revealed when the man of God stretched himself." He called God's people to extend to radical extremes—and referenced the prophet who laid himself over the body of a young man who had died (see 1 Kings 17:21). He said,

> "We want to get possession of the power and use it; God wants the power to get possession of us and use us." —Andrew Murray

"The prophet stretched himself over the dead boy. You couldn't even see the dead boy—the negative circumstance." Death is just about as negative of a circumstance as we could ever have, but if we stretch ourselves and stretch our faith to new levels God can do mighty miracles. When we stretch, we aren't adding anything to what's already present. We're reaching higher and wider and deeper than we were before. We show our faith when we take risks—when we love, speak, give, witness, or pray for someone. God can lead us through doors we've not previously known existed—if we stretch.

Affirming Others

Not only should believers accept and use their own gifts, we should affirm the gifts God gives others. While the Lord desires to build His church, the enemy seeks to break the unity of the body and impede the joint operation of the gifts. Considering the church as a body, we can think of the gifts of the Spirit as the central nervous system that sends sensory information throughout the entire being. Without these impulses, our bodies would be unable to move and would atrophy. We could lose feeling and suffer damage to the affected parts, rendering them immobile.

The gifts of the Spirit in operation serve as a vital support to the wholeness in the body that enables us to do the work of the Lord. God wants to heal the damage done to the spiritual nervous system in His church. To re-sensitize, we must repent of what has desensitized us in the first place. We must have a renewal of the flow of the Holy Ghost to every cell, organ, and member of the body for our health and the health of our mission.

Angelic Assistance

In our divine-human partnership, God dispatches angels to attend to the needs of His people. We don't know how many angels exist, but we do know there are at

Chapter 22: The Divine-Human Partnership

least two heavenly angels for every fallen angel. When we align ourselves with God, we plug in to the realm in which angels operate.

When angels show up, they come with power and purpose. They bring messages or minister to God's people. We don't always know what they're doing or bringing, but one thing is certain, when angels show up, God is at work. Eli Hernandez said, "Something birthed when angels showed up. Redemption and deliverance had been mandated from the throne. The angelic brought it into 'now' what Heaven already declared."

When I see a flash of light or sense the presence of an angel, I stop what I'm doing and try to connect. I ask God to reveal the reason for the visit. Angels have stopped by my prayer room, and I've sensed different purposes for their appearing—comfort, strength, impartation, and even commissioning.

I am not a student of angelology, but I appreciate the assistance available through this divine-human partnership. We welcome angels when we create an atmosphere of worship. And I'll take all the help I can get.

I've heard some people say they've prayed God would send a particular angel to do a work. Specifically, Eli Hernandez once asked the Lord to send the angel that was at the pool of Bethesda to him. He asked God to "stir the waters one more time." In response, Brother Hernandez said the ceiling opened up and light infused his entire body. He fell backwards and realized he was laying in a pool of water. Brother Hernandez believed God wants His people to create environments where the Lord can loose dimensions that have been on hold—dimensions written about in the Word of God. He expressed desire to experience what others had, such as Willie Johnson, whose angel Brother Hernandez believed he came in contact with after her passing.

In one message, he mentioned a woman whose husband gave her a hard time about going to church. At prayer she asked God to send the same angel who shut the lion's mouth to her husband. When she got home, her husband said, "Had a good prayer meeting, didn't you?" In her absence, he'd been visited by an angel. He told his wife that from that moment on, she could go to church whenever she wanted. He wasn't going to say a thing.

You may not have sensed or seen an angel. Neither had Elisha before God opened his eyes and he saw the spirit world. Those who allow God's Spirit to lead and teach them may find their spiritual vision opened as well. As His Spirit leads us, we learn to run straight ahead at the "green lights," slow down at the "yields," and hit the brakes when the reds show up. We must follow the quiet, inner witness that's most often not an audible voice. The discernment we've been talking about—that spiritual insight or knowing—will help us to see the way.

As believers abiding in Christ, what flows through Him—His own divine nature—flows to us (see 2 Peter 1:4). We partner with God. We ask and we receive not just because we prayed in His name, but because our requests agree with His Word, His nature, and His will. Knowing God through His Word, prayer, and consecrations prepares us to minister. The more familiar we are with His Word and His Spirit, the more clearly we receive His instructions and impressions. The more sensitive we are to God spiritually, the more we'll be able to minister to the spiritual needs of others. As Watchman Nee said, "Spirit must touch spirit." And as Willie Johnson exemplified, we must live in the moment—willing to stop whatever we're doing, tune in to the Spirit, and be used as a conduit of His love, healing, and deliverance.

23

Shine!

*Arise, shine; for thy light is come, and the glory of the
Lord is risen upon thee.*
Isaiah 60:1

In Chapter 22, we discussed how God releases various aspects of Himself into the world through the gifts of the Spirit, like the colors of the rainbow shining hope and promise to all who see them. It's time to turn our attention to what "shining" looks like. For our discussion, shining means replicating the ministry of Jesus and acting as He would if He were here in our place. How would Jesus conduct Himself if He was living in our houses, our bodies, our marriages, our churches, or our communities? How would He act if He was you?

Perhaps one of the most famous "shine" verses comes from a book we've referenced often in *Kingdom Come*. Isaiah said, "Arise, shine; for thy light is come, and the glory of the Lord is risen upon thee" (Isaiah 60:1). It's time for God's church to rise up. Arise and walk through the land, for God will give it unto thee (see Genesis 13:17). Arise means to stand, but that's not all. Arise also means to become powerful or to come on the scene. It's time for the men and women of God to rise up and take their places with the boldness and confidence God intended.

Silenced no more by shame, we embrace who God created us to be with our unique purposes and destinies. We use the gifts He's given us. He's called us, and we're headed for victory, signs, and wonders! I believe God is letting His people know through this very book that we should expect more. He's stirring the waters, and we must not hesitate. We must respond and refuse to be held back by any thoughts of limitations or inadequacies. We're complete in Him, and so we cast down any thought that makes itself higher than God—even our own self-perceptions. Instead, we embrace the will of God and believe what He says about us.

The Israelites wandered in the desert for forty years. The carcasses of men and women fell one by one. Those same people buried in the sand could have enjoyed the promises of God, but they didn't agree with His plans for them. They were free, yet they still lived with a slave mentality.

How many saints of God today have been delivered from Egypt (a symbol of bondage to sin), but are still wandering in a spiritual desert not even realizing who they are or the power they have with God and man? It's time to embrace change. Embrace moving in the flow of the Spirit. It's time to arise. We've been appointed by God to shine His glory in the world around us. And I say, "Let His glory cover the earth!" (see Habakkuk 2:14).

We've focused on verse 1 of Isaiah 60, but look at the very next words: "For, behold, the darkness shall cover the earth, and gross darkness the people: but the Lord shall arise upon thee, and his glory shall be seen upon thee" (v 2). We live in a world that's getting darker all the time. When Isaiah wrote these words, he was living in an era when spiritual darkness had shrouded even the land of Zion. But in the darkness, the Lord arose on His people—His light streaming forth. Jesus, the Sun of Righteousness has arisen with healing in His wings (see Malachi 4:2). Our God is a sun and shield. He promised to give grace and glory and withhold no good thing from those who walk uprightly (see Psalm 84:11). These verses beautifully express some of the main points of *Kingdom Come*.

The righteousness, peace, and joy of the kingdom of God come only to those who are "in the Holy Ghost." The light of the world has come and now shines the brightness of His glory in the hearts of those who have received His Spirit (see 2 Corinthians 4:6).

Use it or Lose It

We must use what we've been given, or we'll lose it. Jesus taught a parable to His followers that began, "For the kingdom of heaven is as a man travelling into a far country" (Matthew 25:14). He went on to tell the story of a man dividing coins among his servants. To one he gave five, to one two, and to another, one. The last servant, afraid of his master, buried his coin and had nothing to benefit the man (who represented the kingdom of God) when he returned. The last servant allowed his fear to keep him from investing in the kingdom, and what he had was taken from him. In fact, he was thrown into outer darkness where "there shall be weeping and gnashing of teeth" (v 30).

The teaching in Matthew 25 is frightening to me because I see in it the potential of not only displeasing God, but possibly losing out on salvation. God didn't light our lamps for us to hide the light of His Spirit under a bowl, a basket, or in a clay pot (see Matthew 5:15). God calls us

> "The grace that comes to me each day must flow out to others or I will become like a spiritual dead sea."
> —Marvin Walker

to put our lamps on a lampstand—a place of service—where we can bring light to others. In the tabernacle, the lampstand lit the room for the ministry of the priests. We looked previously at Revelation 2:5 in which the church in Ephesus teetered on the brink of losing their candlestick. God threatened to remove their place of shining service unless they repented from their dispassionate behavior and returned to their first works. God wants us to remember our early days when we were first enlightened—not that we would do "more" or even the same things the same way. But He instructs the church to do quality works born of genuine love and passion for God.

When we don't bear fruit for the Lord, we have reason to be concerned about losing our place. The threat to the Ephesian church wasn't an idle one. The lampstand of the church where Paul labored three years was removed. God has given us so much. We must be careful not to esteem it lightly. Instead we are to be light in our world (see Matthew 5:14). When we shine, others see our good deeds and God receives praise (see Matthew 5:16). By our labor of love, the earth is filled with more and more of God's glory.

In the previous chapter we looked briefly at the work and mission of the church.

> **The mission of the church is to nurture the body of Christ and reach the world with the gospel.**

God gave gifts (ministry and endowment gifts) to equip every believer for this work. We could spend a lot of time on the subject of the works of the church, and we might disagree on the fine details, but we can clearly see in Scripture the primary works of evangelism, discipleship, and benevolence in the early church. This mission is like a three-legged stool. We need all three legs, or we won't have a sturdy seat.

As we discussed previously, God created each of us uniquely with different gifts and callings. Each of us likely has our "candy stick" or favorite issue. But what impassions one should never be used to cause division in the church at large. It's God's design to see His work accomplished, and that requires everyone doing their part. We need Sunday school teachers, outreach directors, musicians, singers, shut-in ministry, bereavement support, recovery groups, and more. As finite human beings, we only have so much time and energy. What's significant to one man or woman from a God-placed burden in his or her life is meaningful to the body at large in that the service of one contributes to the overall health of the church. So while we focus on doing our best in the places God calls us to serve, we support and affirm others, recognizing the contribution of each member.

On the other side of that coin, no matter our primary calling, everyone should have compassion for those in want of basic necessities. Whoever teaches should teach with joy, and that same teacher should also be concerned with the needs of others (see Romans 12:7, James 1:26-27). The benevolence component of the mission of the church includes doing good to all, but especially to those who are fellow members of the household of faith (see Galatians 6:9-10).

Along with compassion ministries, discipleship and outreach comprise the main work of the church. I like to use the word *nurture* in regard to discipleship. When we disciple others, we help nurture their faith through study, communal worship, and fellowship. This includes serving alongside others and helping people develop in their gifts and callings. It includes helping people navigate their "life waves" so they can see God's big picture and grow and thrive as they continue in the way of the Lord.

Outreach means reaching out. We reach beyond the "living stones" of the church walls to share the opportunity of abundant life with others who don't know the Lord. This is another way we reflect God in our world. Each of us shines our light in the candlestick of outreach. It may be a prison ministry, a food pantry, or simply a lunchtime Bible study. It could be a position in church leadership or an international missions work. Whatever we find to do, we should do with all our might to the glory of God knowing He's working in us and through us (see Ecclesiastes 9:10). We work with expectation knowing God's desire for kingdom expansion and multiplication (see Psalm 62:5, Isaiah 54:2-4, 1 Chronicles 4:10).

> "Expectation is the birthplace of the miraculous." —Jeff Arnold

His Shining Jewel

I visited a church in Albion, Michigan, where a man gave a testimony about an angelic visitation. He said the angel was like a diamond reflecting blue light. Eli Hernandez spoke of God as transparent light, which explains how He could be everywhere, but unseen. Although we don't see God's spiritual light manifest continually in our everyday lives, what isn't visible with the human eye can still be seen. How? In the life of the godly who are "full of light and joy" (Proverbs 13:9, NLT).

Like the differing gifts of the Spirit, each facet of our life reflects the light that shines on us. We don't create the light. It comes from another source—from God's Word and Spirit. Today, laboratories can create gems that sparkle from a distance and look, to the untrained eye, like real diamonds. But gemologists tell us that when we look within a man-made diamond, it can't hide its origins—it's not been formed in the earth through heat and pressure. It's not genuine. Even at their best, synthetic stones lack the depth of natural diamonds.

 As kingdom ambassadors, we must be careful to offer what only a genuine experience with God can provide— a reflection of His true light. His authentic luminescence overtakes and consumes Satan's lesser, false lights. The entrance of God's Word gives light (see Psalm 119:130).

I believe we're most like God and most pleasing to Him when we shine the light He has placed in us in this dark world. As we minister—evangelizing, nurturing others, and through our benevolent deeds—we radiate the glory of His goodness, mercy, and love. We shine through something as simple as offering a cup of water in His name, praying for a coworker in a time of stress, volunteering at a child's school, teaching a Bible study, or supporting missions work. We make ourselves willing to be spent—like a candle that burns, its wax melting and rising as a vapor as it emits light.

We make ourselves interruptible (without irritation) to shine on the needs that present themselves throughout our days. We live out kingdom principles and take the lead in bestowing preference to others. We give, love, and bandage. We share our lives, our resources, our gifts, and talents. We use our words to build, nurture, and instruct. We partner with God in the work of delivering and setting captives free. God has entrusted us with His Spirit to do His work in our world. This is the fulfilling of the Great Commission at its deepest level.

As we stay connected to God, assemble ourselves in worship, and continually cleanse the debris of the world from our lives, we take in living water. This water, teaming with life, shines brightly with flashes of heavenly light. And you and I, as Claudette Walker once said, "become a walking well, connected to a deep underground river." A well, she said, that "will overflow to thirsty travelers."

> "God does not have accidents. He has appointments."
> —James Guerrero

Brighter and Brighter

"The road the righteous travel is like the sunrise, getting brighter and brighter until daylight has come" (Proverbs 4:18, GNB). As we walk in the sunlight, it shines brighter and clearer. We've spoken at length about personal, spiritual transformation and growth. Along with our spiritual progress often comes a desire for a position. That may or may not happen. God positions people in the body as He sees fit and in His time. It's not wrong to desire a place of godly service, but we need to ask God to purify our motives and help us find our "right now" place of service in His body.

In some circles there's much talk about "mantles" and taking on the ministry or gifting of someone who has passed away. I've spent some time studying the subject, but the only decisive conclusion I've arrived at is that a Christian should avoid an entitlement attitude. No one in the church should have a "mantle me" attitude (similar to "king me" when playing checkers.) No one deserves what someone else worked for or found favor with God to receive. So while each of us offers ourselves to God for His service, we can't attempt to maneuver or manipulate ourselves into a particular ministry. We're His servants, and so we serve at His pleasure. And this service brings joy.

> "The most infallible proof of the presence of God in a person is joy."
> —Leon Bloy

We've got to have Jesus, not a "ministry." In whatever we do for His kingdom, His light and love should flow through us. That means something different for each of us. For me, it includes writing and speaking and being a mom, neighbor, wife, and faithful believer. You have to hear His voice and determine what that means in your life. Whatever role we play, we must remember the power of any ministry comes from the love of God and the demonstration of His Spirit. As we abide in Him and entertain His presence, the natural outcome should be a demonstration of His nature.

No Fear

"The Lord is my light and my salvation; who shall I fear? The Lord is the strength of my life; of whom shall I be afraid?" (Psalm 27:1). When we fear the Lord and obey His voice, we have light even when darkness pervades all around. When we trust in the Lord, we can rely on Him because as we lean on God, He supports us. In the book *The Prayer of Jabez,* author Bruce Wilkinson said, "God is not scanning the horizon for spiritual giants or seminary standouts. He eagerly seeks those who are sincerely loyal to Him." He said believers are always "one plea away from inexplicable, Spirit-enabled exploits." The power is in His touch. Wilkinson said, "For a Christian, dependence is just another word for power." So while we move forward, we cast our fears upon God and trust Him to do what He said He would do.

> "Progress always comes with fear. Let faith have the last word."
> —Jeremy Burns

We've talked about facing our own fears, but at times, our ministry efforts bring us to confront the fears of others. Because people are afraid of the supernatural or have experienced "church hurt" in the past, some erect barriers and speak contentiously. These fears can exist concurrently in the same heart that longs to experience what our spirits are transmitting to theirs. People might not like everything we say, but many would admit to sensing a peace and joy in us that's absent in their lives. Some long, also, for dignity and purpose and admire righteousness even if they don't want to live it. So, while for some, their body language and vocabulary may scream, "leave me alone," the heart cries out for the love of God.

The gifts of the Spirit are essential in knowing how and when to share with people that are expressing resistance. If God burdens you for a particular person, be patient. Let His love and glory shine through you so others will see our great God and desire Him.

Sunny with a Chance of Healing

We touched briefly above on Jesus; the Sun of Righteousness risen with healing in His wings. Charles Spurgeon wrote on the topic, "The Sun which will arise is of no common sort. It is the Sun—the Sun of Righteousness, Whose every ray is holiness. . .

Light, warmth, joy, and clearness of vision will come, and healing of every disease and distress will follow." Spurgeon closed his message with a call to the congregation to sing Charles Wesley's hymn, "Hail the heav'nly Prince of Peace! Hail the Sun of Righteousness! Light and life to all He brings, Ris'n with healing in His wings."

In the natural world, the sun is the center of our solar system. God designed it that way to reflect the arrangement of Heaven where Jesus is preeminent over all. He's the light and central figure of the kingdom. His light drives away shadows and darkness. His presence brings joy and enlightenment. Isaiah spoke of the rising son, and Zacharias proclaimed his son, John, would prepare the way for the "dayspring from on high" (Luke 1:78). The wings of God speak poetically of the healing available to those who take refuge beneath them. Beautiful parallels have been drawn between the wings mentioned in Malachi 4:2 and the healing power that emanated from the fringes of Jesus's garment (see Mark 5:25-34). The light of the world radiated through Christ and healing came with the light—healing for the inner and outer person.

> The days may be dark, but the forecast is bright and sunny with a chance of healing.

The Old Testament's Sun of Righteousness is the New Testament's Bright and Morning Star. Those who don't know Jesus, even though they may seem happy, possess souls as darkened as a solar system without a sun. They may not even realize it, because they've grown accustomed to coping with life in the dark. So you and I must carefully dispense the light of God's hope and His tender mercy. Heaven's dawn gives light to those who sit in darkness—to guide all who are willing to the path of peace (see Luke 1:78-79).

Maintain Focus

God promised to keep in perfect peace those who keep their minds stayed on Him (see Isaiah 26:3). When our focus is steadfast on the King and kingdom, we have hope—a confident expectation. His kingdom of peace and glory dwells within and shines light in the darkness.

> A firm focus yields mature and complete peace.

Having a right focus impacts the flow of God's anointing. Anointing is what unites Heaven and Earth and breaks yokes of oppression (see Isaiah 10:27). The anointing of the Holy Ghost overrides feelings of inadequacy that would hold God's people back from demonstrating His Spirit and power (see 1 Corinthians 2:4). Remember, what He has shone in us, shines out of us. We must be full of the Spirit. We must take time to refill what life and ministry depletes.

This brings to mind the "blue rooms" I saw in my dream mentioned in Chapter 9. There's a spiritual place of refreshing we can enter any time we take our focus off the world around us and step into spiritual communion with God. A place where the anointing flows. A place where we turn our faces to the face of God, and He shows up with the oil of refreshing and gladness (see Psalm 45:7). He meets us there, and as we saturate in His glow, we experience Him in new ways. When knowing Him more deeply is our greatest desire, I believe we'll find ourselves standing at thresholds into new spiritual dimensions.

Moses received a promise that God's presence would be with him, but he wanted more. He wanted to see the glory of God (see Exodus 33:14, 18). In God's presence, Moses's face began to glow, and it affected the way people saw him as their leader. As we spend time with God and allow Him to fashion His plans and purposes in our lives, our countenances reflect His abiding presence. We experience a greater level of trust that He is leading us exactly where we need to be. We live with contentment and confidence and move with grace to exercise the gifts He gives us to bless others.

Paul wrote to the Corinthians, "But we all, with open face beholding as in a glass the glory of the Lord, are changed into the same image from glory to glory, even as by the Spirit of the Lord" (2 Corinthians 3:18). Some translations refer to beholding in a mirror or glass, and others refer to "reflecting like mirrors." Perhaps we don't need to choose one translation over the other. Whether Paul meant we should contemplate the glory of God, or reflect the glory of God, both renderings ring true. If we look to the example of Moses that Paul was referring to in this passage, we see that Moses both beheld and reflected the glory of God. Beholding begets becoming which begets reflecting. You and I, with unveiled faces, see a reflection of the glory of God that changes us into His very image, from one degree of glory to the next.

> The human job description can be reduced down to one phrase, "reflect God's glory." —Max Lucado

When we spend time in His presence, we can't help but shine. There's an aura around people who abide with God. Those who look to Him are radiant (see Psalm 34:5). Our faces should radiate God's glory and our lives mirror the kingdom as each day, we commit to unveiling the light hidden to those that are lost (see 2 Corinthians 4:3–4).

Shining Land

God leads the way, even choosing those things He plants in you and me. We partner with Him, scattering His seeds in our own fields. Hosea wrote about breaking up our fallow ground—seeking the Lord until He comes and showers His righteousness upon us (see Hosea 10:12). The language of Hosea means more than scattering seed. What the KJV translates "sow" also means to become pregnant or conceive. God plants life in His people—in those people who break up their fallow, uncultivated ground. Fallow ground is soil that at one time had been prepared, but then left unseeded. It represents either abandoned hope or plans for the future not yet acted on. It may at times represent soil that needed recovery time before planting again.

I believe God is calling some people to plow up their fallow ground and plant again the seeds of His Word (see Mark 4:14, Jeremiah 4:3). Consider with me how the plowing of a field turns over dry land, bringing to the surface moist soil that glistens in the sun. The word translated *fallow* is from a root word that means "lamp" and was used in reference to the holy candlestick in the tabernacle (see Exodus 25:37). When we plow and plant in our lives, we release light and life for others (see Galatians 6:7-8). With expectation, we plow in the areas of our calling (see 1 Corinthians 9:10).

People must have light to see. When we shine, God works. He forgives and heals (see Psalm 103:3). Demonic influence departs where it once held ground (see Acts 8:6-8). Devils and unclean spirits are associated with darkness, but the light we share can burn off shadows of doubt or unbelief.

> We make our fields shine by plowing them.

Shine

We opened this chapter with Isaiah 60:1-2. Let's end with an encouragement from verse 3: "And the Gentiles shall come to thy light, and kings to the brightness of thy rising." The Lord is speaking through this prophecy even today. It's time to arise from anything that has depressed or suppressed us spiritually. Arise into a new life and shine, although darkness is all around, the light in us will break through to the "Gentiles," the people who don't know God. They will be drawn to the great and glorious light rising in God's church—a demonstration of Heaven on Earth.

Many of us are familiar with Jesus's words, "My house shall be called the house of prayer" (see Matthew 21:13). Yes, He was angry at the time. He overturned tables and benches, but the true significance of His words are found when we look to their original context. Jesus was quoting Isaiah who in the same setting had previously declared God's intention to do something that had long been forbidden. He would allow eunuchs ("blemished" people) and strangers (non-Jews) the opportunity to worship among His people. With beautiful language the prophet declared the Word of the Lord: "Even them will I bring to my holy mountain, and make them joyful in my house of prayer: their burnt offerings and their sacrifices shall be accepted upon mine altar; for mine house shall be called an house of prayer for all people" (Isaiah 56:7).

The God who gathers outcasts is gathering people of all nations and backgrounds unto Himself. His expressed desire is to make each person who enters covenant with Him joyful in His house of prayer. Those who have experienced Jesus for themselves can attest that God is keeping His promise.

God's goal is to restore glory. He began with Moses and the tabernacle, creating an earthly replica of Heaven. His desire is that His people would be who He made them to be. Irenaeus of Lyons said, "The glory of God is man fully alive." And according to L. R. Knost, the broken things of this world could be mended if we would "love intentionally, extravagantly, unconditionally." He said, "The broken world waits in darkness for the light that is you."

On Earth as it is in Heaven

Thy kingdom come, Thy will be done in earth, as it is in heaven.
Matthew 6:10

God's will originates in Heaven. He desires what's demonstrated there to be lived out by His people on the Earth. When we pray in agreement with Heaven, we speak with the same dominion power Adam and Eve had in the Garden. We can pray with authority and release the kingdom into the atmospheres of our homes, cities, and churches. When we declare His name and His will, our expectant faith activates the hand of God. Being fully persuaded of His promises, we pray that the Spirit of God leads people to the foundational principle of repentance. As Eli Hernandez said, "Repentance unlocks the access of what God wants to give us."

Jesus said the kingdom of God enters with force, and the powerful seize it and carry it away (see Matthew 11:12, Luke 16:16). The precise meaning of this concept is the subject of debate. It can but doesn't necessarily refer to violence or combat. It may refer to eager, zealous believers who refuse to give in to opposition and instead press their way into the kingdom to possess it. Whether it's combat, or zeal to pursue God, the main point, I believe, is that we can't be passive about our walk or our work.

The apostles operated with boldness and power. Peter walked right up to a lame man and without praying for him called out healing (see Acts 3:6). If in our conscience we could grasp that we have the same level of God-given authority the apostles had, what might we see released in our world?

Healing

Physical healing is interwoven with the message of the gospel. We know suffering at times serves a purpose, and we should be willing to suffer as necessary for the advancement of the Kingdom (see John 15:20). Some conditions (such as Paul being struck with blindness on the road to Damascus) serve a higher purpose, but this is usually the exception and not the rule. Believers shouldn't necessarily accept illness as the will of God. During the Covid-19 pandemic, people took opposing views regarding the purpose or origin of the virus. Some assigned the outbreak of the virus as judgment for sin, and others believed it to be a tool in the hand of God. Lacking definitive evidence, we should take care before making assumptions about illnesses—on a broad scale and in personal lives.

Jesus went about healing and doing good. What He did, the church has been commissioned to continue. How did Jesus heal? He spoke directly to a woman's fever (see Luke 4:39). He told a man with a withered hand to stretch it out, and it was restored (see Matthew 12:13). He spoke the words "be open" to a deaf man who had a speech impediment, and the man received his hearing and his tongue was released (see Mark 7:34). He healed the Centurion soldier's servant without seeing him or touching him, but by the request of a man of faith (see Matthew 8:5–13). Another woman was healed by touching Jesus's garment (see Matthew 9:20). There are many examples, but from these few we see that Jesus healed different maladies in different manners. Sometimes He addressed the person, other times the ailment. Sometimes He touched the person, other times He issued proclamations, and in some cases He did both together. Such was the case of the woman who had an infirmity for eighteen years. Jesus both touched her and said, "Woman, thou art loosed," and immediately she was made straight (Luke 13:11–13). As we continue the work of Jesus, we shouldn't be surprised when He persists in using different manners and methods.

Throughout my ministry, I've seen the power of God demonstrated in a variety of ways. After preaching in St. John, New Brunswick, I was contacted with reports of three people who received healings in their bodies. In March of 2014, I received a message of a miracle report from Idaho. A woman I'd prayed with at a recent ladies' conference had been diagnosed with a 100 percent blockage of an artery in her brain. It had been confirmed by two doctors that at any time, she could have a stroke. Fear had so overcome her; she was afraid even to move. After the conference, at a previously scheduled appointment with a specialist, the doctor confirmed that . without any treatment (besides prayer), this elderly woman's blockage reduced from 100 percent to 35 percent. This put her in a range the doctor said was normal for her age.

In 2017 at Bannon Camp in New Brunswick, while seated at a kitchen table, I noticed bilingual labels on some condiment and seasoning packages. The labels were in both English and French. I thought of how people learn new languages. We relate a new word with one we already know. God works in a similar way to teach us Kingdom concepts and culture. Jesus exemplified this often with parables—first showing the natural and then its meaning in the supernatural—words, concepts, and roles.

At that camp, I stepped out of a box and did something I'd never done before or since. I felt impressed that the ladies needed anointing and prayer. I went to the evangelist quarters and found an old pillowcase. I cut it in pieces and during the service anointed the squares of fabric with oil and dispersed them to the ladies. After preaching an abbreviated message, God moved in a powerful way. One woman was delivered from cigarettes and many received emotional healing. Another lady came to me following the service and shared that she'd been asking God for a prayer cloth for two weeks. God ministered to these women on the campground, but they also took prayer cloths home. We soon began receiving reports of the prayers God had answered. The oil on a bit of fabric held no power on its own, but those cloths represented His healing presence.

Miracles, Signs, and Wonders

In addition to physical healing, I've received testimonies of financial miracles, the resolution of painful family situations, and even ongoing land deals being settled overnight. Almost everywhere I go, people who have grown cold in their relationship with God, and even walked away, have been restored. Some who have spent lifetimes seeking Him, and others who just happened to walk in the church doors, have been miraculously filled with God's Spirit.

I once prayed with a woman who was seeking God's direction but was feeling crushed by the burdens of life and disappointments of unmet expectations. When I approached her, even though I didn't know her situation, I perceived her need for prayer. She seemed downcast, and as I stood before her, I felt her posture was not one conducive to receiving. I encouraged her to lift her hands a little higher and to tilt her face upward. As I placed my hand on her forehead, she began to cry. Later she told me that the moment she lifted her face, her mind was filled with a vision of Heaven and she saw the throne room of God. He washed away the feelings of frustration and resentment that she'd felt. Since that time, the Lord has frequently allowed her to revisit that place in prayer.

Emotional healing can come with one divine touch, but it's not always a once-and-done interaction. While some wounds require engaging the help of a professional, God has used me to bring emotional healing and encouragement to hurting people. I pray with both men and women, but so often the Lord leads me to minister to the wounded hearts of His precious daughters. As I look over the congregation, I wait for the Lord to lead me. Most often, I speak to the people before touching them. It prepares them to focus on God, activates their faith and builds expectancy. In noisy or distracting situations, your words announce your presence, so you don't frighten the people you're trying to minister to. Some aren't comfortable with touch, but others are very willing to receive a "laying on of hands" that often transmits a current of power from one person to another (see Acts 8:18, 1 Timothy 4:14). One particular thing that happens while in the altar, when I lay hands on individuals, they often fall to the ground under the power of God. While I'm certainly not pushing them, the Holy Ghost does a work at that moment. When they get up, their entire countenances are changed.

In a ladies' conference in Newark, Ohio, a spirit of deliverance was in the house, and women who had been delivered from fear and shame were laid out all over the sanctuary. The power of God was flowing, and they responded. These types of demonstrations have happened throughout North America as well as in international ministry. God uses everyday people—people just like you and me—as His conduits to release Heaven on Earth.

I remember a time God opened a new level of ministry to me. I was in Elliot Lake, Ontario, in a worship service. We were singing about chains breaking, and I could almost hear them falling. In the Spirit I saw the chains as more than manacles or cuffs that restrict function and mobility. I became aware of a gate that had been closed by a chain, but through worship, had fallen off and the gate swung open. It was a gate within me to an inner chamber. It opened a channel that allowed the Spirit to flow with more force and from a greater depth. Following that event, I noted a significant increase of boldness in my delivery and liberal response among the congregation. I believe God has more for each of us to experience, and I pray that gates swing open for every person reading this book.

When the Answer is No

When God chooses not to answer prayer the way we hope, we must be careful not to assign blame to the person being prayed for—as if their unmet expectation was the result of their lack of faith or a hidden sin issue. One unanswered prayer doesn't mean we shouldn't ask again (see Luke 18:1-8).

The mystery of healing is a mystery, and we should be so careful not to wound people further by prognosticating reasons why they didn't receive their requests.

Chapter 24: On Earth as it is in Heaven

There are times people choose to claim their healing, but as a person praying for another, we should use discretion when encouraging others to claim something they've not yet received if we've not received a direct word from God.

My husband Bill received a chaplain license through the First Responder's Chaplain Association in Michigan. For two years he volunteered weekly at the emergency room of a local hospital. Every shift he served he made himself available to pray for patients, but not everyone wanted prayer. We shouldn't take a refusal for prayer personally. Some people, even though they're hurting, are afraid of the supernatural or changes healing might bring to their day-to-day lives.

Discernment

We discussed discernment at length in Chapter 16. Often discernment precedes demonstration. This is true for all types of ministry, from sharing a testimony to praying for deliverance. We ask God to increase our vision to identify real needs and perceive the root or essence of underlying issues. Often when we seek to minister to others, we may unknowingly face invisible entanglements between physical, spiritual, and emotional issues.

As Kara S. McCoy, a counselor and fellow minister so often tells me, "The thing is not the thing." In other words, what is being requested when a person approaches the altar for prayer may only be a symptom and not represent the entirety of his or her need.

What we hear with our natural ears sometimes needs spiritual interpretation. A person in pain, distress, or shock may not realize or be willing to reveal the root of a problem. It's not always for us to know every detail, but we can be sure God does. He will tell us what we need to know as we need to know it.

> With one ear, listen to requests, and with the other, tune in to the Spirit.

Altar Ministry

Altar ministry is so important. When we serve in this capacity, we should ask the Lord to reveal His will and help us truly see the souls of the individuals before us. How should we pray? Who should we pray for? On one occasion, He may draw us to a certain individual. Another time, He may instruct us *not* to pray. When we first approach someone to minister, we should pay attention to what comes to mind.

The first impression may be what their spirit is projecting outward—their pain, their grief, or a longing in their heart. The most important consideration is to be led by the Lord, not by our human observation or compassion.

As we learn to flow in the Spirit—receiving and releasing from God—we connect with what He's doing in the moment. When God imparts spiritual insight, we should exercise caution before using phrases like, "Thus sayeth the Lord . . ." or "God showed me something about you . . ." Instead, utilize a non-threatening approach, such as, "I felt impressed with something. Is it ok if I share it with you?" As you develop confidence in the use of spiritual gifts, your delivery may become bolder over time. For now, just start praying what you're sensing. I find that many times after I begin praying, God unfolds more specific information that facilitates personal ministry. Sometimes I speak words in English, and other times praying in the Spirit delivers the message they need.

I often begin by acknowledging the faith of the person seeking prayer. I then thank God for being with us and begin to intercede for the need. For those who aren't ready for prayers of healing, salvation, or deliverance, I simply ask if I can pray a blessing upon them. Most people are willing to receive a blessing. A prayer of blessing often opens a door for deeper ministry and almost never fails to touch a person's heart. Love is the key.

I recently had the unique opportunity to baptize a young man at a neighboring minister's church. Following the baptism, my husband, daughter, and I wanted to take him out to celebrate, but we struggled to find an open restaurant. After driving to three locations, we were finally successful, added our name to a list, picked up our buzzer from the hostess, and sat outside with several other patrons that were also waiting for their tables.

> The kingdom of God among us demonstrates in love.

My husband and I sat next to two ladies. The older of the two wore a black mask with gold printing that said, "Jesus, cover me." Bill and I both commented on it, and after some small talk we shared the reason for our celebration dinner. The woman became so excited about the baptism that her hands shot up in the air and she began praising God in front of all the other customers—out loud! The young man we baptized was surprised, being new to church, but everything was happening in God's divine plan.

We learned this dear woman had recently lost her 30-year old daughter—only eight days after she had given birth. But despite the great sorrow she felt, she maintained her faith and praise. My heart went out to her, and I asked, "Can I hug you?" She said yes. I wrapped her in my arms and prayed for her, and God was there. He just showed up. So sweetly.

When we finished, she was beaming, and she told me why. She said that when I hugged her, she felt the love of God flowing from my heart to hers in such a tangible way she was unable to move. And she said her burden immediately lifted. Hurting people are all around us, even people of faith in such need of the love of God. When we reach out to them—although we may not even be aware we are moving in the Spirit—if God is truly flowing through us like a conduit, He will meet needs we don't even see. He will minister to the hearts of hurting people with something as simple as a touch as we give it under His direction. I pray the Lord opens our eyes to see their needs and gives us sensitivity and boldness to reach out to them.

Visualizing

While the idea of seeing a vision during prayer can help us know how to minister, there's an added benefit when we engage our whole selves as we pray. Not only speaking faith-filled words based on someone's need, we can use our minds to "see" the outcome of the prayer as we pray it. For example, if praying for someone with cancer, we can visualize tumors shrinking in our mind's eye and specifically imagine their blood being cleansed.

Visualizing what we ask God seems to heighten faith and bring positive outcomes. Mike Easter testified that when he implemented this type of creative envisioning in prayer, he saw immediate results. He shared his story:

Without a Vision (Proverbs 29:18)

How desperately I wanted my family to experience what had happened to me. I was new to the church and the only one in my family saved. After much prayer and Bible study with Mom, things were going nowhere. Then one night in prayer the Lord spoke to me, *Without a vision, the people perish* (Proverbs 29:18).

I was shocked that God was speaking to me. To my surprise and bewilderment, He spoke again, *Without a vision, your family will perish.*

I tried to comprehend what it meant, but then God made it very clear. *Everything you see around you is a result of Me speaking it into existence. But before I spoke it, I first saw it. You must be able to see it first. Now tell me, what do you see?*

I closed my eyes, and saw my dad in the front row praising God.

What else do you see?

I saw my mom with a tambourine, singing and praising God, and I saw my sisters all filled with the Spirit and singing in the choir.

Do you see it?

"Yes, Lord."

Do you receive it?

"Yes, Lord, I receive it."

So from this moment on, don't ask Me to save your family. From this moment on, thank Me for saving your family.

I received it and believed it. I didn't plead with my family anymore, because it was already done. I could see it. And it happened just like He said it would. About three months later, my dad came into church, and my sister, two months after. A year later, they were followed by my mom and sisters.

Deliverance

In the Old Testament, there's only one "devil" mentioned, but in the New Testament, Jesus referred to fallen angels as devils. I believe it's safe to think of these words interchangeably. There are devils among us. They take up residence in some unbelievers and seek to oppress or demonize God's people. Although Spirit-filled believers can't be possessed, some still suffer with the demonic-inspired feelings of being heavily burdened by worries, troubles, and fears. These effect both mental and physical wellness. Demonic influences work to convince even good-intentioned believers to live in obsessions that suppress and agitate. Another tactic is overinflating legitimate concerns, but where the Spirit of the Lord is, there is liberty. Believers don't have to live under the weight of demonic oppression.

How can we handle these demonic forces? Before we attempt to cast out devils, we need to be prepared, confident, and authorized. Whether praying for people in the church or on the street, we must be sure the enemy has no access into our lives through unrepentant sin. We should never attempt to minister in an area we're struggling, because we won't have authority over it.

As we've discussed, not every gift is given to every believer, but every believer has access to whatever gift God deems necessary in any given situation. This includes spiritual deliverance. When casting out demons, we should never rush to lay hands on anyone (remember the sons of Sceva). We should wait until we feel authorized by God to pray for deliverance in Jesus's name. In fact, we may not want to lay hands at all. When Jesus cast out demons, He spoke directly to them (see Luke 4:35).

For those purposely engaging in deliverance ministry, working as a team is often effective. Team members pray together to prepare their hearts and ask God for His protection from any evil that may present itself. When we pray for discernment, God may reveal to us the identity of a demon that possesses or oppresses. Often, the issue the person has struggled with reveals the demon that troubles them internally or externally: fear, worry, shame, anxiety, and so on. Then, it's simply a matter of commanding it to go in Jesus's name. Sometimes loud screams, coughing, vomiting, or convulsions occur when a demon is cast out of a person. Once it has departed, the vacated place now needs to be filled with God's Spirit. Encourage the liberated person to worship the Lord and pray to be filled with the Holy Ghost. After all, a demon may attempt to return. Everyone needs to be taught to change any habits that grant access to the demonic realm. People also need to know how to rebuke the enemy for themselves.

According to Scripture demonic activity can rule over certain areas (see Ephesians 6). Some demons have territorial boundaries and strongholds over regions. It may seem daunting to consider taking authority over such a large manifestation of evil, but God has given His people power over all of the works of the devil, no matter their scope or size.

I remember a time I was engaged in a spiritual battle in my community. I found myself in a head-to-head battle with forces that had been revealed to my pastor years previously. They were operating through city employees

> "You don't have to wrestle with demons. Operate in faith and the devil will take flight." —B. H. Clenendan

and interfaith religious leaders. For two months, I stood my ground and refused to give way to intimidation, deception, and manipulation. I'm not saying I'm a spiritual superwoman. I had a lot of backup, including my husband who came through like a champ when a hostile "minister" attempted to isolate me (in front of the media). When the decision finally came down, a spiritual stronghold broke, and I gained power to identify and defeat it. Now, in other areas of ministry and life, I perceive the Jezebel spirit that works behind the scenes attempting to manipulate, twist, and deceive. I know the tactics, and I know I have the power to stand up, refuse to engage in useless dialogue, and say no. And the enemy has no power to make me say or do otherwise.

Sometimes simply observing the chaos in the world reveals the identities of the spirits at work, but with or without this information, believers still have authority to rise up and stand against them. We can prayer walk and prayer drive through our cities, pull down strongholds, cast down principalities, and release the light and glory of God. One thing I've done to prepare to minister in other regions, is to pull up maps of the city, state, or country and prayer walk the region via the internet. I've also researched the history of a location which arms me with information regarding the kinds of spiritual influences that have been present in that area in the past. This helps me minister more effectively when I arrive. For those who minister locally, these same principles apply.

 As believers, we may not be assigned to a spiritual inquisition to capture and bind every demon active in the world, but we absolutely have authority in the church. And we certainly have authority over our own lives. Anyone can get the devil off their own back. Those who want to be delivered, God is able to deliver. God wants His people free from anything that restrains their function in the body.

T. F. Tenney delivered a message in 1988 titled "A Nightmare in the Enemy's Camp." In it he gave the account of a demented woman right out of the bush country of South Africa. She'd been tormented out of her mind for years, and it took five men to literally drag her to missionary Bug Freeman. Brother Freeman looked at the woman and then to those who brought her and asked, "Does she speak English?"

"No." they answered.

"Does she speak Bhakti?"

"No." The woman spoke no language known to the men.

Suddenly one of the lady's arms broke free from the men's grip. She pointed it right at the minister's face and said, "E. L. Freeman, I know you and I'm not afraid of you."

Brother Freeman looked back and said, "I know you know me, and I know you're not afraid of me, but you're afraid of a name I've got. In the name of Jesus, come out of her."

And the devil departed.

> "It's going to take the supernatural to change the world."
> —Kenneth Haney

Our Inheritance

Miracles transcend the common course of nature. They are *super*natural—beyond nature. The last words recorded in the Gospel of Mark give us some insight into God's plan for His followers. After Jesus had spoken with the apostles and was received up into Heaven, "they went forth, and preached every where, the Lord working with them, and confirming the word with signs following. Amen" (Mark 16:20). God worked with them, confirming the words they spoke on His behalf by the miraculous!

Jesus moved in supernatural power. He brought Heaven to Earth—the supernatural into the natural with healings, deliverances, signs, and wonders wherever He went. The church today is called to do what He did in our generation.

> Our inheritance in the kingdom includes the miraculous.

I once heard Eli Hernandez speak on the miraculous. He used the word "metabolize," and I couldn't stop thinking about it. In my spirit, the word "metabolize" kept connecting to the word "miracle." Metabolism has to do with organic function, which is interesting considering our earlier discussion of the organic origin of supernatural gifts. Metabolism is a process within an organism by which its material substance is produced, maintained, or destroyed. As organisms, the miraculous could metabolize in your life or mine at any moment. When we're in an atmosphere charged with the presence of God and His holy angels, we, at any instant, could be a moment away from a miracle.

I believe God wants His church to have a picture of the miraculous! And I believe Pete Kalajian's painting of the pool of Bethesda is one that encapsulates this concept. God is willing to move on behalf of His people. Of course, we can't force His hand to do what contradicts His will, but even in the Scripture, the Lord changed His mind for His friend (see Exodus 32:14). Abraham, the father of the faith, wasn't without his faults. He lied about his wife more than once and he had a few weaknesses. That didn't change the fact that God called him His friend. He stood by Abraham even when he made mistakes and rescued him. Jesus calls His followers not only His servants, but also His friends (see John 15:15).

God works the miraculous in response to our obedient faith that operates in love (see 1 Corinthians 13:2). What kind of faith could move mountains and release miracles?

> If we're friends of God, we can expect God to move on behalf of our requests.

A mature, confident faith. A faith that fully relies on the power of God to work wonders. A faith as simple as a child who believes God keeps His Word.

It is Written

Satan tells us that true freedom is impossible, but Jesus said, "You shall know the truth, and the truth shall make you free" (John 8:32). Satan tells us we're alone in our struggles, but Paul wrote that every temptation we face is no different from what others experience (see 1 Corinthians 10:13). In fact, they all find their roots in the lust of the flesh, the lust of the eyes, and the pride of life (see 1 John 2:16, and the temptations of Jesus recorded in Luke 4:1-13). We don't stand alone in our temptations and trials. Everyone faces the same core issues.

One of Satan's greatest lies is that those he has blinded, will never see. He wants us to give up praying and reaching and preaching to others.

If God saved us, He can save them (see 2 Corinthians 4:6). If He made His light to shine in our hearts, He can do the same for our unsaved family members, coworkers, and friends. Any seeds of doubt planted in our hearts must be uprooted by God's Word, "It is written."

Jesus used words to release miracles. He spoke and water turned into wine. People were healed. Those who live in agreement with kingdom principles are empowered to speak life (see Proverbs 18:20-21). Our mouths are gateways for the miraculous. With our lips we affect the spiritual atmosphere and release the Word of God. The Lord used words to create the world, and His Word spoken through us brings healing (see Proverbs 12:18). The power to pierce through darkness. The power to tear down, build up, and transform. The sounds we utter usher in moves of God. With our words, we position ourselves for Holy Ghost outpourings.

God's Word is living and active, so we keep it before our eyes and in our hearts. It's powerful—as powerful as He is. He used it to create the world, and it is the sword yet in His mouth destined to destroy His enemies. When we internalize the Word of God, the fire of the indwelling Spirit can forge an undefeatable weapon. And that weapon is your voice and mine—an anointed, truth-speaking voice that releases the Spirit of God in our world.

Development

God wants to prepare us for a greater work. He will mentor, train, and shift us into position for a higher calling, but we must engage and learn to move with the pulse of His Spirit. Wait until He speaks. Respond when He enters. Billy Cole said, "Learn to recognize the voice of God. He will tell you what, where, and when . . . and you show up with a right attitude and message."

With the training, we will face opposition. I found several quotes to inspire and help us navigate adversity and opposition. Dean Byfield said, "With advancement comes adversity, but hold on to God, and you will make it." Nathan Scoggins said, "You step into adversity when God wants you to be a deliverer." Billy Cole said, "There is great sacrifice and suffering for those called to a special dimension in God to minister to the broken."

On the front end of battle, we pray against sabotage and for courage. On the back side, we pray against retaliation and discouragement. My pastor, Marvin Walker, refers to this as the whip of the dragon's tail after he's taken a hit. Especially after a great victory, the enemy, though wounded, makes one last swing. He attacks with accusations and attempts to paralyze with fear and doubt, but God will restore our souls from the weariness and expenditure of ministry (see Isaiah 40:31).

Revival

God's Word proclaims that in the last days the love of many would grow cold. Amidst great social decay, lawlessness, and rebellion against God's ways, the church must stay hot and proclaim the gospel of the Kingdom throughout the whole world (see Matthew 24:12-14). While some are growing cold, we must rise with faith and fan the flame of revival. We must have a revival of faith that comes with the demonstrations of faith. We must know more than just the Word, but also be led by and obedient to His Spirit.

> "The Holy Ghost is coming upon us like He did the first church so we can do the works of the first church." —Eli Hernandez

You may never stand behind a pulpit, but you have a part to play in the end-time revival. The anointed messages you deliver will make a difference to those willing and hungry in your *metron*—your circle of influence. Be encouraged and keep at it. Paul's preaching delivered the Ephesians from the ruling occultic power of the goddess Diana, but it happened over time as he faithfully shared the Word (see Acts 19). And as you faithfully share your testimony, the powerful love of God will chip away, bit by bit, at walls others have built around their hearts. Trust God to lead your way as He did for Israel in the desert. God works through people who listen, agree with His kingdom purposes, and move out on His promises. We can take new lands and recover lost ones. We can advance the kingdom when we shine the light of God in our world.

We must be willing to take risks. When we're frightened or worried, we can turn to God in prayer. He gives power, and as we speak words in faith, we set in motion the plans God has placed in our hearts. As we work with Him, we pray until something happens. We pray until we feel God's presence and love—an active moving of His Spirit that releases power. We won't know the solution for every problem, but as Rema Duncan said, our "job is to do what He says. We just need to hear what He says, then we will know what to do." He also said to "get comfortable with the ignorance of what to do next." When we don't know what's coming next, we rely on God and remain willing to step out as He directs.

God invites us to be eyewitnesses to the same signs, wonders, and miracles exhibited in the New Testament church. His hand works through ours. His words spoken from our lips touch people's hearts. There's nothing more powerful than the anointing that flows through words of truth to liberate those held captive by sin, suffering, or strongholds. We must live out the power of the doctrines in our lives and demonstrate the Spirit. Then the light of God's love will flow through us and draw thirsty people to the fountain of life.

C. Peter Wagner said, "God is moving with power in the world today. From the operational role of the Holy Spirit to warfare worship, from prophecy to miraculous healing, from demonic deliverance to powerful prayer and the new power levels taking place." God is at work, and we must take an active part in the manifestation of His Spirit in the Earth. Let's do what Jesus did, touching, caring, teaching, loving, delivering, and just being with the people. Listening, being attentive to others, and resisting the impulse to monopolize conversations.

What's in Your Hand?

When God calls us to serve and brings new opportunities for growth and change, it's normal to have questions. Did you know God has questions, too? Of course, He already knows the answer, but when God called Moses, He asked him anyway: "What do you have in your hand?"

Moses had only an ordinary rod or staff. He had no idea how God would use it, but God knew. He already saw him lifting his rod to perform the miraculous. Moses's rod became a snake. Surely, he felt vulnerable picking it up by the tail, but Moses obeyed, and when he did, what had been a common piece of wood transformed into the rod of God (see Exodus 4:20). When we, like Moses, obediently serve God, He blesses and multiplies what He placed in our hands.

One Sunday, as I was praying before a service, I asked the Lord, "What do I have in my hand?" I had not noticed when I asked the words that I had both arms wrapped around my Bible holding it close to my heart. I realized what I had in my hand, and what you also have in yours. It's the Sword of the Word of God. We have something amazing and wonderful and supernatural in our hands. God delivered the Israelites out of Egypt with a rod in Moses's hand. What can He do when His Holy Ghost-filled believers wield the sharp, two-edged sword of His Word in His name? We have something powerful!

What's in your hand? If it's the Word of God, it will flow into your heart and out of your mouth as a powerful weapon and tool. What's in your hand could also be the very sword of your defeated foe. David used Goliath's sword to win victory over his enemies, and the word of your testimony will bring victory in your life . . . and in the lives of those you minister to.

> Samson used a donkey's jawbone. David used a sling. Abigail used her kitchen and common sense. Jael used her tent peg and hammer. What's in your hand?

There's really nothing in your hand or mine that God didn't give to us or enable us to have. No, individuals don't come to the Kingdom with equal resources and opportunities, but we give what we have, and make the most of it—honing, sharpening and developing every gift and resource. No matter what else we may have to offer, if in our hands we hold the Word of God, we have everything we need. God's Word tells us we shouldn't covet, but Paul told believers they should covet earnestly the best gifts (1 Corinthians 12:31). Time is short, and there's no time to waste. God is no respecter of persons. He looks for the willing and selfless (see Romans 12:1).

I remember a particular service I wasn't scheduled to do anything. I prayed, "God, I'm not doing anything this service—preaching or singing or leading—but let me minister." During the altar service, when I prayed for a young man and placed my hand on his head, he immediately received the Holy Ghost. It was amazing! Afterwards I talked with another man who had been undecided for at least twenty years about baptism, and he was baptized in Jesus's name.

Whether we speak to the masses around the globe or to those in our very own communities, God's voice is heard through ours. His love extends through us—our hands, our acts of service, our eyes of compassion, and in the power and demonstration of the supernatural. This is the time. This is the place. We are the people. Feel the intensity of the hour and let us together redeem the time.

Today is the day to take the keys God gave the church and unlock doors for others. Tune in to the spiritual world and personally experience a greater dimension of liberty and power that sets others free. The Spirit of the Lord is already upon us! We unite with Him and He works with us as conduits to bring healing to the broken, comfort to the grieving, and to shine His light in the darkness.

Throughout *Kingdom Come* we've examined many concepts, and I've attempted to provide useful tools to help people live out their faith in the real world. I pray at the conclusion of this book, you feel better equipped to be God's temple—to open yourself to see the unseen and to respond right away when God moves. I pray that you develop a greater sensitivity to the supernatural and demonstrate the gifts of God as He flows through you. May God richly bless you as you move forward strengthened and inspired for your journey.

The kingdom of Heaven is not meat and drink, but righteousness, peace, and joy in the Holy Ghost. The most important words in this phrase, "in the Holy Ghost," establish the greatest key of all: Everything is experienced "in Him." As we abide in God in righteousness and peace with joy, His favor flows in us and through us. We live and minister from a place of overflow as we connect at the throne and receive power from on high. We simply reflect His glory, and may His glory cover the earth.

For thine is the kingdom, and the power, and the glory, forever and ever. Amen.

End of Section 3

APPENDIX I:
Kingdom Come Diagram

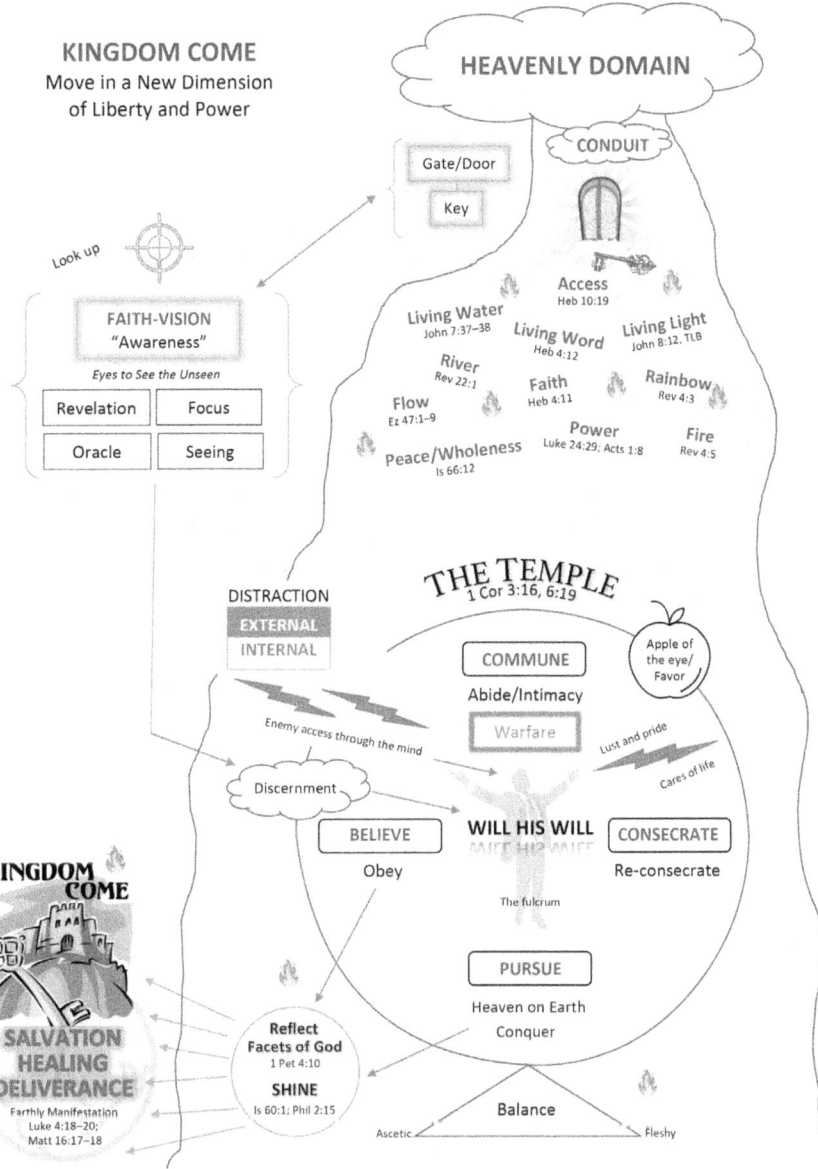

APPENDIX II:
Diagram Explanation

Developing the flow for the book, *Kingdom Come,* required a compilation process I've never used before. The complexity demanded a graphic that not only offered a quick visual reminder of its content, but also a reference guide to keep the composition true to the concepts.

Simply put, the diagram begins in the heavenly domain. It reveals components of the kingdom of God and how to access them through faith. Secondly, the temple portion represents you and me as we abide with God, in God, and live out His will. It addresses not only our identities and purposes, but also the challenges we face in dealing with common distractions and enemies from without and within. At the center of the work, and core to effectively living out *Kingdom Concepts,* is the greatest battleground, the will of man. Only when we will what God wills, are we able to complete the work of the Great Commission and reflect the love and supernatural power of God in our world.

Finally, when our temples are "whole" in such a way that we now serve as uninhibited conduits of God's kingdom, we unite in the purpose of God to see salvation, healing, and deliverance manifest in the earth. All for His glory. All in His name. As He moves us into a greater dimension of liberty and power.

ADDITIONAL WORKS BY LORI WAGNER

Ministry Resources
Preach Like a Lady: A Handbook for Women in Ministry
Gender & Ministry: A Biblical and Historical Investigation of Women in Ministry
Insight on Ministry from a Christmas Tree Farm

Topical Study
Wisdom is a Lady (Small Group Resource Pack)
The Scent of Hope: New Life from Dead Dreams
Holy Intimacy: Dwelling with God in the Secret Place

Biography
Through the Waters: The Life and Ministry of Evangelist Willie Johnson

Fiction
The Briar Hollow Trilogy: *The Rose of Sharon, Buttercup,* and *Marigold*
Gateway of the Sun

Discipleship/Christian Growth
Gates & Fences: Straight Talk in a Crooked World
Christian 101: Biblical Basics for New Believers and Youth
The Pure Path Series: *The Girl in the Dress, Covered by Love, Unmasked,* and *The Pure Life*

Prayer/Devotion
ABC Essentials on a Path of Prayer
Arise! Walk in the Sunrise!
The Eight Days of Christmas

Inspirational
Quilting Patches of Life
A Patchwork of Freedom

Miscellaneous
Bachik, the Birthday Kiss
Pete's Passage
Orbis: The Fun Family Game You Win by Blessing Your World

ENDNOTES

1. *Coram Deo* harmonizes with greatest and second greatest commandments taught in the Old Testament and affirmed in the New Testament by Jesus, "The first of all the commandments is, Hear, O Israel; The Lord our God is one Lord: And thou shalt love the Lord thy God with all thy heart, and with all thy soul, and with all thy mind, and with all thy strength: this is the first commandment. and the second is like, namely this, Thou shalt love thy neighbor as thyself. There is none other commandment greater than these" (Matthew 12:29–31, see also Deuteronomy 6:4–5 and Leviticus 19:18). https://www.coramdeoassociation.org/meaning-of-coram-deo/

2. Kohler, Kaufmann Kohler and Ludwig Blau. "Shekinah." In *Jewish Encyclopedia*, 1906. http://www.jewishencyclopedia.com/articles/13537-shekinah.

3. The term was used by rabbis in place of the word "God" and is connected with the tabernacle, the burning bush (Deuteronomy 33:16) and the glory on Mount Sinai (Exodus 23:16).

4. The Greek word *christos* translated "Christ" translates "anointed." "The single title *Christos* is sometimes used . . . to signify the One who by His Holy Spirit and power indwells believers and molds their character in conformity to His likeness, Rom 8:10; Gal 2:20; 4:19; Eph 3:17." *Vine's Expository Dictionary of New Testament Words* "christos."

5. See Revelation 19:20. According to Vine's, the word "brimstone" originally denoted "fire from heaven" and the word is connected with sulfur. "Places touched by lightning were called *theia*, and, as lightning leaves a sulphurous smell, and sulphur was used in pagan purifications, it received the name of *theion*."

6. James Strong. Strong's Exhaustive Concordance of the Bible, (Peabody, MA: Hendrickson, 1988), s.v. "Dikaiosuné."

7. W. E. Vine, *Vine's Expository Dictionary of New Testament Words*, Unabridged (McLean, VA: MacDonald Publishing Company, 1989), s.v. "righteousness."

8. "To whom also Abraham gave a tenth part of all; first being by interpretation King of righteousness, and after that also King of Salem, which is, King of peace" (Hebrews 7:2).

9. Scott B. Noegel, and Brannon Mitchell Wheeler. *Historical Dictionary of Prophets in Islam and Judaism.* Lanham (Md.): The Scarecrow Press, 2002. p. 301.

10. Hebrewic teaching says Abraham received the priesthood from Melchizedek. Joshua Garroway, "Who Assumed Melchizedek's Priesthood?" *TheTorah.com* (2016). https://thetorah.com/article/who-assumed-melchizedeks-priesthood

11. Brown-Driver-Briggs Hebrew and English Lexicon, Unabridged, Electronic Database. Copyright © 2002, 2003, 2006 by Biblesoft, Inc.https://www.biblehub.com/hebrew/3389.htm

12. David A. deSilva, *An Introduction to the New Testament: Contexts, Methods, and Ministry* (Downers Grove: InterVarsity Press, 2018), 637.

www.ingramcontent.com/pod-product-compliance
Lightning Source LLC
Chambersburg PA
CBHW071224080526
44587CB00013BA/1494